INCOME DISTRIBUTION IN A CORPORATE ECONOMY

NEW DIRECTIONS IN MODERN ECONOMICS

Series Editor: Malcolm C. Sawyer,
Professor of Economics, University of Leeds

New Directions in Modern Economics presents a challenge to orthodox economic thinking. It focuses on new ideas emanating from radical traditions including post-Keynesian, Kaleckian, neo-Ricardian and Marxian. The books in the series do not adhere rigidly to any single school of thought but attempt to present a positive alternative to the conventional wisdom.

A list of published titles in this series is printed at the end of this volume.

INCOME DISTRIBUTION IN A CORPORATE ECONOMY

RUSSELL RIMMER

Reader
Department of Information and Numerical Sciences
Deakin University
Australia

Edward Elgar

Published by
Edward Elgar Publishing Limited
Gower House
Croft Road
Aldershot
Hants GU11 3HR
England

Edward Elgar Publishing Company
Old Post Road
Brookfield
Vermont 05036
USA

A CIP catalogue record for this book is available from the British Library

Library of Congress Cataloging-in-Publication Data
Rimmer, Russell.
    Income distribution in a corporate economy / Russell Rimmer.
        p.   cm. — (New directions in modern economics)
    Includes bibliographical references and index.
    1. Income distribution—Mathematical models. 2. Industrial
organization—Mathematical models. 3. Prices—Mathematical models.
4. Stock-exchange—Mathematical models. I. Title. II. Series: New
directions in modern economics series.
HB523.R56 1993
339.2—dc20   92–36098
                                                                    CIP

ISBN 978 1 85278 695 3

Printed and bound by CPI Group (UK) Ltd, Croydon, CR0 4YY

Contented wi' little, and cantie wi' mair.

R. Burns, *Contented wi' Little*

Contents

Figures and Table

Figures

Table

Acknowledgements

I am indebted to many people. Robert Dixon, in many conversations, encouraged my interest in theories of income distribution and directed me to the literature on the neo-Pasinetti theorem. It has been my good fortune to have had the generous intellectual support of Geoffrey Harcourt at the University of Cambridge, John King, Sheila Rimmer and Michael Schneider at La Trobe University, and several anonymous referees. Deakin University allowed me to take periods of leave at the University of Glasgow. There David Vines and Andrew Stevenson were very encouraging. I am also thankful to the School of Economics and Commerce at La Trobe University for help in preparing the typescript. Robyn Kress of Deakin University generously provided technical advice on graphics and layout. Rosemary Moore expertly prepared the typescript and provided excellent suggestions for the correction of grammar and algebra.

Academic Press charitably gave permission to reproduce from the *Cambridge Journal of Economics* the material in Section 3.4.

For the International Economic Association Macmillan Ltd gave permission to redraw Figures 13 and 14 from F. A. Lutz and D. C. Hague (eds) 1961, *The Theory of Capital*, as Figures 3.1 and 3.2 on pages 65 and 67 below.

1. Introduction

This book is about theories of income distribution. First those theories which were the subject of intense debate between neoclassical and Keynesian scholars during the 1950s and 1960s are reviewed. The neoclassical approach (set out in the first three sections of Chapter 2) emphasizes the importance of the technical parameters specifying the production function. On the other hand, the Keynesian theories of Chapter 3 promote planned investment and savings propensities as the important determinants of distribution. The approach preferred here has evolved from dissatisfaction with attempts to synthesize the neoclassical and Keynesian approaches; the goals of incorporating more recent developments in investment theory and industry economics into short-run theories of distribution; and the urge to understand how activities in securities markets might affect income shares.

In the neoclassical theory producers are price takers and factors of production are rewarded according to their marginal products. Opponents of the neoclassical school have been critical of the logic of the approach, the theoretical framework, the techniques of analysis, and the ideology that might underlie interest in this form of theorizing. Some of the attacks on neoclassical theory by Keynesian scholars are reviewed in the later sections of Chapter 2. These economists were especially dissatisfied with the notion of a perfectly competitive microeconomy as the basis of a theory of distribution.

Chapter 3 is focused on the contributions of Nicholas Kaldor, who associated his work with Keynes by appealing to the passage in the *Treatise* on the widow's cruse. To Keynes the incomes of entrepreneurs were the result of their own expenditures – even those on 'riotous living'. Provided entrepreneurs continued to spend, profits, like the widow's cruse, would not be exhausted. In the theory proposed by Kaldor in the mid-1950s, the owners of enterprises could generate greater profits by planning greater expenditures on investment. This model is set out in Section 3.1 and, because a subsequent model devised by Kaldor is central to the arguments presented here, the model of the 1950s is referred to as his 'earlier' or 'initial' model (of distribution). Pasinetti (1961–2) subsequently claimed to correct a logical slip in Kaldor's formulation, although the perception of a slip depends on what is assumed about the savings propensity applied by wage and salary earners to the return flowing from their savings (Section 3.2). With his model Pasinetti was able to provide a rigorous derivation of the Cambridge distribution equation for the profit share,

$$\frac{P}{Y} = \frac{1}{s_P} \frac{I}{Y},$$

where I denotes investment and s_P is the propensity to save out of profits. Kaldor had only been able to obtain the Cambridge equation on the assumption that the savings propensity from wages and salaries was zero.

Pasinetti's analysis exposed two areas of concern to neoclassical scholars. First, even though Pasinetti allowed workers the prospect of saving and so sharing in profit income, his analysis appeared to Samuelson and Modigliani (1966) to be of an economy in which there were hereditary classes of capitalists and workers. Second, they seized on a mathematical restriction which precluded the possibility of solutions other than the Cambridge equation. In his reply to this marginalist critique Kaldor (1966) dismissed each of the objections with a 'neo-Pasinetti' theory in which the main features of the Cambridge equation were preserved. The neo-Pasinetti model represents a world in which enterprises are organized as corporations, and which pay a portion of profit as dividends to households holding corporate securities. Households make available to corporations their labour and, via the securities market, a portion of their incomes. Together with retained profits this portion of household income constitutes aggregate savings. This is the framework adopted in later chapters to investigate the role of securities markets in the determination of distribution.

Another strand of the post-Keynesian literature begun by Boulding is integrated into the neo-Pasinetti framework in Chapter 3. This balance sheet approach preceded Kaldor's initial work, Pasinetti's revision, and the neoclassical attack of Samuelson and Modigliani.

When two obvious assumptions are added to Boulding's model of a developed economy the neo-Pasinetti result may be obtained. With this approach the problems which preoccupied Samuelson and Modigliani do not arise, suggesting that, if Kaldor, Pasinetti and the neoclassical critics had interpreted Boulding appropriately, one aspect of the debate between the Keynesian and neoclassical schools might have been avoided. The balance sheets of Boulding are of interest for more than their age and their capacity to break a deadlock between factions in dispute. With them it is shown in Section 3.4 that income shares are responsive to pressures tending to crowd out business investment in favour of household expenditure on durable assets.

By settling on the neo-Pasinetti environment, the models developed in later chapters depart from the literature emanating from Kaldor's earlier model. That is, rather than regarding society as composed of groups defined by type of income, questions of distribution between households and corporations are addressed. This is a different philosophical perspective from the conception of society as two classes. Within the neo-Pasinetti paradigm two extensions or modifications are made here to the post-Keynesian approach to distribution. One goal of the book concerns the investigation of the role of industrial organization in determining distribution. Kaldor proposed an industry base for his growth theories in which each firm may be taken as a representative of the whole microeconomy. The representative firm employed a fixed fraction of the available labour force, and up to full employment set price as a mark-up on average direct cost. This industry structure was a central component of Kaldor's argument that a Keynesian equilibrium with under-employment is not consistent with an equilibrium state of steady growth. The representative firm and how Kaldor reached this view are discussed in Section 3.5. This section also contains an account of the critique by Harcourt which suggests that it is implausible to use the representative firm in Keynesian analyses of the short run. With the emphasis being on the short run here, it is therefore reasonable to seek another microeconomic basis for the neo-Pasinetti model. Guidance on this extension of the neo-Pasinetti framework may be sought from the literature which developed from Kaldor's initial model. In Chapter 4 some examples of this literature are set out. This survey is intended to provide insight into the ways in which post-Keynesian theory might be extended to incorporate recent developments in industry economics. Some writers have attempted to integrate a perfectly competitive microeconomy into the earlier approach. Extensions of this type have been researched by Sen (Section 4.1) and Riach (Section 4.2). These contributions have added to our understanding of short-run processes, and they provide a synthesis of the Keynesian approach of the *General Theory* with neoclassical mechanisms. Neither approach was considered appropriate for the microeconomy of the neo-Pasinetti model. Another approach to the industry base was taken by Harcourt (Section 4.3). He put forward a price rule in which corporations linked the mark-up directly to the level of planned investment. This was proposed as a way of illustrating how investment plans would lead to the required savings.

In line with the goal of incorporating theories of investment into the neo-Pasinetti approach, two adaptations of Kaldor's earlier model to allow for endogenous investment are also reviewed in Chapter 4. Usually post-Keynesians insist that investment be exogenously determined, although Kaldor did not adhere strictly to this principle. In the mid-1950s he thought that it was the ratio of investment to income which should be fixed (albeit when national income was constrained by full employment); in 1961, however, he theorized that investment is induced when the average cost curves of firms lie below the supply schedule and normal profits are being realized. In the synthesizing model proposed by Riach (Section 4.2) investment varies directly with income, with the constant of proportionality being sensitive to changes in the profit share. His purpose was to promote the importance of the reverse of the causal linkage investigated by Kaldor, that is the causality from distribution to demand. King and Regan (Section 4.4) have considered a direct link between investment and consumption. This approach suggests the possibility of employing an accelerator theory. None of these approaches is taken up. Rather faith is kept with Kaldor to the extent that investment remains exogenous with respect to the commodity-market variables normally included in Keynesian theories of distribution. The inclusion of a securities market in the neo-Pasinetti model allows the possibility that variations in a securities-market valuation indicator might be taken into account by managers when deciding investment strategies. One candidate is Tobin's q, which Tobin and Brainard have suggested impinges on planned investment

(Section 5.1). Accordingly, a component of the short-run investment rate is made responsive to variations in q, the ratio of the securities market valuation of the capital stock relative to its replacement cost. The type of industrial base included in the neo-Pasinetti model of Chapter 5 is drawn from the theory proposed by Harcourt. Prices are set in relation to investment plans, but with the addition that the mark-up is not permitted to fall below a minimum level. For Kaldor this component of the margin was required to account for the influence of the market power of the representative firm (Section 5.2). Combined with the q theory of investment, the price rule provides a mechanism by which households may influence planned investment and the price level. In the q theory a component of investment depends on the assessment of corporate assets by securities markets. Variations in this assessment depend in part on the perceptions of households. If changed perceptions lead to a variation in the level of the induced component of investment, then price is also affected via the mark-up mechanism. While the managers and boards of directors of corporations do not have sole control over these macroeconomic indicators, they can exert some influence on activities in the securities market. For example, they might influence household expectations by raising the levels of dividends. In the version of the neo-Pasinetti paradigm set out in Chapter 5 the profit share varies inversely with the price elasticity of investment demand, but never falls below a minimum value associated with market power. When q, the ratio of the market valuation of securities to the replacement cost of the assets they represent, is held fixed, expansions of planned autonomous investment induce increases in profits and income, with profits growing relatively more. On the other hand, when the economy-wide margin is expanded by more than is required to support investment expenditures, profits are unaffected, while there is a tendency for national income to contract. Shareholders are not disadvantaged by these changes, but households not receiving dividend income must adjust to the full effect of increases in the commodity price, producing a tendency for output to contract in the short term.

A deficiency of the model analysed in Chapter 5 is that Tobin's q is determined exogenously. How activities in securities markets affect income shares would be better expounded in a model where this linkage between financial and commodity markets is endogenous. The literature on the structure, conduct and performance of markets provides specific roles for the microeconomy in the determination of the mark-up and Tobin's q. In Chapter 6 this literature is reviewed, along with empirical studies of the investment – q relationship and mark-up theories of price formation. The decision is taken to replace the price rule of Chapter 5 with a profit-maximizing theory of oligopoly associated with Cowling and Waterson (1976) and Clarke and Davies (1982). This approach, like Kaldor's representative firm, has parallels in the work of Kalecki. Skott (1989, pp. vii–viii) has observed that one may have reservations concerning the assumptions underlying the theoretical developments on oligopoly, but they 'deserve serious consideration'. He was optimistic that rigorous results, like those of Cowling and Waterson and Clarke and Davies, would provide a means of integrating the Keynesian and Marxian perspectives 'without the dogmatism which on occasion has afflicted both traditions'.

In Chapter 7 the approach of Clarke and Davies is exploited to represent an economy consisting of profit-maximizing oligopolists who collude to preserve their output shares. The mark-up is then an increasing function of industry concentration and the extent or intensity of collusion. Tobin's q is endogenized by regarding firm-level qs as indicators of the extent to which enterprises capture non-competitive rents. By using a simplified version of the approach of Lindenberg and Ross (1981) it is shown that, when securities markets take account of the above-normal rents which oligopolists receive, the economy-wide q is a function of the short-run profit rate. A version of the neo-Pasinetti model involving these linkages is solved to study the effects of an increase in the Herfindahl index of industry concentration. As a result of this change price rises and income is redistributed towards profits while wages and national income contract. In a model in which the macroeconomic structure consists of an imperfectly competitive market organized as a circular product space, with units of the commodity being distinguished by their distance from the customer, Weitzman (1982) and Solow (1986) have obtained similar outcomes. Their concern was unemployment and they concluded that it might not be eliminated by the unfettered operation of the price mechanism. But further Solow (1986, p. 313) was of the view that 'Small scale myopic adjustments might be self-frustrating'. The parallel between the simulation of Chapter 7 and the analyses of Weitzman and Solow can be seen if the increase in concentration is thought of as arising during a slump when an enterprise closes its doors and dismisses its workforce. The insulation of profits from the effects of such a slump stimulates activities in the securities market, the price of securities rises, and capital gains can be realized. In this short-run simulation the capital gain is shown to include a component accounting for the inflationary effects associated with the increase in concentration. Even though the securities price rises it is possible that Tobin's q will decrease. In particular, when q is initially greater than its long-run value of unity, q is projected to fall relative to the value it would have attained had all firms continued to operate. That is, the market value of securities does not rise as much as the replacement cost of capital. However q does not fall below one. The extent to which q exceeds its long-run value in the new equilibrium is the outcome of a multiplier-like process, in which the favourable influence in the securities market of planned nominal investment bids up q, which in turn induces further nominal investment expenditure. If initially q is less than its long-run value, it is projected to increase as households build into their estimations of the securities price the enhanced rents available to the more concentrated industrial sector. In the long run q is unaffected by an increase in concentration.

This book is intended to be read by students beginning study or research in income distribution, and therefore there are a number of entry or starting points. Obviously in using the book in this way there will be times when the background material of earlier chapters will need to be consulted. The contents of Chapters 2 and 3 were written to serve as introductions to neoclassical and post-Keynesian theories of distribution. For readers already familiar with the basic material in the early chapters, a suitable starting point might be Chapter 4, which was included as a reference to theoretical studies which suggest new directions for the elucidation of Keynesian distributive processes. In Chapter 5 is set out a neo-Pasinetti model motivated by the analyses in Chapters 3 and 4. Another entry point is Chapter 6, which contains a review of empirical and theoretical topics in investment theory, price theory and industry economics which might be employed to broaden or augment the quantitative analysis of distribution. The model of Chapter 7 draws on the theoretical developments discussed in Chapter 6. Approaches to further research are suggested in the conclusion. One obvious direction for further activity is the refinement of the modelling of securities and other financial markets to improve on the analysis presented here of their roles in the distribution of income and wealth.

2. Income Distribution in a Perfectly Competitive Economy

Neoclassical theorizing on the distribution of income stretches back into the nineteenth century. Production was thought to be carried out by independent small firms whose activities had no effect within the industry and the market in which each agent sold its output. In later chapters this assumption is abandoned, and firms are assumed to have degrees of market power and the capacity to collude with competitors to improve their performances. In Section 2.1 the basic assumptions of the one-good neoclassical model are assembled to show that there exists an economy-wide production function. The neoclassical resolution of the problem of 'adding up' factor shares is discussed in the next section. In Section 2.3 it is shown that the relative shares of labour and capital depend on properties of the technology. Post-Keynesian criticisms of perfect competition and the neoclassical approach are reviewed in Section 2.4. Within the confines of the one-good model, an analysis is undertaken in Section 2.5 of the pivotal role sometimes ascribed to capitalists in the production process. The strands of post-Keynesian theory which will be followed in building models of distribution in a corporate economy are presented in Chapter 3.

In neoclassical macroeconomics all factors of production are rewarded according to their marginal products. Suppose that one good is produced using quantities of two factors: labour, denoted L, and capital, K. If there is a production function, F, specifying the volume of output, $F(K,L)$, then the partial derivatives of this aggregate production function, where they are defined, measure the marginal products of each input. The first partial derivative, $D_1F(K,L)$, is the marginal product of capital. Similarly, $D_2F(K,L)$ is the marginal product of labour. If there is perfect competition in both the market for inputs and the market for output, and if profit is maximized, then each factor is employed up to the level which equates its marginal product with the corresponding real return to the input. In terms of the production function,

$$D_1F(K,L) = r/p \quad D_2F(K,L) = w/p , \qquad (2.1)$$

where r and w denote the rental rate on capital and wage rate respectively, and p is the price of a unit of output.

Clark, in 1899, discussed distribution using a model in which both factors are rewarded with their marginal products. Influential studies came from Hicks in 1932, Solow in 1957 and 1958, Bronfenbrenner in 1960 and Johnson in 1973. In the early work marginal productivity and perfect competition were associated with the equitable distribution of income: 'Where natural laws have their way, the share of income that attaches to any productive function is gauged by the actual product of it. In other words, free competition tends to give to labour what labour creates' (Clark, 1899, p.3). This approach is often described as 'marginal productivity theory'.

2.1 The neoclassical microeconomy

The macroeconomic production function relates the level of aggregate output to the usage of the aggregate factor inputs. But F is not simply a computational black box; it is meant to capture the essence, if not all the detail, of the (perhaps) many firms that contribute a share to aggregate output. When is it valid to use this black-box notion? That is, what sort of industry structures are consistent with the existence of an economy-wide production technology? One structure consists of a collection of firms, each having the same competitive properties as was assumed for the whole economy, and, except for size, each is indistinguishable from its competitors. Distinction between firms on the basis of size is unimportant in neoclassical theory as all firms are assumed not to have market power: firms are atomistic, price-taking agents. To construct an aggregate production function for this type of microeconomy requires some of the properties of homogeneous functions. These are introduced as the construction proceeds.

For the economy producing only one commodity, suppose that each firm has the same (microeconomic) production function. As there is only one produced good, once a unit of measurement is settled, the quantities made by each firm may be added to obtain aggregate output. If there are *n* firms each producing amount, Q_i, then total output is:

$$\sum_{i=1}^{n} Q_i \tag{2.2}$$

Because each firm uses the same production function then:

$$Q_i = F(K_i, L_i) \tag{2.3}$$

where K_i and L_i denote the quantities of capital and labour used by firm *i*. Obviously the single commodity is used both for consumption by households and by firms to accumulate stocks of capital. Often grain is cited as the commodity type possessing simultaneously the dual properties of both a consumption and an investment good. In one-good models it is the only factor with which labour can work. Grain does not have this property, as it must be augmented with other goods, such as the services of machinery (including perhaps, livestock) and land, before labour can produce new crops. Nevertheless, having only one type of capital means that for each firm K_i is a quantity of the same good.[1] Similarly, with labour assumed to be a homogeneous service, L_i represents a quantity of the same type of labour for each firm.

The common production function is assumed to display the property of constant returns to scale (also known as linear homogeneity). That is, if the quantities of the inputs are each increased by the proportion λ then output grows by this same proportion. This is often paraphrased as: 'Doubling each input, doubles output.' Formally this is

$$F(\lambda K_i, \lambda L_i) = \lambda F(K_i, L_i) \quad \lambda > 1 \tag{2.4}$$

An important property of constant returns production functions emerges if λ is set at $1/L_i$. For then:

$$F(\frac{K_i}{L_i}, 1) = \frac{1}{L_i} F(K_i, L_i), \tag{2.5}$$

$$F(K_i, L_i) = L_i F(\frac{K_i}{L_i}, 1), \tag{2.6}$$

and the marginal products of capital and labour are given by

$$D_1F(K_i, L_i) = D_1F(\frac{K_i}{L_i}, 1),$$

$$D_2F(K_i, L_i) = F(\frac{K_i}{L_i}, 1) - \frac{K_i}{L_i} D_1F(\frac{K_i}{L_i}, 1).$$
(2.7)

The marginal products clearly depend only on the capital to labour ratio K_i/L_i. If each competitive firm maximizes profit then it will employ capital and labour so that (2.1) is satisfied. When the amount of capital in use is fixed, as will be assumed in the short run under consideration in later chapters[2], each firm must operate with the capital–labour ratio which satisfies

$$D_2F(K_i, L_i) = w/p.$$
(2.8)

Because the technology, F, and the real wage, w/p, are the same for each firm, K_i and L_i will be combinations which give the same capital–labour ratio for each firm. For historical reasons, firms might have accumulated different sized stocks of capital for use during any particular short-run period. Also, as the capital–labour ratio is the same across firms, the demand for labour by each is proportional to the quantity of its capital stock in use. But firms are otherwise not remarkably different. In common with every other firm, any one 'representative' firm is competitive, profit-maximizing, faces the same production technology, and operates with the same capital–labour ratio.

It is now easy to see that F may also be used to determine aggregate output, Q. For

$$Q = \sum_{i=1}^{n} Q_i = \sum_{i=1}^{n} F(K_i, L_i) = \sum_{i=1}^{n} L_i F(\frac{K_i}{L_i}, 1),$$
(2.9)

the last equality being (2.6), which is true because F has constant returns to scale. Now for each firm K_i/L_i is the same as the economy-wide ratio, K/L, and from (2.9)

$$Q = \sum_{i=1}^{n} L_i F(\frac{K}{L}, 1)$$
(2.10)

Because the term in F is now independent of i, (2.10) may be simplified to

$$Q = F(\frac{K}{L}, 1) \sum_{i=1}^{n} L_i = F(\frac{K}{L}, 1) L = F(K,L) \qquad (2.11)$$

and the last equality is valid because F again has constant returns to scale. Thus there is an aggregate production function for the model: it is simply the linearly homogeneous function describing the technology common to each perfectly competitive, profit-maximizing firm. Other industrial structures are consistent with the existence of an aggregate production function. For example, in any single-firm economy where production is described by a relation assigning each input combination to a unique output level, the technology is independent of the practices of the firm. But in general the distribution of income will not be the same as in the case of purely competitive firms. The analysis of income distribution in imperfectly competitive economies is taken up in Chapters 5 and 7.

2.2 Does marginal productivity exhaust the product?

To arrive at the profit-maximizing conditions (2.1), it was assumed that *both* factors of production are rewarded with their marginal products. This is a departure from Ricardian analysis, in which the income of one factor (land) is the surplus or deficit remaining after labour's marginal product has been paid out. The neoclassical extension raises the problem that, where the incomes of both factors are so determined, they may not exactly add up to the value of the available output. From (2.1) the shares of capital and labour, S_K and S_L, are given by

$$S_K = \frac{rK}{pQ} = D_1 F(K,L) \frac{K}{Q} = \frac{\text{marginal product of capital}}{\text{average product of capital}}$$
$$\qquad (2.12)$$
$$S_L = \frac{wL}{pQ} = D_2 F(K,L) \frac{L}{Q} = \frac{\text{marginal product of labour}}{\text{average product of labour}}$$

To ensure that the ratios of marginal to average products sum to unity, one of two assumptions is required: either globally (for all values of K and L) the production function has constant returns to scale, or the economy operates where locally this same property is observed.

When the production function has constant returns globally, the factor incomes guaranteed by marginal productivity always exactly exhaust the product.[3] Consider the example of the Cobb–Douglas technology which has been widely used in aggregate studies. The constant returns version of this function is

$$F(K, L) = aK^{1-\alpha}L^{\alpha} \quad 0 < \alpha < 1,$$

where a and α are constants. It is easy to establish that α and $1-\alpha$ are the shares of labour and capital in output. For labour, calculate the marginal product:

$$D_2F(K, L) = \alpha a K^{1-\alpha}L^{\alpha-1} = \alpha\frac{aK^{1-\alpha}L^{\alpha}}{L} = \alpha\frac{Q}{L}$$

That is, the marginal product of labour is a constant multiple of the average product for this function. So from (2.12), the share of labour is simply α. Similarly S_K can be shown to be $1-\alpha$, and so factor shares add to unity.

More generally, by appealing to Euler's theorem, production functions having constant returns to scale may be shown to exhaust the product. This theorem ensures that, if the production function has constant returns to scale, then

$$Q = D_1F(K, L)K + D_2F(K, L)L. \tag{2.13}$$

When each factor is rewarded with its real return this becomes

$$Q = \frac{r}{p}K + \frac{w}{p}L,$$

and division of this equation by Q shows that factor shares add to one. Production functions which have increasing or decreasing returns to scale do not satisfy (2.13), although they may satisfy a generalization of the theorem. Suppose that F has the homogeneity property,

$$F(\lambda K, \lambda L) = \lambda^j F(K, L)$$

for j not equal to one. The theorem similar to (2.13) for these functions is

$$jQ = D_1F(K, L)K + D_2F(K, L)L \qquad (2.14)$$

(see Smith, 1982, p.52). When $j = 1$, this result turns into (2.13). When j is greater than one, F has increasing returns to scale and the factors together receive more than the product. When j is less than 1, there are decreasing returns to scale, and some output remains after the factors are paid.

The second condition ensuring that functional shares add to 1 was advanced by Robinson (1933). She showed that the product is exactly exhausted when the economy operates in perfectly competitive equilibrium at the bottom of a U-shaped long-run average cost curve. This happens because, for small variations in the levels of capital and labour around the equilibrium values, returns to scale are constant. The Robinson condition places less emphasis on the properties of the production function, but focuses attention on the location of perfectly competitive, profit-maximizing equilibria. Following Hicks and Samuelson, Johnson (1973, pp.21–2) has argued that

[The local condition] is a requirement imposed by the assumption of market conditions of perfect competition, which imposes the absence of both profits and losses. If the logic of factor-utilization choice implies payment by marginal productivity and the logic of perfect competition implies zero profits, the competitors in the market must choose points on their production possibility technology such that both requirements are fulfilled.

The assumption of perfect competition implies that the market clears. That is, overall revenue must equal the costs of production. Implicit in this is the assumption that there are no 'pure' or 'above normal' profits: there can only be the returns which accrue to the factors. Hence

$$pQ = pF(K, L) = rK + wL, \qquad (2.15)$$

and, because rewards are decided by marginal productivity,

$$pF(K, L) = pD_1F(K, L)K + pD_2F(K, L)L. \qquad (2.16)$$

Thus simultaneous satisfaction of the requirements of market clearing and marginal productivity means that the product is exhausted. If p is cancelled from both sides of (2.16) then (2.13), the constant-returns version of Euler's theorem, emerges. The difference with the global condition is that now (2.16) only applies locally, and is only valid within the collection of market-clearing combinations of inputs. When the industry structure is not competitive but is, say, monopolistic, constant returns are not required to ensure that distributive shares add to one. For then 'the monopoly profit is a surplus that can absorb any excess of total product over factor payments, or in the case of increasing returns monopolistic price-fixing will ensure that factors do not receive the values of their marginal products' (Johnson, 1973, p.21).

2.3 Technology and substitution

We have already seen that if the production function is of Cobb–Douglas form then functional shares are given by a constant associated with the technology. With other production functions, too, the relative shares of labour and capital can be shown to depend on properties of the technology. To do this, the elasticity of substitution is introduced.

For a production function the collection of all combinations of inputs which may be used to produce a particular level of output is known as an *isoquant*. Along the isoquant the elasticity of substitution is a measure of the ease with which the factors of production may be substituted for each other in producing the given volume of output. In Figure 2.1 the isoquant corresponding to combinations of K and L which may be used to produce output Q is labelled QQ. The slope of the isoquant at any point indicates the extra amount of capital required to compensate for the loss of a unit of labour in the production of Q. This is called the *marginal rate of substitution*, and is given by the negative of the ratio of the marginal products of the factors.[4] As L/K increases along the isoquant (or, more familiarly, as the capital–labour ratio decreases), the slope becomes flatter. The marginal rate of substitution is *diminishing*.[5]

Also shown in the figure are two isocost lines. Each straight line shows the combination of inputs which may be purchased for a given outlay or level of total cost. The slopes of the isocost lines vary with the wage–rental ratio, w/r.[6] For the same wage–rental ratio, total cost is smaller on C_1C_1 than on C_2C_2. In perfect competition

Figure 2.1   Cost minimization

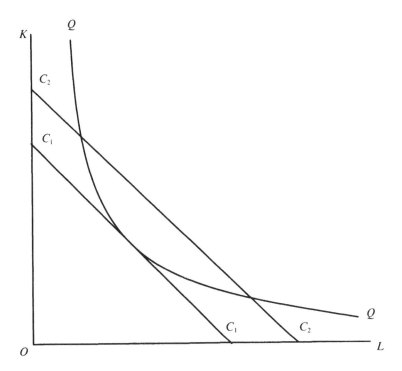

profit is maximized at the level of output prevailing along the iso-quant QQ, where cost is minimized. Geometrically, cost is mini-mized on the isocost line closest to the origin O, which has a point of tangency or contact with the isoquant. In Figure 2.1 this occurs at the point where the isoquant QQ and the isocost line C_1C_1 are in contact and have common slope.

With these preliminaries over, the elasticity of substitution may be defined. Figure 2.2 shows two isocost lines tangent to the isoquant, QQ. On C_2C_2 the wage rate is higher relative to the rental rate than is the case on C_1C_1. If initially the wage–rental ratio and total cost are such that the isocost line is C_1C_1, then K_1 units of capital are in use and L_1 units of labour are employed. But when the wage–rental ratio increases to that of C_2C_2 , employment of labour falls to L_2 and usage of capital rises to K_2. Capital is substituted for labour as the

Figure 2.2   Factor substitution

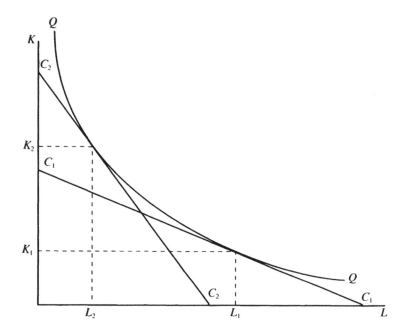

former becomes relatively cheaper. It is apparent that along the isoquant is mapped out a direct relationship between w/r and K/L: increases in the wage–rental ratio result in an increase in the capital–labour ratio. Therefore in perfect competition when profit is maximized, the degree to which one factor may be substituted for the other might be measured by the ratio

$$\sigma = \frac{\text{proportional change in } K/L}{\text{proportional change in } w/r} \qquad (2.17)$$

This is the *elasticity of substitution.* It is defined so that the *greater* the value of σ, the *easier* it is to substitute between capital and labour.

There is a link between the value of the elasticity of substitution and the effect of changes in the wage–rental ratio (w/r) on the share of labour relative to capital (wL/rK). Labour's relative share can be written as

$$\left(\frac{w}{r}\right)\bigg/\left(\frac{K}{L}\right) \tag{2.18}$$

When $\sigma = 1$ a change in w/r is matched by a proportional change in the capital–labour ratio, and the quotient (2.18) is not changed by variations in w/r. The constant-returns technology having unit elasticity everywhere is the Cobb–Douglas functional form.[7] It was shown above that this production function generates constant functional shares. When σ is greater than unity, then from (2.17) the capital–labour ratio must increase by a larger proportional amount than the wage–rental ratio. In this case it follows from (2.18) that labour's share decreases relative to that of capital. If σ is less than one, the capital–labour ratio increases proportionately less than w/r, and labour's relative share grows. A class of constant returns production functions for which the elasticity might be other than unity is given by

$$F(K, L) = \{aK^{-\beta} + bL^{-\beta}\}^{-1/\beta} \quad \beta > -1, \ \beta \neq 0 . \tag{2.19}$$

Given β, each has *c*onstant *e*lasticity of *s*ubstitution (hence the name CES) given by

$$\sigma = \frac{1}{1+\beta} \tag{2.20}$$

For β greater (less) than 0, σ is less (greater) than one. The CES and Cobb–Douglas functions have been widely used in empirical work. Two polar cases occur. When the isoquants are straight lines, σ is said to be infinite, reflecting the idea that the factors are perfect substitutes. At the other extreme, $\sigma = 0$, and substitution between factors is impossible. Factors are then used in fixed proportions to produce any level of output, and labour's relative share adjusts in line with variations in w/r.

The elasticity of substitution may be used to explain the considerable degree of constancy in the functional shares of the US, Britain and other developed countries. It was pointed out earlier that changes in the wage–rental ratio are matched by the same proportional change in the capital–labour ratio when $\sigma = 1$, thus ensuring that relative shares are constant. There is doubt, however, that σ always has this value, and the explanation was dismissed (notably by Kaldor, 1957, p.592). Bronfenbrenner (1960) attempted to build a quasi-proof by contradiction to show that neoclassical theory contained an explanation which did not depend on σ being unity. His proof was valid when σ was assumed to be greater than one, but it was not effective for σ less than one. Using the assumptions of marginal productivity, he derived a formula which may be written as

$$\frac{\text{proportional change in } W/Y}{\text{proportional change in } K/L} = -\left(1 - \frac{W}{Y}\right)\left(\frac{\sigma - 1}{\sigma}\right), \quad (2.21)$$

where W/Y is labour's share, $W = wL$ and $Y = pQ = pF(K, L)$.

When σ = 1 the right hand side of (2.21) is zero and labour's share is insensitive to variations in the capital–labour ratio. But to set up all the hypotheses of Bronfenbrenner's method, suppose that a discernible change occurs in the share of labour. Following Bronfenbrenner, it is assumed here that 5 per cent is a modest, discernible change that is probably not due to error in the techniques of statisticians. When σ is greater than unity it can be demonstrated that the rule (2.21) derived from marginal productivity, together with the assumed change in labour's share, leads to a very unlikely outcome (if not a contradiction) in the short run. Equation (2.21) may be rearranged to

$$k = -\frac{l}{(1 - W/Y)}\frac{\sigma}{\sigma - 1},$$

where k and l denote proportional changes in the capital–labour ratio and in labour's share. For a developed economy, a reasonable value for labour's share is 0.7. Now when $l = 5$ per cent

$$k = -\frac{5}{0.3}\frac{\sigma}{\sigma - 1}.$$

An unlikely, implausible, outcome emerges when σ is set at 1.2, for in this case

$$k = -\frac{5}{0.3}\frac{1.2}{0.2} = -\frac{30}{0.3} = -100.$$

That is, for labour's share to grow by 5 per cent the capital–labour ratio must fall to zero when σ is only slightly greater than unity. In terms of Figure 2.2 this means that no capital is used and the economy operates at a point very far to the right along the horizontal axis, not only stretching the imagination, but also the region of validity of the mathematics underlying the derivation of (2.21). Try now a much larger value of σ, say 100. In this case

$$k = -\frac{5}{0.3}\frac{100}{99} = -16.67\,(1.01) = -16.84.$$

For larger and larger values of σ the term, σ/(σ-1), is very close to one and so the magnitude of *k* can never be smaller than 5/0.3 = 16 2/3 per cent. Even this lowest magnitude seems greater than might usually be expected in the short or medium term, especially with technical change ruled out. This outcome seems contradictory and so the hypotheses from which the argument began cannot simultaneously be true. That is, for Bronfenbrenner neoclassical theory must be consistent with a fair degree of constancy of relative shares – at least when σ > 1.

The procedure does not produce such a clear-cut result when σ is very much less than one. Consider the case where σ = 3/7 and the share of labour is again set at 0.7. A 5 per cent change in labour's share is now associated with the capital–labour ratio changing by

$$k = -\frac{5}{0.3}\frac{3/7}{(3/7-1)} = \frac{5}{0.3}\frac{3}{4} = 12.5 \text{ per cent.}$$

An even smaller change in *k* is required when σ = 1/7:

$$k = -\frac{5}{0.3}\frac{1/7}{(1/7-1)} = \frac{5}{0.3}\frac{1}{6} = 2.8 \text{ per cent.}$$

Hence when σ is very much less than unity only a modest change is required in *k* and the quasi-proof by contradiction fails. Bronfenbrenner tested a number of other values of σ using a slightly smaller value for labour's share. His conclusion was much the same: 'We may conclude that conventional marginal distribution theory does in fact imply considerable constancy of relative shares, provided only that the elasticity of substitution between capital and labour is not well below unity' (*ibid.*, p.287).

The analysis may also be easily set in a formal comparative statics framework. Differentiation of (2.21) with respect to σ gives

$$\frac{\partial}{\partial \sigma} \left(\frac{l}{k}\right) = -\left(1 - \frac{W}{Y}\right)\frac{1}{\sigma^2}.$$

When σ is sufficiently greater than one and labour's share is large, the expression on the right is small, implying that, proportionately, labour's share, l, varies little with the capital–labour ratio, k.

2.4   The post-Keynesian critique of neoclassical distribution

Opponents of the neoclassical paradigm have been critical of the logic of the approach, the theoretical constructs, and the techniques of analysis. In addition there is suspicion of the ideology that might motivate the building of neoclassical models. In the later chapters of this book, models are built which incorporate and extend post-Keynesian ideas. In this section the main objections advanced by post-Keynesians to the one-sector, neoclassical theory of distribution are reviewed. An appreciation of the diversity of views among post-Keynesians may be gleaned from Hamouda and Harcourt (1988). In accounts of the debates on growth and distribution, post-Keynesians are sometimes also collected under the heading of the 'Cambridge (England) School'. They have been called other names, including 'Italo-Cantabridgians' by Samuelson (1973, p.852). It is not geography or ethnicity which is common to the group, but rather a 'dislike of mainstream neoclassical theory and IS/LM general equilibrium versions of "Keynesian" theory [and] also their attempts to provide coherent alternative approaches to economic analysis' (Hamouda and Harcourt, 1988, p.2). Here the particular post-Keynesian or Cambridge line which is developed in later chapters is most closely identified with Kaldor.

Post-Keynesians are deeply suspicious of the aggregate production function: 'the [aggregate] production function, like Alice's flamingo, will not keep still but wiggles about and regards us with an injured expression, as soon as we attempt to make use of it' (Champernowne, 1961, pp.223–4). In Section 2.1, it was shown that, if there exists an aggregate production function, the one-sector neoclassical theory of distribution rests on a foundation consisting of perfectly competitive, profit-maximizing firms, all using the same technology.

These specialized assumptions about the nature of firms, which imply that any perfectly competitive firm 'represents' the operation of the supply side, are felt by post-Keynesians to be too removed from reality to be useful in analysis or policy prescription. For Hamouda and Harcourt (1988, p.25), perfect competition and profit maximization are unlikely to be the 'horses for the courses' of most issues in economics. Post-Keynesians do not necessarily agree on the methods and techniques (the horses) to use for a problem (the course). For example, looking ahead to Section 3.5, the representative firm proposed by Kaldor, albeit a very different one from that of the neoclassical school, was dismissed as untenable by Harcourt.

Post-Keynesians dispute the process of aggregation. Aggregation was required in Section 2.1 to prove the existence of the economy-wide production function. There the adding up of factor inputs and outputs across firms presented no difficulty. This was because all firms were assumed to produce the same homogeneous product, using only two inputs, each consisting of homogeneous units, and used by each firm in the same proportions. When aggregating across dissimilar industries, which might not form a mosaic consisting of replicas of a representative activity, inputs and outputs are not likely to be homogeneous. The most potent and widely accepted Cambridge School criticism lies in the challenge to the neoclassical conception of aggregate capital, and the construction of aggregate capital indices to feed into the aggregate production function.[8] There are now many excellent reviews of this debate, and the interested reader is referred to Jones (1976, Section 6.2) and Harcourt (1972, Chapter 4).

In essence Robinson (1953–4, p.83) recognized that the neoclassical insistence on an aggregate capital index led to a circularity of argument: 'we have to begin by taking the rate of interest as given, whereas the main purpose of the production function is to show how wages and the rate of interest (regarded as the wages of capital) are determined by technical conditions and the factor ratio'. In a one-good economy, the commodity satisfies both consumption and investment demands, and homogeneity ensures that output, capital and labour are measured in the same units, and the rate of profit can then be determined from the production function by 'calculating' the marginal product of capital. But problems arise when there are different production techniques, each employing a different capital good to produce just one consumption commodity. Examples may be constructed in which a production method, rejected at a lower rate of interest as unprofitable, might emerge again at a higher interest rate as the most profitable. This may occur even though the technique has a lower capital–labour ratio than the alternatives. Such 'reswitching' contradicted the neoclassical view that firms involved in profit maximizing would not revive less capital-intensive methods of production. That is, it was thought firms would always want to acquire more capital to raise output per worker. The process of 'capital deepening' is discussed in the next section. For the problems on Robinson's agenda, the solution was to measure capital 'in terms of the *labour time* required to produce the different heterogeneous items of capital equipment, with a given rate of interest being used to reflect the different gestation periods of different items' (Jones, 1976, p.127). Economists such as Samuelson (1962, 1966), Solow (1955–6, 1957) and Swann (1956) subsequently rectified their theoretical positions. By 1966, Samuelson (p.583) had moved some way towards the 'horses for courses' pragmatism: 'If all this causes headaches for those nostalgic for the oldtime parables of neoclassical writing, we must remind ourselves that scholars are not born to live an easy existence. We must respect, and appraise, the facts of life.'

Difficulties also emerge in the estimation of economy-wide production functions. Econometricians may be forced to use inappropriate or, at best, rough indices of output and the flows of factor services. For capital, whether or not aggregation is appropriate logically precedes the issue of choice of index. This apart, weighting schemes used to aggregate factors may not allow for variations in the intensity with which different units of the input are used. Another problem is that estimation procedures may be confounded by identification and specification problems. King and Regan (1976, p.49) reach an emphatic conclusion: 'Cobb–Douglas or CES functions fitted to aggregate data do not confirm marginal productivity theory or the existence of a particular type of aggregate technology.' A review of recent developments in the modelling of production techniques and the demand for inputs is given in Berndt (1991, Section 9.1). His summary (p.460) is:

Because of the desire to account for possible heterogeneity of production technologies among industries, many econometricians today prefer to work with more disaggregated data in which prices rather than quantities are exogenous. As a result most recent econometric studies of substitution

relationships among inputs employ general cost or profit functions, . . .
rather than production or transformation functions . . . .

Proponents of marginal productivity have devised multisector
models in which relative price shifts between consumption and
investment goods, the final demands for each type of commodity,
and relative factor rewards all interact in the determination of equilibrium supply and demand. In this Walrasian general equilibrium
configuration, the distributional consequences of a change consist of
components attributable to the effects of substitution between
factors, and to the effects of output adjustments. Variations in
distribution associated with demand adjustments may be more substantial than those associated with substitution possibilities. Rimmer (1989b) reports a quantitative general equilibrium analysis in
which the effects of substitution between factors due to relative wage
changes are small, but output-related adjustments are many times
greater.

Aggregation and the aggregate technology became matters for
intense debate when neoclassical scholars extended to the whole
economy the microeconomic principle of equating factor rewards
with marginal products. Why was this attempted? One suggestion is
that in microeconomic problems the mathematics falls out conveniently, and the implications are well understood, so the temptation
to apply the methodology in macroeconomics is irresistible: 'The
analysis was not at all clear but the metaphysic was pleasantly
soothing' (Robinson and Eatwell, 1973, p.42). Another answer to
the question raises suspicions about the ideology which might motivate the reliance on marginal productivity. This is taken up in the
next section.

2.5 Capital deepening, the importance of capitalists and reswitching

Howard (1979, pp.94–5) points out that capitalists occupy pride of
place on some interpretations of the one-sector neoclassical model.
Capitalists are those who forgo the pleasures of current consumption. Through this self-denial a supply of output is reserved for use
in the next production cycle. The scarce capacity for deferral of
consumption, or 'waiting', may then be regarded as a factor, just like
the labour input:

'Waiting' came to be seen as a genuine factor service on par with labour. As such it also represented an important aspect of ideology. In particular it allowed the argument that the capitalists performed the scarce and costly service of abstaining from current consumption so that interest represented a 'reward' to a factor service commensurate with the effort rewarded by wages. (Howard, 1979, p.94).

Put another way: they also serve who wait. What elevated the inactivity of waiting to its central position was the beneficial effect thought to flow to labour from additions to the capital stock.

The argument is as follows. The process of providing more capital for labour to use, known as *capital deepening*, raises output per worker. However, because of diminishing returns to labour, at some stage additional units of capital will not be associated with increases in output as large as were earlier additions. Capital deepening eventually reduces the output–capital ratio, drives down the marginal product of capital and drives up the marginal product of labour. With profit maximizing and perfect competition this corresponds to an increase in the wage–rental ratio. The importance of factor-augmenting technical change has been ignored in this account, giving the analysis a short-run flavour where the techniques of production are regarded as exogenously fixed, and capital deepening is determined by exogenous forces.

From the earlier discussion of relative shares and the elasticity of substitution, it might be suspected that capital deepening does not always improve labour's share of income. First consider the possibility that a constant output level, Q, is maintained, but more capital is used in production. This situation is shown in Figure 2.2. Assume that initially output Q is produced with the quantities K_1 and L_1. When additional capital is made available, production takes place with inputs K_2 and L_2. In moving between combinations (K_1, L_1) and (K_2, L_2) there is an increase in the wage-rental ratio as represented by the change in the slopes of the isocost lines between C_1C_1 and C_2C_2. As previously noted, if the elasticity of substitution is unity then the proportional change in the capital–labour ratio is equal to the proportional change in w/r, and there will be no change in labour's relative share. In this case the substitution of capital for labour matches the increase in the wage relative to the rental rate: labour may be displaced, but those remaining in employment are (relatively) better rewarded. The result that relative shares are unchanged may be strengthened when the production function has constant returns to scale. In this case the production technology is Cobb–Douglas, each factor's share is constant, and so capital deepening may reduce employment and raise the relative wage, all with no effect on the distribution of income. This Cobb–Douglas-dependent analysis suggests that the owners of the capital stock should be indifferent, on distributional grounds, to whether the work force is smaller or larger. Figure 2.3 shows a similar situation, but here output expands with capital deepening. If the isoquants in this figure are unit elastic then, as before, the relative share of labour will be preserved while employment declines. By appealing to Bronfenbrenner's result (2.21) it can easily be seen that (in both Figures 2.2 and 2.3) capital deepening will cause the share of labour to rise when the elasticity is less than unity and fall when the elasticity is greater.

Figure 2.4 illustrates the case where, at a higher output level, the employment of labour is maintained at its original level, L_1, which might be thought of as full employment. In this situation capital deepening generates an increase in labour's income, $W = wL$.[9] For this to happen the wage rate must increase. If the elasticity of substitution is not greater than one then labour's share of income will not be reduced by capital deepening.[10] When labour and capital are more easily substitutable, then in moving to the higher output level Q_2 there is a fall in the labour–output ratio and a rise in the capital–output ratio. These effects outweigh the increase in the wage–rental ratio and capital's share increases, and so the income of capitalists must also grow.

Capital deepening is now seen to be good for everybody involved in production: when the elasticity is greater than unity, capitalist income grows more; when σ is less than one, the wage bill grows faster. Return now to the case where labour may be displaced by capital deepening. For the constant-returns technologies, it can be shown that the total income of labour remaining in employment will increase by a greater amount than occurs when all jobholders retain their employment.[11] These cases have demonstrated that capital deepening may be beneficial to workers but, contrary to the claim reported at the beginning of this section, it need not always be so. Indeed the last point on the incomes of those remaining in employment may well be a stimulus to those in work to seek to maintain a pool of unemployment.

The relevance of capital deepening was undermined by the phenomenon of capital reswitching. With capital deepening, more

Figure 2.3   Capital deepening with both factor inputs variable

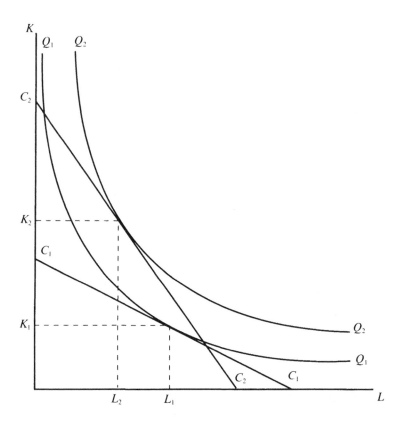

capital-intensive production methods are used as the rate of return falls. So, in neoclassical thinking, firms would not switch back to production techniques which had been superseded by more profitable ones. But under plausible assumptions it can be shown that there might arise values of the rate of return at which firms would revert to using less capital-intensive methods. Obviously the associated reductions in capital intensity, output per worker and the capital–output ratio have implications for the distribution of income. The capital-reswitching debate is reviewed in detail in Harcourt (1972, Chapter 4). The central issues of this book were not motivated by this part of the debate between neoclassical and post-

Figure 2.4   Capital deepening with fixed employment

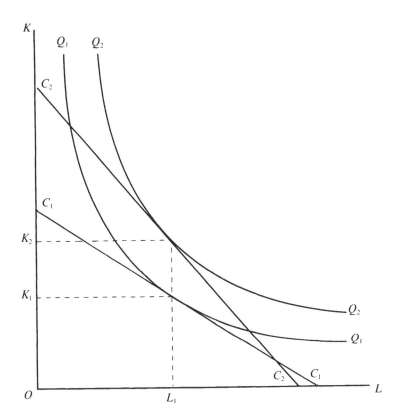

Keynesian scholars; rather, the issues raised in their arguments about the savings propensities of agents and about microeconomic structures are taken up directly. In the next chapter a post-Keynesian theory of income distribution and different assumptions about savings behaviour are investigated.

Notes

1. Further, no distinction is drawn between quantities of the capital good of different vintages. Alternatively, it might be assumed that all grain produced, and not consumed, in one period is used in the production of the next crop.

2. Sargent (1987, p.8) makes the point that 'Regardless of how the assumption is rationalized, ruling out trading of existing stocks of capital is a fundamental feature of the class of 'classical' and 'Keynesian' models that [he is] describing'. The short-run assumption that capital is fixed to each firm overrides the need for temporal assumptions about the possibility of trade between firms in existing units of capital.
3. This result depends on Euler's theorem, which is discussed later in the text.
4. To see this, fix output at Q and differentiate $Q = F(K, L)$ with respect to L to obtain

$$0 = D_1F(K, L)\frac{dK}{dL} + D_2F(K, L),$$

where

$$\frac{dK}{dL} = -\frac{D_2F(K, L)}{D_1F(K, L)}.$$

5. This property is required to ensure that, in the case of two inputs, solutions (2.1) to the profit-maximizing problem are sufficient as well as necessary (see Smith, 1982, p.37).
6. Total cost, $C = wL + rK$, and so the equation of any isocost line is

$$K = \frac{C}{r} - \frac{w}{r}L.$$

The slope of this line is $-(w/r)$.
7. See Allen (1968, pp.51–2) who shows that the production function with constant returns to scale and unit elasticity of substitution everywhere is the Cobb–Douglas technology.
8. There are results which set out the conditions required to ensure that index number aggregates may be constructed for capital similar to those used for output. See the resume in Stiglitz and Uzawa (1969, pp.124–5). Alternatively the properties of the production technology may be further restricted (see Solow, 1955–6, pp.286–7).
9. W is given by

$$W = D_1F(K, L)L = F(K, L) - D_1F(K, L)K,$$

and the change in W induced by capital deepening is

$$\frac{dW}{dK} = D_1F(K, L) - D_2F(K, L) - K\left\{D_1^2F(K, L) + D_2D_1F(K, L)\frac{dL}{dK}\right\}$$

$$= -K\left\{D_1^2F(K, L) + D_2D_1F(K, L)\frac{dL}{dK}\right\}, \tag{2A.1}$$

where $\frac{dL}{dK}$ = the change in employment induced by capital deepening. When L is unchanged, the second term inside the { } brackets is zero and

$$\frac{dW}{dK} = -KD_1^2F(K, L).$$

As there are diminishing returns to capital $D_1^2 F(K, L) < 0$, the change in the income of labour is positive. That is, labour's absolute income is raised by capital deepening when employment is maintained.

10. This is just another application of Bronfenbrenner's result (2.21).
11. Equation (2A.1) of note 9 describes the change in the income of labour caused by a deepening of capital. Now when F has constant returns to scale,

$$D_1^2 F(K, L) = f''(k)/L \text{ and } D_2 D_1 F(K, L) = -kf''(k)/L,$$

where

$$k = K/L, f(k) = F(\frac{K}{L}, 1) \text{ and } f'(k) = D_1 F(K, L)$$

(see Dixon, Bowles and Kendrick, 1980, pp.224–9). Hence

$$\frac{dW}{dK} = -kf''(k)\left\{1 - k\frac{dL}{dK}\right\}. \tag{2A.2}$$

$f''(k)$ is negative because of diminishing returns, and so:

(i)   if $\frac{dL}{dK} < 0$ then $\frac{dW}{dK} > 0$; and

(ii) if $\frac{dL}{dK} > 0$ then $\frac{dW}{dK} \gtrless 0$ as $\frac{dL}{dK} \lessgtr \frac{1}{k} = \frac{L}{K}$.

Notice from (2A.2) that in case (i) where labour becomes unemployed, W increases by more than when all existing jobs are retained. When capital deepening produces a net expansion of employment (case (ii) above) W may grow, depending on the relative sizes of the marginal and average labour–capital ratios.

3. Some Post-Keynesian Approaches to Distribution

During the 1950s, dissatisfaction with the marginal productivity theory of distribution motivated Cambridge School scholars such as Boulding (1950, 1953), Champernowne (1958), Kahn (1959), Kaldor (1955–6), Kalecki (1954) and Robinson (1956) to propose alternative formulations. Naturally there was cross-fertilization of ideas. For instance, Kaldor (1955–6, p.94, n2) acknowledged intellectual debts to both Robinson and Kalecki. The analysis in this chapter is devoted to the contributions of Boulding and Kaldor. The contributions of the former to distribution theory have languished relative to the attention paid to the latter – yet the two have a close relationship. Both willingly embraced the widow's cruse and Danaid jar notions of the *Treatise*:

If entrepreneurs choose to spend a portion of their profits on consumption (and there is, of course, nothing to prevent them from doing this) the effect is to increase the profits on the sale of liquid consumption goods by an amount exactly equal to the amount of profits which have thus been expended. ... Thus profits, as a source of capital increment for entrepreneurs, are a widow's cruse which remains undepleted however much of them may be devoted to riotous living. When on the other hand, entrepreneurs are making losses, and seek to recoup these losses by curtailing their normal expenditure on consumption, i.e. by saving more, the cruse become a Danaid jar which can never be filled up; for the effect of this reduced expenditure is to inflict on the producers of consumption-goods a loss of an equal amount. Thus the diminution of their wealth as a class is as great, in spite of their savings, as it was before. (Keynes, 1930, Vol. I, p.139)

This last quotation is precisely the one used by Kaldor (1955–6, p.94, n1) to validate the description of his theory as Keynesian in spirit. The treatment of entrepreneurial incomes as being the result of their expenditure, in preference to the reverse causation, is common to most post-Keynesians. Allusions to the widow's cruse occur in four chapters in Boulding's *Reconstruction of Economics*, in which is introduced a balance sheet approach to macroeconomics. Classical economists had tended to assume that saving was undertaken only by entrepreneurs and the recipients of property income. It appears from the quotation taken from the *Treatise* that Keynes drew a similar distinction between the earners of different types of incomes – the levels of the cruse and the jar were only affected by entrepreneurial savings intentions. Kaldor (1955–6, p.94, n2) chose to depart from the 'restrictive assumption that savings are entirely supplied out of profits'. Rather, those who worked for wages and salaries saved part of this income, but the propensity to do so was not as great as the desire to save from profits. Saving was no longer a scarce predilection, to be found amongst only the patient capitalists described in Section 2.5. Boulding did not explicitly include savings propensities in the equations of his theory of distribution, nor did he attempt to model differences in these propensities for the main actors. This was done much later (see Rimmer, 1989). Had Boulding done so, one issue of ferocious debate between Keynesian and neoclassical theorists might never have arisen, or at least might have proceeded along other lines.

To appreciate this point, the chronological order of developments must be clear. Boulding's initial account was published in 1950, whereas Kaldor's model was unveiled in 1955–6. Five years later, Pasinetti (1961–2) announced a model which corrected what he saw as a flaw in Kaldor's account. After another four years, Samuelson and Modigliani (1966) objected to the Pasinetti approach on mathematical grounds, because it overlooked the possibility of other 'dual' outcomes; and they objected from an historical perspective, because it assumed the existence of immutable classes of workers and capitalists. Simultaneously with Samuelson and Modigliani, Kaldor (1966) published a rebuttal which redeemed the validity of Pasinetti's result in a slightly modified form. But if two obvious assumptions had been added, Boulding's theory would have taken all of these researchers directly to this neo-Pasinetti result, saving a lot of paper and unnecessary mathematical analysis. Interest in the Samuelson–Modigliani dual solutions has persisted (see recent contributions to the *Oxford Economic Papers*, 1991).

This chapter begins with an account of the Kaldor and Pasinetti approaches. The first two sections provide a comparison of the effects of different assumptions about savings propensities. In

Section 3.2 the objections of Samuelson and Modigliani are raised. The neo-Pasinetti theorem is developed in Section 3.3. The chronological short-cut apparent in Boulding's work is presented in Section 3.4. In the final section the microeconomic structure implicit in Kaldor's analysis is investigated, and his preference for full-employment equilibria is explained.

3.1 The basic Kaldorian model

The exposition by Kaldor of his first theory of income distribution was in terms of a model in which total income Y, was assumed to consist of the two components, aggregate wages W, and aggregate profits P, so that

$$Y = W + P. \tag{3.1}$$

Pasinetti (1961–2) emphasized the assumption that there are two classes, one of which earns wage and salary income and potentially receives a return P_N on its savings, while the other, a class of entrepreneurs, has only one source of income, namely P_C generated as a return on its savings. Aggregate profits may then be written as

$$P = P_N + P_C. \tag{3.2}$$

Savings out of wages, denoted by S_W, wage-earners' savings out of non-wage income S_N and saving by the one-income class S_P are each assumed to be given by

$$
\begin{aligned}
S_W &= s_W W \\
S_N &= s_N P_N \\
S_P &= s_P P_C,
\end{aligned}
\tag{3.3}
$$

where s_W, s_N and s_P are savings propensities. The level of total savings is given by

$$S = S_P + S_N + S_W. \tag{3.4}$$

Assume that the economy is closed to trade and there is no government. Equilibrium requires the equality of planned saving and planned investment (I):

$$S = I. \tag{3.5}$$

A formal analysis of this system of equations is undertaken in the next section. Before that we look first at the Keynesian mechanism at work in Kaldor's version of equations (3.1)–(3.5). His distribution result may be derived from the national income identity (3.1), the equilibrium condition (3.5), and the savings equations on the assumption that wage and salary earners accumulate savings from the interest paid on earlier savings at the same rate as entrepreneurs. That is, assume

$$s_N = s_P,$$

so that total savings out of profits is given by

$$S = s_W W + s_P P_C + s_N P_N = s_W W + s_P(P_C + P_N) = s_W W + s_P P \tag{3.4a}$$

Suppose now that entrepreneurs or capitalists decide to raise expenditure on investment. When the economy is operating at full employment – an assumption central to Kaldor's analysis – investment rises as a proportion of real income. This can only happen if disposable income is diverted from consumption to raise the ratio of savings to income. From Kaldor's savings equation (3.4a)

$$S = s_W W + s_P P = s_W(Y - P) + s_P P = s_W Y + (s_P - s_W)P,$$

and the savings ratio is given by

$$S/Y = s_W + (s_P - s_W) P/Y. \tag{3.6}$$

When savings propensities are constant and $s_P > s_W$, the planned savings ratio can only be increased by a redistribution of income in favour of profits. The assumption that $s_P > s_W$ is crucial, for if s_P were less than s_W then an increase in S/Y could only be brought about by a reduction in the capitalist share. (Consider the rigidity imposed by the possibility that $s_P = s_W$. Then, with fixed savings propensities, the savings ratio would be unresponsive to the distribution of income.)

Because there is full employment, a planned increase in investment does not raise activity and real income, but *nominal* income adjusts. For the increase in investment, price must be flexible and, crucially for the redistribution, it must also be assumed that the money wage rate is fixed. When there is full employment, denoted L_f, an increase in nominal income translates into an increase in nominal profits. Real wages and the wage share fall, inducing a redistribution to profits and a rise in real profits. The analogy with the widow's cruse is obvious: by spending more the one-income class has increased both its real income and its share.

In 1961, Kaldor firmly rejected the neoclassical approach: . . . Marshall, Clark, Wicksell and Böhm-Bawerk . . . had tried to show how factor prices and distributive shares depended on the production function and [Kaldor] thought this was all nonsense. . . . The difficulty was that the neoclassical school tried to apply a generalised marginal productivity theory to the economy as a whole, a job which [Kaldor] now felt simply could not be done. (Report by Lutz of Kaldor's comments, see Lutz and Hague, 1961, p.294)

It is not surprising, therefore, that Kaldor eschewed the use of a neoclassical production function in his theory of distribution. On the problem of aggregation of capital, he was more ambivalent:

It was true that it was hard to measure capital, yet in Mr Kaldor's model . . . the quantity of capital also played an important role despite the difficulties of measuring it . . . Mr Kaldor did not feel that [these] difficulties of measurement should lead us to abandon all attempts at measurement. The possibility depended on the purpose for which the measure was required. For some purposes, the measures needed to be more exact than for others. (*ibid.*, p.299, 305)

The unambiguous rejection of a role for production functions and marginal products in determining distribution has often been criticized. Kaldor countered with a microeconomy consisting of firms with constant average cost over most of their output range, and which set price using a mark-up rule. This representative firm has an important role in Kaldor's rationalization for investigating full-employment equilibria (see Section 3.5).

A Keynesian approach in the sense of the *General Theory* might be formulated using neoclassical concepts to determine the level of national income as well as distribution. But some argue this was not intended: 'Keynes rejected the notion that either the income of labour or the amount of employment could be determined by marginalist principles operating at the microeconomic level in the labor market' (Kregel, 1979, pp.49–50). Others argue, that in the short run, employment is determined by aggregate demand, and then the real wage and labour's share is determined from the marginal product. (See, for example, Riach, 1969, pp.551–2.) Johnson's view (1973, p.173) was that, after the influence of aggregate demand has been exerted on employment, and provided a weather eye is kept on the influence of the fixed money wage rate, the neoclassical mechanism will operate. Whatever Keynes intended, there is an opening for the use of marginal productivity. Specifically, a production function can be introduced for which, in the short run, the real marginal productivity of labour falls as output rises. With the money wage fixed this implies that prices rise with output. What happens to the wage share then depends on the substitution possibilities in the sense of the discussion in Chapter 2 of neoclassical theory. Integration of neoclassical production functions and perfect competition with Kaldor's theory of distribution is discussed in Chapter 4.

Kaldor applied his distribution theory to modify Harrod's condition that balanced growth is only possible when the values of the overall average savings propensity s, and the capital–output ratio v, desired by capitalists, bring the 'warranted growth rate of capital' ($= s/v$) into equality with the 'natural rate of growth', that is the sum of the growth rates of the labour force l, and of labour productivity r. In his analysis Harrod assumed that s ($= S/Y = I/Y$), v, l and r are independent of each other, so that the equality

$$v (I/Y) = l + r$$

is only accidentally satisfied. But if we substitute into Harrod's condition the equation for I/Y,

$$I/Y = s_W + (s_P - s_W)P/Y,$$

derived from (3.6) by setting $S = I$, then

$$v \{s_W + (s_P - s_W)P/Y\} = l + r.$$

It is now clear that, within the region where Kaldor's equation for the savings ratio is valid, the warranted rate can adjust to reach equality with the natural rate when the profit share is flexible.

3.2   Savings behaviour and income shares

The system (3.1)–(3.5) consists of seven equations in 13 variables, so that to solve the model six variables must be exogenously determined or further structural equations added. Before investigating closures proposed during the 1950s and 1960s, the system (3.1)–(3.5) is first condensed into just one equation. If equation (3.3) modelling the accumulation of each component of saving is substituted into (3.4), and the result substituted into the equilibrium condition, (3.5), then

$$I = s_W W + s_N P_N + s_P P_C. \tag{3.7}$$

When Pasinetti's disaggregation of profits in (3.2) is substituted into the national income identity, (3.1), and rearranged, then

$$W = Y - P_N - P_C. \tag{3.8}$$

Substitution of (3.8) into (3.7) gives

$$I = s_W Y + (s_N - s_W)P_N + (s_P - s_W)P_C, \tag{3.9}$$

although this is often written as

$$I/Y = s_W + (s_N - s_W)(P_N/Y) + (s_P - s_W)P_C/Y.$$

Equation (3.9) involves seven variables and is a convenient vehicle for the discussion of a number of closure options. Common to the closures analysed here is the assumption that

$$s_W, s_N \text{ and } s_P \text{ are constant,} \tag{3.10}$$

which means that (3.9) is a relationship among four variables. It now follows from (3.3) that savings out of the three types of income accumulate in simple proportions to the levels of these three incomes.

Pasinetti (1961–2, p.97) proposed that workers save out of all forms of income at the same rate. That is,

$$s_N = s_W, \tag{3.11}$$

in which case (3.9) simplifies to

$$I = s_W Y + (s_P - s_W)P_C. \tag{3.12}$$

According to Pasinetti (1961–2, p.96) there is implicit in Kaldor's (1955–6) paper a closure with

$$P_N = 0. \tag{3.13}$$

This assumption also serves to simplify (3.9) into (3.12). Pasinetti claimed Kaldor's implicit or supposed use of (3.13) to be a 'logical slip'. Condition (3.11) means that workers are indifferent to the sources of their income in deciding their consumption–savings patterns, whereas Pasinetti's condition (3.13) occurs when workers receive no return on savings or have never saved, which is the case when s_W is taken to be zero in all periods. A determination of s_N cannot then be made. Sen (1963, p.54) assumed that 'if a worker earns some income from property as profits, his savings behaviour out of that income is the same as that of the capitalists proper'. That is, Sen's view appears to be that workers' attitudes to savings out of wages and salaries and out of profits may be different, and that

$$s_N = s_P. \tag{3.14}$$

This is the assumption made in the previous section to derive Kaldor's savings equation. The reduced form equation (3.9) for the model then simplifies to

$$I = s_W Y + (s_P - s_W)(P_N + P_C), \tag{3.15}$$

which may be written as

$$I = s_W Y + (s_P - s_W)P. \tag{3.16}$$

P represents 'the income of property owners generally, and not only of entrepreneurs' (Kaldor, 1955–6 p.95). This view was put more forcibly in 1966, when Kaldor had moved completely away from the division of society into two classes. The theories resulting from the savings behaviour assumed in each of (3.11), (3.13) and (3.14) are summarized in the following tableau:

Pasinetti	*Pasinetti on Kaldor*	*Sen*
$s_N = s_W$	$P_N = 0$	$s_N = s_P$
$I = s_W Y + (s_P - s_W)P_C$	$I = s_W Y + (s_P - s_W)P_C$	$I = s_W Y + (s_P - s_W)P$
$P = P_N + P_C$	$P = P_C$	$P = P_N + P_C$

To see conveniently the effects of these different assumptions, we first introduce one more constraint. In line with the importance to Keynes of 'animal spirits' in the determination of investment, Kaldor (1955–6, p.371) assumed that 'investment, or rather, the ratio of investment to output can be treated as an independent variable, invariant with respect to the . . . savings propensities'. Here it is assumed that

$$I = \bar{I}, \qquad (3.17)$$

the level $\bar{I}$ being exogenously determined, and the investment equations in the tableau above now involve two endogenous variables (either the pair P_C and Y, or the pair P and Y). If

$$s_P \neq s_W$$

then these equations may be rearranged to obtain either

$$P/Y \text{ or } P_C/Y = (\bar{I}/Y - s_W)/(s_P - s_W). \qquad (3.18)$$

Equation (3.18) for P/Y explains the share of total profits in income, whereas as an equation for P_C/Y it explains the share of income received by capitalists (the one-income class). In either version of the equation, the share is determined by the same expression involving savings ratios and the ratio of investment to income.

Kaldor argued that the entrepreneurial savings rate exceeds that of workers, because 'the bulk of profits accrues in the form of company profits and a high proportion of companies' marginal profits is put to reserve' (*ibid.*, p.96, n1). When

$$s_P > s_W \qquad (3.19)$$

the profit shares vary directly with (a) the investment-income coefficient, I/Y; and (b) the capitalists' propensity to consume, $(1 - s_P)$.

Point (a) is consistent with the stylized fact that there is a high correlation between the share of profits in income and the share of investment in output. Coupled with the assumptions of full employment and flexible prices, relative to the nominal wage, point (b) is the widow's cruse or Danaid jar. With $s_P > s_W$, the values of the shares given in (3.18) will be positive only if s_W is less than $\bar{I}/Y$, while the shares accumulating to workers (that is, $1 - P_C/Y$) and to wages and salaries (that is, $1 - P/Y$) will be positive only if s_p is greater than $\bar{I}/Y$. This last inequality is also the condition which ensures that the profit shares are not greater than one. Unlike Kaldor, Pasinetti was unable to determine the share of all profits from the system of relations and assumptions used so far. Recall that the system is

$$I = s_W Y + (s_N - s_W)P_N + (s_P - s_W)P_C, \qquad (3.9)$$

$$s_W, s_N \text{ and } s_p \text{ are constant}, \qquad (3.10)$$

$$s_N = s_W \text{ or } P_N = 0 \text{ or } s_N = s_P,$$
$$(3.11) \text{ or } (3.13) \text{ or } (3.14)$$

$$I = \bar{I}, \qquad (3.17)$$

and

$$s_P > s_W. \qquad (3.19)$$

This collection is here referred to as the 'basic Kaldorian model'. To obtain the share of total profits, Pasinetti (1961–2, Sections 3 and 4) added to this system the equations

$$K_W/K = S_W/S \qquad (3.20)$$

$$P_W = r\,K_W \qquad (3.21)$$

$$r = P/K, \qquad (3.22)$$

where equation (3.20) relates the ratio of the total stock of capital owned by wage and salary earners, K_W, to the proportion of total savings accounted for by workers; (3.21) is a formal statement of the assumption that workers' returns are calculated using the prevailing rate of interest (r); and the identity (3.22) is a formal statement of the long-run assumption that the rate of interest and the profit rate are equal (*ibid.*, p.98). Equations (3.20) and (3.21) are long-run in spirit. The first is valid only if we assume that the entire capital stock in use at the conclusion of the period did not exist at the commencement of the analysis, that it was acquired from savings generated throughout the period, and that a state had been reached in which the stocks of capital owned by workers and capitalists grew at the same steady rate. Equation (3.21) abstracts from the short-run diversity of returns on different investments, and to different classes of investors. In particular, no account is taken of the generally lower rates of return available to investors placing small amounts of savings.

With the additional equations the system can be manipulated to obtain:[1]

$$(1 - s_W \, Y/\bar{I})\frac{P}{K}\frac{s_P}{s_P - s_W} = (1 - s_W \, Y/\bar{I})\frac{\bar{I}}{K}\frac{1}{s_P - s_W}. \qquad (3.23)$$

Provided that $(1 - s_W \, Y/\bar{I})$ is non-zero, that is if

$$\bar{I} \neq s_W Y, \qquad (3.24)$$

(3.23) may be simplified to

$$r = P/K = (1/s_P)(\bar{I}/K),$$

and the profit share is given by

$$\frac{P}{Y} = \frac{1}{s_P}\frac{\bar{I}}{Y}. \qquad (3.25)$$

This last equation contains a surprising message: when workers save the same proportion of their profit income as of their wages and salaries, in the long run the distribution of income between total profits and wages is independent of this savings propensity. But, as can be seen from (3.18), s_W influences the distribution of income between *classes* in the theories of Pasinetti, Kaldor and Sen. The theories of Kaldor and Sen also yield Pasinetti's result when s_W is negligible. Pasinetti's result is again the widow's cruse or Danaid jar.

However, the validity of Pasinetti's long-run theory of the profit share depends on the assumption (3.24) that $\bar{I} \neq s_W Y$. We have already seen that the share of capitalist income, given by equation (3.18), will be positive only if $\bar{I}$ is greater than $s_W Y$, which is just a particular case of (3.24). Samuelson and Modigliani (1966, Sections 5 and 10) found that, corresponding to the case $\bar{I} = s_W Y$, there is a 'dual' solution which Pasinetti had ignored. In this case the capitalist share of income is zero, rentiers own none of the current capital stock and are unable to invest, so that the added equation (3.20) reduces to

$$S_W = S, \tag{3.26}$$

(as now, in the long-run steady state, $K_W = K$). Workers' savings are given by

$$S_W = s_W(W + P_N) = s_W Y,$$

while if the capital stock is growing steadily at rate g then

$$S = I = gK,$$

and the dual condition implies

$$K/Y = s_W/g.$$

Therefore Samuelson and Modigliani arrived at a 'golden age' in which only the savings propensity of workers matters and the capital–output ratio settles at a value consistent with the exogenously given growth rate g and savings propensity s_W. In Kaldor's estimation (1966, p.311) 'the end of it all is not a violent revolution *à la* Marx, but the cosy world of Harrod, Domar and Solow, where there is only a single savings propensity applicable to the economy'.

Samuelson and Modigliani offered two criticisms: the first challenged the reality of the Pasinetti inequality $\bar{I} > s_W Y$, and the second challenged the class structure underlying the assumptions made about savings propensities. For Pasinetti the inequality $\bar{I} > s_W Y$ guaranteed the existence of a golden age with

$$\frac{P}{Y} = \frac{1}{s_P} \frac{\bar{I}}{Y}$$

when the level of investment is consistent with full employment.

Samuelson and Modigliani (1966, p.274, n1) also objected that 'Pasinetti's [inequality] can not hold for s_W any higher than a modest 0.05', this statement being based on numbers which are 'econometrically reasonable for a mixed economy like the U.S., U.K. or Western Europe'. Thus the investment–income coefficient could be quite small; in fact, just greater than 0.05. In a developed economy a value so low for the ratio of gross investment to income does not seem plausible. The second line of attack expressed dissatisfaction

with the assumption of 'permanent' classes of pure profit and mixed income receivers with given and unchanging saving propensities . . . [because] . . . in a modern industrial society the capitalist class is not a hereditary caste: its membership at any point of time is far from limited to people who were born into it by virtue of inherited wealth. (*Ibid.*, p.297)

In analysing the first criticism, Kaldor (1966, p.312) suggested that, in a world where enterprises are organized as corporations and profit income is paid as dividends, the appropriate measure of the savings propensity of wage and salary earners should be derived from the savings of the working class made available to the corporate sector. In particular, workers' investment in consumer durables (other than housing) should be deducted from workers' savings before s_W is estimated. Kaldor did this using US and UK data for 1966 and found values of s_W smaller than Samuelson and Modigliani's 'modest 0.05'. On the second criticism, Kaldor's response was that he had

always regarded the high savings propensity out of profits as something which attaches to the nature of business income, and not to the wealth (or other peculiarities) of the individuals who own property. It is the enterprise, not the particular body of individuals owning it at any one time which finds it necessary, in a dynamic world of increasing returns, to plough back a proportion of the profits earned as a kind of 'prior charge' on earnings in order to ensure the survival of the enterprise in the long run. . . . Hence the high savings propensity attaches to profits as such, not to capitalists as such. (*Ibid.*, p.310)

This more forceful statement of the high savings propensity being associated with individuals and not classes is consistent with Kaldor's view in 1955–6 (quoted above).

Nevertheless, Samuelson and Modigliani had the mathematical advantage of having located alternative solutions to the Pasinetti theory. One way of countering Samuelson and Modigliani's criticisms is to appeal to Kaldor's neo-Pasinetti formulation. We turn now to a discussion of the neo-Pasinetti theorem and then add the aggregate balance sheets for businesses and households devised by Boulding (1950).

3.3 The neo-Pasinetti theorem

Kaldor swiftly and decisively dealt with the criticisms levelled at post-Keynesian theory by Samuelson and Modigliani. This was accomplished in a comment published at the same time as their critique. In an appendix to his comment, Kaldor developed a model which preserves the distinguishing features of the post-Keynesian framework and which does not have the defects seized on by the critics. Here we examine how in this model the main features of Pasinetti's distribution result are sustained. The model is extended to the short run and, in place of the valuation ratio, Tobin's q is introduced to the analysis. Later in this book the version of the model developed in this chapter is extended to incorporate an imperfectly competitive industrial sector.

Kaldor considered an economy with corporations owned by shareholders. The corporations were controlled by managers and directors, who financed investment plans from retained profits or from the issue of new securities. A 'household' sector was included which received income in the form of wages and dividends, and with its only savings avenue being the purchase of corporate securities. Corporations cannot acquire securities, nor is money explicitly included. Both groups' savings could be valued and these values could be added if the model was expanded to include a role for money. Skott (1981, pp.569–72; 1989, Chapter 5) has developed this line of research.

In the aggregate, households are assumed to save the same fraction (s_h) of wage and property income, while corporations retain a proportion (s_c) of current profits. Taken together, total wage income, W, and total dividends, $(1 - s_c)P$, create a *demand* for securities given by

$$s_h \{W + (1 - s_c)P\}.$$

Households contribute to the *supply* of securities by selling those purchased in earlier periods. This happens in the households of inactive workers and entrepreneurs who dissave to fund current consumption. By comparison, the demand for securities is generated by households in a different position in the life cycle, namely households with employed workers saving for retirement, or active entrepreneurs attempting to build valuable portfolios. In realizing capital gains, shareholders also contribute to the supply of securities. Shareholders might expect that a proportion of retained profits will generate further dividends in the future, which they realize now by disposing of some of their portfolios. More directly, shareholders might perceive that their personal incomes should include retained profits. Given the saving propensity, s_h, they are able to maintain a level of spending from non-wage income consistent with these perceptions by realizing capital gains. Probably the most important consideration in households' decisions to realize capital gains is the uncertain nature of this type of income.

In the initial version of the neo-Pasinetti theorem, Kaldor (1966, p.317) combined the contributions to securities demand from distributed profits with the supply of securities coming from consumption out of capital gains, and called the difference the shareholders' net consumption out of capital. He modelled this as a proportion c of capital gains G contributing to the supply of securities. Here we follow the version of the model developed in a footnote (*ibid.*, p.318), in which the contributions of households to supply and to demand in the securities markets are treated separately. The proportion c of capital gains will now be used to model the aggregate household contribution to the supply of securities. When c is set at $1 - s_h$, the model then corresponds to the version developed in Kaldor's footnote.

The contribution to the supply of securities made by corporations is postulated to be a proportion i of total business investment expenditure. Thus equilibrium in the securities market occurs when

$$s_h \{W + (1 - s_c)P\} = cG + iI. \qquad (3.27)$$

Gross economy-wide savings are given by

$$s_c P + s_h \{W + (1 - s_c)P\}$$

where $s_c P$ is corporate savings or retentions, and $s_h \{W + (1 - s_c)P\}$ represents total savings out of wages and distributed profits. But there are possible re-sales of securities which were purchased by households in earlier periods. This activity reduces economy-wide savings by the amount of the realized capital gain. Therefore (net) aggregate savings are

$$S = s_c P + s_h \{W + (1 - s_c)P\} - cG. \quad (3.28)$$

Together with equation (3.27) this expression for aggregate savings implies

$$S = s_c P + iI. \quad (3.29)$$

Thus the condition for equilibrium in the securities market determines the net savings of the household sector in terms of two corporate policy variables which reflect the decisions taken with respect to profit retention, and the external financing of investment. Any role in the determination of savings plans for the savings propensity of the household sector or the levels of wages and capital gains has been eliminated by the financial system postulated by Kaldor. Skott (1981, p.568) also derived this result from the equations of the neo-Pasinetti model, but failed to notice that only the equilibrium condition for the securities market was required.

Equation (3.29) and the condition that *ex ante* savings is equated with *ex ante* investment,

$$S = I, \quad (3.30)$$

yield

$$s_c P = (1 - i)I, \quad (3.31)$$

and division by national income, *Y*, gives

$$\frac{P}{Y} = \frac{(1 - i)}{s_c} \frac{I}{Y}.$$

This is a result similar to Pasinetti's original theorem. In the neo-Pasinetti result the savings behaviour of the household sector has no influence on the share of profits in national income. Further, this share does not depend on the especially high savings propensity of

an hereditary caste of capitalists, but rather on the corporate retention rate. In addition, the share of profits now depends on i, the
propensity of enterprises to seek finance from the household sector.
Should $i = 0$ (meaning that corporations do not offer new securities)
we obtain an equation which, save for the interpretation of the
symbol s_c, is Pasinetti's original result. In both models the profit
share depends on investment expenditure. In the neo-Pasinetti
model, investment generates a level of current profits which include
retained earnings equal to the investment expenditure financed by
previously retained profits. Again the widow's cruse analogy
emerges.

Variations in capital gains (G), which measure the change in the
market valuation of securities, are part of the adjustment to equilibrium. Kaldor saw G varying with changes in dividends, earnings
per share, and with fluctuations in the valuation ratio v. The latter is
the ratio of the market value of securities to the book value of the
capital employed by the corporations. The system consisting of
(3.27), (3.28) and (3.30) may be solved for v as well as the distribution of income. To introduce the valuation ratio into the model,
Kaldor proceeded as follows. If

$$p_s = \text{price per share,}$$
$$N = \text{number of shares already issued, and}$$
$$K = \text{value of the capital stock}$$

then

$$v = \frac{p_s N}{K}. \tag{3.32}$$

From this definition the equation

$$G = \bar{N} \Delta p_s = \bar{K} \Delta v + v \, \Delta K - p_s \Delta N \tag{3.33}$$

may be deduced.[2] In it the occurrences of N and K refer to initial
values of these variables, prior to the sale of the number ΔN of new
securities, the variation, Δp_s in share prices, and the change in the
capital stock, ΔK. For this reason the occurrences of N and K have a
superscript bar, making clear the definition of G in terms of the
increase in value of existing shares held by households. In (3.33)
Kaldor assumed

$$p_s \Delta N = iI, \qquad (3.34)$$

so that the value of investment financed from the sale of new securities (that is, iI) was equated with the value of the ΔN new securities at the price prevailing when they were issued. With i and I fixed, this implies that the volume of a new issue is determined endogenously by (3.34). In particular, ΔN is removed from direct management control as it cannot be exogenous in this formulation of the model. Rather, the implicit time ordering of decisions is from the determination of the value of planned investment, I, to the number of shares or securities which must be sold, at price p_s, to finance the proportion iI, of investment expenditure. The assumption that I is exogenously fixed is relaxed in Chapter 5.

Also in (3.29) Kaldor set

$$I = \Delta K \qquad (3.35)$$

where, it has already been noted, K was taken to be the historical book value estimate of the value of the capital stock. For the extensions of the model proposed in later chapters, it is convenient to transfer attention from the valuation ratio to Tobin's q, which differs from v in the use of replacement cost to evaluate capital assets. Consequently (3.35) cannot be used.

> In the absence of direct price quotations or a ready market for capital assets in stock or in use, market values are approximated by simple procedures such as applying straight-line depreciation to the original cost of fixed capital and then converting the undepreciated balance from historical cost to replacement cost by use of price indices applicable to broad classes of plant and equipment. (Von Furstenberg *et al.*, 1980, p.397)

For a one-good model a unit of new capital has the same price p as a unit of the good sold for consumption. If M denotes the number of units of this single commodity used for capital purposes, then the replacement cost of capital is

$$K = pM.$$

Suppose that at the end of the previous period the existing $\bar{M}$ units of capital are valued at price p, and that these $\bar{M}$ units do not depreciate. Then I_R units of the commodity are added to the capital stock when price is $\bar{p} + \Delta p$. The market valuation of capital becomes

$$\bar{K} + \Delta K = (\bar{M} + I_R)(\bar{p} + \Delta p)$$
$$= \bar{K} + I_R(\bar{p} + \Delta p) + \bar{M}\Delta p$$
$$= \bar{K} + I + \bar{M}\Delta p,$$

and the equation for ΔK comparable to (3.35) is

$$\Delta K = I + \bar{M}\Delta p. \tag{3.36}$$

One way of reconciling (3.36) with (3.35) is to introduce an allowance for depreciation, D, as the reduction in value of existing items of capital by exactly the amount Δp per unit. That is, write

$$D = -\bar{M}\Delta p.$$

Realistically, depreciation and price changes are not necessarily so intimately connected. The first is a function, for example, of accounting regimes, taxation allowances and changes in valuation caused by technological obsolescence. On the other hand, in this model the price p is one of the equilibrating variables which adjusts to produce equilibrium in the commodity and securities markets. Moreover, such a depreciation allowance negates the process described above in the quotation from von Furstenberg, as being used to calculate replacement cost. In fact, setting $D = -\bar{M}\Delta p$ would recover the valuation of capital appropriate in the previous period.

Substitution of equations (3.35) and (3.34) into equation (3.33) for G produces

$$G = \bar{K}\Delta v + (v - i)I, \tag{3.37}$$

while with (3.36) and v replaced by q, G is given by

$$G = \bar{K}\Delta q + (q - i)I + q\bar{M}\Delta p. \tag{3.38}$$

The form of G does not influence the derivation of the neo-Pasinetti theorem. That is, the method used to value the capital stock has no impact on the theory of distribution obtained from the model.

Kaldor was interested in discovering golden age equilibria in which the valuation ratio is not disturbed from the value consistent with the capital stock growing at a constant rate g. He therefore set

$$\Delta v = 0. \tag{3.39}$$

With this condition the model can be solved to obtain the steady state value for v which ensures that household sector savings are sufficient to take up new issues from the corporate sector. Kaldor's steady state value is obtained by substituting the neo-Pasinetti result (3.31) into the securities market equilibrium condition (3.27), and then using equation (3.37) for G. In doing this, it is assumed that $c = (1 - s_h)$. That is, households have the same savings propensity for capital gains as for wages and for dividends. The expression obtained for v is

$$v = 1 - \frac{1 - s_h(Y/I)}{1 - s_h} = s_h \frac{Y/I - 1}{1 - s_h}. \qquad (3.40)$$

When the capital stock in the golden age is growing at the constant rate g, $I = gK$, and the valuation ratio v, remains unchanged so long as the capital output ratio is constant. This will happen when national income also grows at the rate g. From (3.40) it can be seen that v is a function of household savings behaviour and the inverse of the ratio of investment to income. Also note that the valuation ratio is in the long run independent of either of the corporate policy variables s_c and i which were seen above to determine aggregate savings. When G is given by (3.38), and in place of (3.39) it is assumed the change Δq in Tobin's q is zero, the model may be solved to obtain

$$q = \{s_h(Y/I - 1)\}/(1 - s_h)(1 + p'\bar{M}/I_R)$$

Here p' denotes the rate of growth, $\Delta p/p$, in the price of the commodity. For q to remain at a steady state value, something must be assumed about the growth rates of price and of the real capital stock, I_R/M. An obvious assumption is that these rates are constant and equal. Interestingly, this may be deduced when the neo-Pasinetti model is augmented with a pricing rule such as the one proposed by Harcourt (see Section 4.3). It is not possible to take $p' = 0$, as price must be free to adjust to a value consistent with a new equilibrium. In later chapters, q is used in preference to v. Now, following Kaldor, the valuation ratio is used as the indicator of market value relative to the cost of assets, so that (3.37) is the appropriate equation for G.

In the paper introducing the q ratio, Tobin (1969) took as a condition of long-run equilibrium that $q = 1$. That is, he assumed that in long-run equilibrium the capital stock would be valued at its replacement cost. Setting the valuation ratio v to be one means that eventually the titles to units of capital come to be valued at the historical cost of the physical units. Solutions of the neo-Pasinetti model with this property satisfy the Samuelson and Modigliani condition, $I = s_h Y$. This follows directly by letting $v = 1$ in (3.40). Further, the imposition of the Samuelson and Modigliani criterion can only yield solutions with $v = 1$.

To see this, return to the initial equation for aggregate savings

$$S = s_c P + s_h \{ W + (1 - s_c) P \} = cG, \tag{3.28}$$

and, for the moment, make no assumption about the value of v. With the national income identity, equilibrium is given by

$$I = s_h Y + s_c (1 - s_h) P - (1 - s_h) G,$$

for $c = (1 - s_h)$. When $I = s_h Y$ this may be simplified to

$$0 = (1 - s_h) (s_c P - G).$$

That is, when $I = s_h Y$ then *either* the household propensity to acquire securities is one, *or* capital gains exactly reflect retained profits (that is, $G = s_c P$), *or* both of these conditions are satisfied. When $s_h = 1$, the equilibrium condition for the securities market,

$$s_h Y - s_h s_c P = iI + (1 - s_h) G, \tag{3.27}$$

becomes $Y - s_c P = iI$, which is just another way of saying that households save all of their income. As $I = s_h Y = Y$ in this case,

$$s_c P = (1 - i) I.$$

That is, the neo-Pasinetti theorem is preserved in this special case, but the profit share is now constant and is given by

$$\frac{P}{Y} = \frac{(1 - i)}{s_c} \frac{I}{Y} = \frac{(1 - i)}{s_c}.$$

Further, when $s_h = 1$ the solution for v,

$$v = \frac{(Y/I - 1)s_h}{(1 - s_h)},$$

is not valid. Not surprisingly, v cannot be determined in this case. As for the case $s_h = 1$, we may show that when $G = s_c P$ and $s_h \neq 1$ the neo-Pasinetti relation between profit and investment is preserved. With $G = s_c P$ the equilibrium condition for the securities market (3.27) simplifies to

$$s_h Y - s_c P = iI.$$

Using the dual condition $I = s_h Y$, this may be simplified to $s_c P = (1 - i)I$. Thus the Samuelson–Modigliani dual condition again generates the neo-Pasinetti theorem. To see that $v = 1$, recall that the capital gain G is given by $G = (v - i)I$. In this case G is retained profit, so that $G = s_c P = (1 - i)I$ from the neo-Pasinetti result. Hence comparison of the previous two equations for G implies that $v = 1$. Now recall that setting $v = 1$ in equation (3.40) implies $I = s_h Y$. In summary it now follows that the conditions $s_h \neq 1$, $v = 1$ are equivalent to the requirement that $I = s_h Y$ in this long-run model.

Thus the model produces a golden-age solution in which capital gains match retained profits and aggregate net savings are equal to the amount which would be saved at the rate s_h from national income. Notice that there is no implication here that all saving is undertaken by households, with corporations contributing nothing. Rather, aggregate saving is the sum of household and corporation savings, and the dissavings of households following their realization of capital gains. This follows from the golden age expression for capital gains given by (3.37). With $\Delta v = 0$,

$$G = (v - i)I.$$

Taking $v = 1$, and using the neo-Pasinetti expression for retained profits (3.31), leads to

$$G = s_c P.$$

If this is so, owners of securities will in aggregate realize capital gains equal to the stream of retained earnings used to finance new investment. Capital gains and share prices are therefore adjusting in line with retained profits in a precise way. In particular, the holders of securities will sell when the price is set so that they realize an income (dividends plus capital gains) equal to the corporate sector's total profits. This result is comparable with the golden age microeconomic theorem proved by Miller and Modigliani (1961, p.426). This intriguing result is taken up again in Chapter 8.

Other authors have developed results similar to the neo-Pasinetti theorem. One approach is to integrate the macroeconomic balance sheets developed by Boulding in 1950 with the neo-Pasinetti equations. This topic is taken up in the next section. In a footnote Odagiri (1981, p.108) claimed to derive the neo-Pasinetti theorem using nothing more than the corporate sector budget constraint, which limits actual investment spending to the level which can be funded from retained profits and new issues. That is, Odagiri began with

$$I = s_c P + p_s \Delta N = s_c P + iI.$$

This is an *ex post* analysis, so that $S = I$ is identically true. On the other hand, Kaldor's view is of an *ex ante* theory in the Keynesian tradition involving the adjustment of savings to the desired investment level. Wood (1975, pp.105–11) derived a result which may easily be reduced to the neo-Pasinetti result for the profit share. He devised a long-run microeconomic theory of the firm, and from it a 'finance frontier' for the entire company sector which is described by the equation

$$s_c \frac{P}{Y} = (1 + f - i) \frac{I}{Y},$$

where f is the ratio of the company sector's acquisition of financial assets to its investment expenditure. Kaldor (1966, p.314, n2) observed that in 'Anglo-Saxon countries' companies maintain a high value for f, enabling them to maintain their long-run growth strategies unhindered by short-term financial difficulties. For the UK, Benzie (1988, pp.80–81) presented evidence to support the notion that firms maintain a liquidity buffer which they use to cope with 'the differing time profiles of income and expenditure flows'. Benzie reported that, between 1970 and 1986, industrial and commercial companies nearly doubled the ratio of their holdings of gross liquid assets to their capital base. However, in the development of the neo-

Pasinetti theorem, Kaldor took $f = 0$. With this assumption the equation for Wood's finance frontier reduces to the neo-Pasinetti equation describing the distribution of income. A summary of Wood's theory is given in the appendix to this chapter.

One line of criticism of the neo-Pasinetti theorem is contained in the footnote of Odagiri reported above. Another criticism was advanced by Davidson (1968). He observed that Kaldor's derivation apparently relied on a neoclassical mechanism to generate equilibrium in the commodity market. The long-run scenario of the neo-Pasinetti theorem entails the assumption of full employment, and in this environment a mechanism must exist to adjust aggregate consumption to the gap between the given level of investment and the level of output. Davidson thought that the mechanism which produces equilibrium in the securities market might also be required to establish equilibrium in the commodity market. In the securities market households are induced by variations in the valuation ratio to forgo consumption to the extent necessary to purchase the supply of securities. However, the rate of return on securities is also dependent on the valuation ratio, implying a dependence of aggregate consumption on the rate of return. Thus Davidson concluded, having incorrectly fixed the distribution of income, that it was 'the *deus ex machina* of the classical system', the rate of interest, which was the equilibrating mechanism in the commodity market (*ibid.*, p.258).

Skott (1981, p.567) pointed out that no such neoclassical mechanism is required: 'The valuation ratio (the "interest" rate) serves to adjust the level of personal net saving to the amount of new securities issued by companies ... it is variations in the distribution of income which bring about the full employment equilibrium between savings and investment.' This, too, is a misinterpretation of Kaldor's model. For in general equilibrium terms there is a reduced system consisting of two equations (obtained by various substitutions into the equilibrium conditions for the model's two markets) and two endogenous variables (the distribution of income and the valuation ratio). This system is solved simultaneously for values of the endogenous variables. The process of simultaneous solution does not assign each variable to one market and then rely exclusively on that variable to produce equilibrium in the market. Nevertheless, variations in the valuation ratio have a greater impact in the securities market than do changes in the distribution of income, whereas variations in the distribution of income have the greater effect in the commodity market. To see this formally, we require the reduced-form equations of the neo-Pasinetti model.

Substitution of equations (3.37), (3.39) and $W = Y - P$ into the equilibrium condition for the securities market (3.27) gives

$$s_h - s_h s_c P/Y = \{i(1-c) + cv\}I/Y. \qquad (3.41)$$

Similarly, using the equation (3.28) for net aggregate savings and the equilibrium condition (3.30), yields

$$s_h + s_c (1-s_h) P/Y = \{(1-ci) + cv\}I/Y. \qquad (3.42)$$

By taking finite changes (denoted with a Δ) equations (3.41) and (3.42) reduce to

$$-s_h s_c \Delta(P/Y) - c(I/Y)\Delta v = \{i + c(v - i)\}\Delta(I/Y) \qquad (3.43)$$

and

$$s_c (1 - s_h)\Delta(P/Y) - c(I/Y)\Delta v = \{1 + c(v-i)\}\Delta(I/Y). \qquad (3.44)$$

The relative magnitudes of the coefficients of the changes in the distribution of income and the valuation ratio may be estimated by taking values imputed for the savings propensities by Kaldor (1966, pp.301–4) for the US and Great Britain. To do this, assume as before that $c = 1 - s_h$.

First, Kaldor assigned s_c a value based on the propensity to save out of gross profits, inclusive of capital consumption allowances, net of tax. For the US and Great Britain this was around 0.7. In the neo-Pasinetti model, s_h is the propensity of households to lend to businesses. Estimates of aggregate personal savings contain components reflecting investment in residential housing. With these components netted out, Kaldor proposed that, for the US and Great Britain, s_h lies in the range 0.01 to 0.03. Here we take $s_h = 0.02$. In 1966, the investment–income coefficient for both the US and Great Britain was around 0.18 (see Norton and Garmston, 1984, p.213) so that in equation (3.43) the coefficients of Δv and $\Delta(P/Y)$ are respectively

$$-c (I/Y) = -0.98 \quad 0.18 \cong -0.18$$

and

$$-s_c \, s_h = -0.02 . 0.7 \cong -0.01.$$

Hence for any given change in the investment coefficient the adjustment to equilibrium in the securities market is more sensitive to changes in the valuation ratio than to changes of the same size in the distribution of income. For the commodity market the coefficients of Δv and $\Delta(P/Y)$ are

$$-c(I/Y) \cong -0.18$$

and

$$s_c \, (1-s_h) = 0.7 \; 0.98 \cong 0.7,$$

so that the establishment of equilibrium in the commodity market is more sensitive to changes in the distribution of income. Further, provided that i is less than 1, the coefficient of I/Y in the $I = S$ condition is greater than the coefficient in the securities market equation (3.43). Therefore changes in I/Y have a greater impact in the commodity market than in the securities market.

We turn now to a discussion of the neo-Pasinetti theorem in the context of aggregate balance sheets for businesses and households devised by Boulding (1950).

3.4 Boulding's theory of distribution in a neo-Pasinetti framework

As we have seen, the criticisms of post-Keynesian growth and distribution theory raised by Samuelson and Modigliani were immediately shown by Kaldor to be extraneous in a model which preserved the main features of Pasinetti's result. This neo-Pasinetti theory may be extracted easily from the research of Boulding. The variant of Boulding's balance sheet approach used for this purpose does not need the assumption of differences in savings propensities, nor is it necessary to postulate that there are hereditary classes of income receivers.

Boulding (1953, pp.478–9) accumulates for one accounting period the balance sheets of all businesses, to obtain total profits as

$$P = I + dM_b + dK_b - I_e + D,$$

where dM_b is the increase in the stock of money held by all businesses, dK_b is the change in the debts of households to businesses, I_e is the component of investment financed from the sale of securities, and D denotes distributions. To Boulding's formulation we add the assumptions that firms obtain finance for a proportion i of total investment from the sale of securities, giving

$$I_e = iI, \qquad (3.45)$$

and as dividends are determined as the proportion $(1 - s_c)$ of total profits,

$$D = (1 - s_c)P. \qquad (3.46)$$

Therefore the balance sheet identity becomes

$$P = \frac{(1 - i)I + dM_b + dK_b}{s_c}.$$

When $dK_b = dM_b = 0$ or when $dK_b = -dM_b$, division by income Y gives

$$\frac{P}{Y} = \frac{(1 - i)}{s_c} \frac{I}{Y}. \qquad (3.47)$$

This is the neo-Pasinetti result. When $i = 0$, that is, when no part of corporate investment is financed externally, (3.47) is just Pasinetti's original result.

   Enterprises hold liquid assets (here, money and the promise of a future stream of payments from households) against the uncertainty of the stream of profits from accounting period to period. In this way they ensure a source of finance for that part of their long-term investment activity which is to take place in any particular accounting period. A possible justification for the assumption that $dK_b = dM_b = 0$ is that, in the long run, when it might be expected that investment plans are realized out of retained profits, there is no need to suppose that businesses hoard retained profits as additions to their holdings of liquid assets. This is in the spirit of Kaldor (1966, p.314, n2) who observed that corporations operate with a liquidity cushion sufficient to prevent frustration of long-run corporate expansion. The alternative equilibrium condition requires that contractions (expansions) of the money supply of corporations are accommodated by expansions (contractions) of household indebtedness to business.

In *A Reconstruction of Economics* (Boulding, 1950, pp.247–8) there is presented a balance sheet for the determination of the net worth of all households. This aggregate balance sheet for households may be combined with Kaldor's theory of the securities market. The net worth of businesses was seen by Boulding as ultimately belonging to households, and it made its way into the households' balance sheet via individual or household holdings of shares in enterprises. The change in the net worth of households, dG_h, is given by

$$dG_h = d(M_h + M_b) + d(Q_h + Q_b),$$

where M_h and Q_h represent aggregate household holdings of money and real assets, while M_b and Q_b denote the same entities for the business sector.

Defining I^* to be the aggregate (household and business) expenditure on new items of capital,

$$I^* = dQ_h + dQ_b = dQ_h + I,$$

then from the household balance sheet it follows that

$$I^* = dG_h - dM,$$

where $M = M_h + M_b$. Increases in the stocks of capital items are financed from savings by households and by businesses, and so

$$I^* = s'_h W + s'_h(1 - s_c)P - cG + s_c P, \tag{3.48}$$

where, as in the previous section, G denotes capital gains, $W + (1 - s_c)P$ is gross household income, and now s'_h is the proportion of household income saved for the purpose of acquiring consumer durable assets and company securities. To proceed, a model of the market for business securities is required. Without modification, Kaldor's securities market fits exactly into this model. If this equilibrium condition, equation (3.27), is subtracted from (3.48) and $W = Y - P$ is used to eliminate wages and salaries, then

$$I^* - iI = [s'_h - s_h]Y + s_c[1 - (s'_h - s_h)]P. \qquad (3.49)$$

Reorganization gives

$$\frac{P}{Y} = \frac{((I^* - iI)/Y - [s'_h - s_h])}{s_c[1 - (s'_h - s_h)]} \qquad (3.50)$$

It is clear in this approach that $s'_h \geq s_h$ and $I^* \geq iI$. In the event that the only form of investment is business accumulation, that is, $I^* = I$ and $s'_h = s_h$, then (3.50) collapses to the neo-Pasinetti result (3.47). Provided $s'_h - s_h$ is less than one, the denominator of (3.50) is positive and we can conclude that the profit share will be greater than zero when

$$I^* - iI > [s'_h - s_h]Y. \qquad (3.51)$$

That is, the profit share is positive when households' savings plans for the accumulation of capital items are insufficient to finance both household investment and investment from retained profits out of national income. The condition which ensures that the profit share given in (3.50) is not greater than one is

$$I^* - iI \leq [s_c + (1 - s_c)(s'_h - s_h)]Y.$$

That is, aggregate savings by households and corporations out of national income for the purchase of physical capital items, net of household lending to businesses for this purpose, exceeds $I^* - iI$, the actual level of aggregate investment, net of business investment financed with funds raised from households.

The interesting feature of this theory is that the share of profits is seen to depend on $I^* - iI$. If we model the distribution of investment between households and businesses with an equation of the form

$$I^* = \gamma I$$

then,

$$\frac{P}{Y} = \frac{[(\gamma - i)I/Y - (s'_h - s_h)]}{s_c[1 - (s'_h - s_h)]} \qquad (3.52)$$

The ratio γ will depend on the investment decisions made by households and by the managers of corporations. Household preferences for fixed assets are reflected in the difference between the savings propensities s'_h and s_h, whereas business investment decisions are reflected in I, i and s_c. In this model, business investment I and the parameters i, s_c, s'_h and s_h are exogenous. There are also other factors, not explicitly part of this model, which will influence γ. These include demographic variables such as the number, structure and the rate of formation of households, and geographic considerations influencing the types of capital items required by the household and business sectors. In (3.52) we see that an increase in γ holding fixed the investment–income coefficient will raise the share of profits in national income. This result can be understood from (3.49). An increase in γ raises I^*, so that profits P must grow to provide households with the necessary income to finance their purchases of fixed assets. The increase in γ represents increased demand by households relative to demand by businesses for capital items, and also implies increased competition between households and businesses for the resources required to form units of capital. With a mark-up pricing mechanism, the relative price increases which accompany these changes in the composition and level of demand induce increases in profit margins. When nominal wages are fixed, real wage rates are reduced so that, if the economy is operating at full employment, the real value of the wage bill falls as profits and dividend incomes grow.

We have been discussing two macroeconomic models of the distribution of income. What ensures that the two approaches are consistent? When in the long run $dM_b = dK_b = 0$, this question may be answered by equating the right-hand sides of the neo-Pasinetti equation (3.47) and the new distribution equation (3.50) to produce

$$I^*/Y - (s'_h - s_h) = \{(1 - i)[1 - (s'_h - s_h)] + i\}I/Y,$$

which can be transformed into

$$I^* - I = (s'_h - s_h)[Y - (1 - i)I].$$

Assume now that, in the long run, profits are retained only for current investment purposes. Therefore the two explanatory equations produce the same result provided households' acquisitions of fixed assets are financed by household savings for these purposes, from that part of national income received by households (that is, $Y - (1 - i)I = Y - s_c P$).

This approach to the preservation of post-Keynesian distribution consists of adding equations (3.45) and (3.46), that is, $I_e = iI$ and $D = (1 - s_c)P$, to the aggregate balance sheet identity for businesses. These equations determine the level of external financing of investment and the value of dividends. For one accounting cycle they are purely identities, as it is easy in any one period to choose values of i and s_c (supposing observations of I_e, I, D and P are all possible) so that the additional equations are valid. It is the imposition of a model of i and s_c which changes the character of the balance sheet approach. Up to the introduction of (3.45) and (3.46) (and the long run assumptions $dM_b = dK_b = 0$), Boulding's work is definitional, or more accurately, composed of a number of definitions and a small number of identities between them. If it is assumed that s_c and i are constant then, from period to period, the validity of our extension depends on the stability of the observed values of i and s_c. In line with Boulding's view that his theory highlights 'a whole complex of decisions . . . relating to dividend distribution and business investment and finance', i and s_c might be postulated to depend on parameters measuring business confidence and expertise[3]. For the current model these variables are effectively exogenous and would require the inclusion of a theory of management behaviour, so that i and s_c might be determined before the new behavioural equations can be tested. These remarks are not solely criticisms of the balance sheet approach, as similar equations are also components of other post-Keynesian theories and have the same status there.

The balance sheet approach might equally well be applied to both long- and short-run scenarios. As we have seen in part, and will see more fully later, the neo-Pasinetti theory may also be cast in the short-run mode where unemployment solutions might be investigated. But in his original Keynesian theory of distribution, Kaldor adhered to full-employment outcomes. Part of this preference may have been to do with remaining close to the spirit of the *Treatise*. Alternatively, it may have been to exclude any role for the tools of marginal productivity theory. With certainty we know that the only *stable* solutions resulting from the interactions of microeconomic agents and macroeconomic forces in Kaldor's world were those with full employment. In the next section we examine Kaldor's representation of all firms.

3.5 Kaldor's representative firm and a two-sector extension

In his analysis of growth theory and distribution Kaldor (1957, p.594; 1955–6, pp.94 and 99) insisted that the assumption of full employment was appropriate because 'A state of Keynesian underemployment equilibrium is . . . inconsistent with a dynamic equilibrium of steady growth.' An understanding of how this opinion was formed can be obtained by expanding the basic model to include Kaldor's (1961, pp.197–210) theory of investment and of the industry structure responsible for supply. Antecedents of Kaldor's representative firm are to be found in the horizontal average variable cost schedule of Kalecki and, of course, Keynes's demand function. The research on manufacturing business by Andrews in 1949 precedes and closely parallels Kaldor's thinking. A cogent account of Andrews's theory of the firm is given in King and Regan (1988, pp.82–5). In this section Kaldor's representative firm is introduced and the stability of its equilibria analysed. Harcourt (1963, 1965) pointed out severe shortcomings in the use of the representative firm in macro-models having multiple sectors. These difficulties are assessed.

Kaldor assumed that:

1. money wages w are fixed at $\bar{w}$;
2. the economy consists of a number of fully-integrated firms with price-making power;
3. firms can employ no more than a fixed fraction of the available labour force;
4. there is sufficient capacity to support the productive employment of all labour (that is, labour is the effective bottleneck to production);
5. average direct costs are constant up to the point of optimum utilization of capacity and rise thereafter; and
6. there is a certain minimum margin of price, p_0, over average direct costs a, that cannot be eliminated by competition.

Assumption (2) means that producers do not purchase raw materials (either domestic or imported), so that each firm's average direct and marginal costs consist only of the costs of employing labour. Up to the point at which labour is fully employed or the point at which optimum capacity use occurs (whichever comes first), assumptions

(5) and (6) imply that the firm's supply curve is horizontal, and lies above the average direct cost curve. In Figures 3.1 and 3.2, the horizontal portions of the cost curves extend up to the full-employment output level Y_f/n. Up to this output level the firm's supply schedule SS is also shown as horizontal. When firms are operating at their employment-constrained maxima, the price at which this output level is supplied is arbitrary but, from assumption (6), not less than the price consistent with the maintenance of the minimum margin. At Y_f/n the supply schedule is shown as vertical in the figures.[4]

A function relating price and demand for the representative firm's product can be derived from the economy-wide condition

$$I/Y = s_W + (s_P - s_W)P/Y. \qquad (3.53)$$

When output from the representative firm is Y, the firm's level of real profit is given by

$$P = Y_r - (a/p)Y_r,$$

and the share of profits in output for the representative firm is

$$P/Y_r = 1 - a/p = (p - a)/p. \qquad (3.54)$$

If P/Y in (3.53) is replaced by (3.54) and also if the occurrence of Y on the left-hand side of (3.53) is replaced by D, the level of effective demand for the firm's output, then

$$I/D = s_W + (s_P - s_W)(1 - a/p). \qquad (3.55)$$

This may be rearranged to obtain the equation

$$p = (s_P - s_W)a/(sp - I/D), \qquad (3.56)$$

for the price required to equate demand to the firm's output level, at the given average direct cost a. That is, (3.56) shows the relationship between price (and hence the profit share for the firm) and demand which ensures that $S = I$. Haache (1979, pp.212–13) referred to this schedule as an IS curve. Here it is simply called the 'demand schedule'. Haache's function is comparable with Hicks's IS function of

Figure 3.1 Supply and demand schedules for Kaldor's representative firm

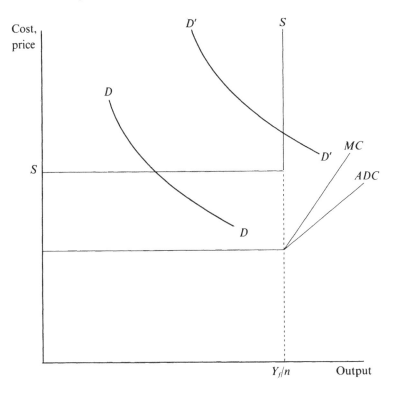

combinations of income and the rate of interest which ensure equilibrium in the commodity market. Kaldor's demand function does the same job, using combinations of income and the profit share.

When I is autonomously determined and $s_P > s_W$, then it follows that the schedule given by (3.56) is a monotonically decreasing function of D, since

$$p'(D) = -(\bar{I}/D^2)(s_P - s_W)/(s_P - \bar{I}/D)^2 < 0.$$

Two demand curves of this type are shown in Figure 3.1 as DD and $D'D'$. Intersection of DD with SS occurs with under-employment. In this case the supply price is p_0 and (3.56) can be solved for the equilibrium level of demand. Also the share of profits (that is,

$(p_0 - a)/p_0)$ is known independently of the equilibrium level of demand, and so the level of profits can be obtained from (3.54). Alternatively the demand curve intersects the vertical segment of the supply schedule (as happens for $D'D'$) and a full employment equilibrium is obtained. Output is fixed at Y_f/n and p is determined from (3.56) as

$$p = (s_P - s_W)a/(s_P - \overline{I}/D) = (s_P - s_W)a/(s_P - n\overline{I}/Y_f).$$

Compared with the under-employment case, the price is now greater, and it follows from (3.54) that at full employment profits are a greater share of income. Therefore this version of Kaldor's model implies that it is in the interests of agents receiving incomes in the form of profits to strive for full employment.

Kaldor extended this analysis to cope with endogenously determined investment. Once the average cost curve lies below the supply schedule, where the price per unit exceeds average cost and a normal profit is being earned, it may be argued that increases in production induce investment in plant and equipment in addition to the autonomously determined level. The point at which the average cost curve AC crosses the horizontal portion of the supply schedule is shown as N in Figure 3.2. To the right of N, I is growing. If the profit share (and hence price) is given, the level of savings,

$$S = (s_P - s_W)(1 - a/p)Y + s_W Y,$$

is sufficient to fund, at output Y, the exogenously determined component of investment. The extra savings required to finance the induced component are generated by an increase in price. That is, equilibrium is re-established in the commodity market by an increase in p, so that beyond N the demand schedule slopes upwards. To the left of N investment is still considered to be independent of the level of activity, and so, up to N, the demand schedule is downward-sloping. Therefore Kaldor's demand schedule is U-shaped.

For the curve drawn in Figure 3.2, the three points labelled E_1, E_2 and E_3, are the points of intersection of the U-shaped demand schedule with the supply schedule. E_1 and E_2 represent under-employment equilibria. For $Y < Y_f/n$, aggregate savings are given by

$$S = s_W Y + (s_P - s_W)P = [s_W + (s_P - s_W)(1 - a/p_0)]Y. \quad (3.57)$$

Figure 3.2 Kaldor's representative firm when there is induced investment

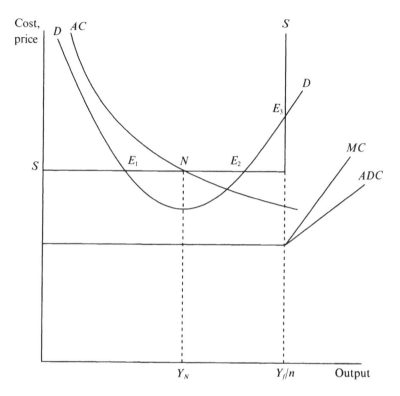

This form of the equation for S can be used to investigate the stability of E_1 and E_2. To the left of E_1 the supply price p_0 is too low for investment–savings equilibrium but, as E_1 is also to the left of N, investment is determined independently of income. When a disturbance reduces output to a level lower than that attained at E_1, saving is less than planned investment and there is excess demand, which is eliminated by the tendency for Y to grow. Output will continue to increase until the level is reached where savings are again equated with investment. This occurs at E_1. When output lies between the values corresponding to E_1 and E_2 the price p_0 is too high to realise equality of investment and savings. Here saving exceeds planned investment. Output will contract until E_1 is reached. Therefore E_1 is a stable equilibrium. But E_2 is unstable as, for output levels to the right of this point, p_0 is again too low to ensure investment–savings equilibrium. Saving is again less than planned investment and income increases to accommodate the excess demand. On Kaldor's theory then, under-employment equilibrium is stable only in conditions of 'slump', that is, at E_1, where the level of induced investment is zero.

As has already been noted, Kaldor preferred the full-employment equilibrium at E_3. To see that E_3 is stable, note first that the savings function is now

$$S = [s_W + (s_P - s_W)(1 - a/p)]Y_f \qquad (3.58)$$

where p is flexible. When income is greater than at E_2, saving is less than investment and income will increase. Once the limit Y_f is attained, there is still excess demand, and from (3.58) it follows that increases in p (and so in the profit share) will bring savings to the same level as investment. If p is greater than the price corresponding to E_3, savings exceed investment and at this price there is excess supply. Equilibrium is restored by reductions in price.

In two papers Harcourt (1963, 1965) investigated two-sector models of distribution and provided important insights into the mechanisms underlying Kaldorian analyses of the short run. These papers are logical ancestors of the models developed in Chapters 5 and 7 of the present volume. Both approaches explore the importance of non-competitive pricing strategies, microeconomic structures and macroeconomic forces in the explanation of the short-run distribution of income. Harcourt's research has exposed a deficiency of Kaldor's microeconomic structure: 'The concept of a "representative firm" which is a replica of the whole economy is shown to be untenable when the analysis is extended to a two-sector model' (Harcourt, 1963, p.21).

In Harcourt's earlier (1963) paper a derivation is presented of the entrepreneurial pricing rule which ensures that Kaldor's distributive mechanism works in the short run. At full employment, the mechanism ensures that a change in demand causes prices to adjust relative to the money wage, redistributes income and so leads to a change in aggregate savings. By 'work in the short run', Harcourt means that changes 'in planned investment at the beginning of a short period [are] so accompanied by movements of resources, prices and the distribution of income, that the investment planned at the beginning of the period becomes actual investment by the end' (*ibid.*, p.26). He concluded: 'there is no guarantee that planned investment will become actual investment and whether it does or not depends on entrepreneurs in the [consumption] sector following significantly different pricing policies to those in the [investment] sector' (*ibid.*, p.33).

To reach this conclusion, Harcourt investigated a number of scenarios, each involving full employment. Here we investigate only one of these. The 1965 paper was not restricted to full employment. Unemployment in the previous period was postulated to have an influence on the current money wage in the consumption sector. This wage rate was thought to be set before, and to provide a floor for, the money wage in the investment good sector. In this model the previous state of the labour market was then able to influence current employment and output in the consumption good sector, aggregate employment, income and its distribution. Generalization of the 1963 model to a system allowing for unemployment did not violate the Keynesian analysis of the short run, nor did it cause any difficulty in solving the model for its endogenous variables. 'The main conclusion of the paper is that the traditional Keynesian analysis of short-period equilibrium can be easily adapted to include decisions concerning price-making and choice of technique, with the result that the distribution of income as well as the level of employment can be determined' (Harcourt, 1965, pp.116–17).

In the 1963 model, a consumption good, bread, and an investment good, steel, are produced. Wage earners do not save and entrepreneurs do not consume. That is, $s_W = s_N = 0$ and $s_P = 1$ (in the notation used earlier). This is Kalecki's more restrictive position, where all savings are supplied out of profits, which are now the exclusive property of capitalists. Quantities of steel, once installed as units of capital, are not mobile or transferable to another sector, whereas labour is perfectly mobile and responds immediately to shifts in sectoral wage relativities. In any period there is excess capacity and, following Kaldor, it was assumed that labour was the scarce resource. Harcourt identified four conditions which had to be fulfilled if investment plans were to be realized, and if the Kaldorian distributive mechanism was to operate. For the realization of investment plans, Harcourt noted (1963, p.27, n6) that only the first condition is required. This strong condition requires that the capital goods sector always has sufficient labour to meet investment demand. For any short-run period the wage of a steel worker, w_i, relative to that of a baker, w_c, was assumed to induce steel workers to remain in that type of employment for the entire period. Thus a definite relative wage structure was associated with each level of employment and output. In the 1965 paper, it is postulated that the money wage, w_c, in the bread sector is exogenous and its value is decided at the beginning of the period. Momentarily after, the wage is set in the steel sector at a level which is not less than w_c, and does not exceed an upper bound which is a function of labour demand. Production levels are given by X/N and x/n, where x and X denote the numbers employed in the bread and steel sectors respectively, and n and N are the corresponding fixed technology coefficients.

Second, it is postulated that in any period the price of bread is set so that the market for the consumption good clears. Because only wage earners consume, the demand for bread is $w_c x + w_i X$ and so the price of bread, p_c, satisfies

$$w_c x + w_i X = p_c x/n$$

or

$$p_c = w_c n \left(1 + \frac{w_i X}{w_c x}\right). \tag{3.59}$$

The labour costs of the steel sector are the profits of the bread industry, so that the mark-up factor is just the profit–cost ratio in the production of bread. Bread entrepreneurs cautiously set the price once the wage bill in the steel industry is known. Under the assumptions made in the 1965 paper, this is possible only after the wage rate w_i has been announced and the required labour force for the steel sector assembled.

When prices, wages, employment and output shares are expected in the next period to have the values of the current period, then the expected profit rates flowing from one extra unit of investment in the current period are

$$\frac{(p_i X/N - w_i X)}{p_i M} \text{ and } \frac{(p_c x/n - w_c x)}{p_i m},$$

where $p_i M$ and $p_i m$ are the expected replacement costs of the capital stocks, M and m, p_iX/N and p_cx/n are projections of expected revenues, and w_iX and w_cx are the expected wage bills. The third condition is that these anticipated rates should be equal,

$$\frac{(p_i - w_iN)X}{p_iMN} = \frac{(p_c - w_cn)x}{p_imn},$$

and so, from the equation for the price of bread, (3.59), the price of steel is

$$p_i = w_iN(1 + \frac{M}{m}). \qquad (3.60)$$

Thus entrepreneurs in the steel sector also mark up costs in setting price. But, whereas in the bread sector this is done cautiously, only after the steel industry has declared its wage and employment levels, entrepreneurs in steel confidently take the pricing decision which ensures they can afford to pay the workforce required to produce planned investment and of course allow the industry's investment plans to be realized. When full employment prevails, which was Harcourt's fourth condition, bread producers are necessarily also passive in determining their production and employment levels. Depending on the magnitude of planned investment, managers in the steel industry willingly raise w_i to attract labour, and equally vigorously reduce w_i or dismiss workers when their wage bill must be reduced; producers of bread can only vary output to employ residual workers. Given the technology, the baking of bread is constrained by the size of the remaining workforce. It is therefore difficult to see the negotiating position which might be adopted by bread entrepreneurs in a collective bargaining process to arrive at the sector's money wage (1965, p.106). Alternatively, w_i might be arbitrated. This seems to fit more easily with the other assumptions set out in the two papers. In the 1965 paper (pp.106 and 111), where the assumption of full employment is relaxed, it is theorized that w_c is a lagged function of the price of bread, productivity changes, the money wage in the sector, and the economy-wide unemployment rate.

The sequence of events set in train by an increase in planned investment is as follows. With fixed technology in the steel sector, the size of its workforce will be known, and therefore so will be the change in the sector's money wage rate. This determines profits in the bread sector (provided its technology is known) and also prices for the period. When there is full employment, a redeployment of labour to the steel sector causes a reduction in the size of the labour force engaged in the production of bread. With the money wage, w_c, fixed, this means that the wage bill of the steel sector rises relative to the wage bill in the bread sector. Thus the price of bread increases, so that an increase in planned investment is inflationary. The price of steel also rises as a consequence of the change in the money wage, w_i, required to induce labour to leave the manufacture of bread. For the steel sector, the mark-up in (3.60) is fixed over the short run, when the physical stocks of capital in use, M and m, are fixed. Thus the ratio of unit cost to unit price,

$$w_i/p_i = N^{-1}(1 + M/m)^{-1}, \qquad (3.61)$$

is constant.

Nominal savings are just the profits of the two sectors,

$$
\begin{aligned}
S &= (p_i X/N - w_i X) + (p_c x/n - w_c x) \\
&= (p_i/N - w_i)X + (p_c/n - w_c)x \\
&= (1 + \frac{M}{m})w_i X,
\end{aligned}
$$

(from (3.59) and (3.60)). Savings deflated by the cost of a unit of capital are given by

$$\frac{S}{p_i} = (1 + \frac{M}{m})\frac{w_i}{p_i}X, \qquad (3.62)$$

and this measure of real savings grows with employment in the steel sector over the short run. Equation (3.61) for w_i/p_i and the relation $X = N\bar{I}$ may be used to simplify (3.62) to

$$\frac{S}{p_i} = \bar{I}$$

Therefore, as Kaldor envisaged, an increase in planned investment induces changes in prices relative to the money wage. This causes a redistribution of income, which induces the growth in real saving necessary to fund investment.

It is now clear that very different behaviour must be assumed of entrepreneurs in the two sectors if the Keynesian mechanism is to work. A similar result may be extracted from a two-sector model proposed by Kregel (1977), when the consumption sector is constrained by the supply of labour and the investment sector has slack capacity (see Rimmer, 1990, Section 2.3 and pp.23–4). In this chapter we have investigated a class of post-Keynesian theories of distribution closely associated with Kaldor. Particular attention has been given to the assumptions which might be made about savings propensities. To arrive at the Cambridge theorem,

$$\frac{P}{Y} = \frac{1}{s_c}\frac{I}{Y},$$

Pasinetti made different assumptions from Kaldor about the class structure of society (as well as extending the basic Kaldorian system with three essentially long-run equations). The Cambridge result was discovered by Pasinetti in his investigation of what he thought was a logical slip made by Kaldor. As has been shown in Section 3.2, no such slip occurred – different assumptions about the savings propensities of wage and salary earners may produce different distribution results. However, Pasinetti's theorizing, as distinct from other post-Keynesian distribution theories, is vulnerable because of the faults detected by Samuelson and Modigliani. Kaldor found a reincarnation of the Cambridge theorem by extending his basic system to include a securities market. To fashion this outcome, the evidence suggests that Kaldor persisted with the savings hypotheses he had made a decade earlier in founding his class of distribution theories. The intensity of the debate on these problems undoubtedly proved productive, but it is also clear that, as early as 1950, the modified Cambridge theorem could have been unearthed, easily and without rancour, from the work of Boulding.[5] As has been shown in Section 3.4, the balance sheets of Boulding are a very fruitful research resource. In that section a role in distribution was found for the competition between households and corporations in capital markets.

Finally, in the present section, we discussed the type of representative firm Kaldor thought operated in his macroeconomy. There is no role in its normal operation for the concepts of production function and marginal productivity. For Kaldor firms colluded, so that a degree of monopoly power was important in determining the minimum profit margin. This theme is taken up again in Chapters 5 and 7, there the models diverge from Harcourt's analysis and criticism of Kaldor's representative firm, in that investment is endogenous. The emphasis on microeconomic structures and non-competitive behaviour shifts from the level of the firm to the analysis of industries. There is, in the industries, collusion on output and pricing. While Chapters 5 and 7 are about the neo-Pasinetti theory and its extension to short-run, imperfectly competitive settings, the next chapter is a review of extensions of the basic Kaldorian model, two of which include elements of perfect competition.

Notes

1. The aim is to obtain equation (3.23), where the factor $(1 - s_W Y/\bar{I})$ appears on both sides of the equation. Manipulation of the model to reach this state highlights the roles played by Pasinetti's new equations, the first of which may be written as

$$K_W/K = S_W/S = s_W(Y - P_C)/\bar{I}.$$

With the expression for $PC/\bar{I}$ derived from the distribution result (3.18) this yields

$$K_W/K = s_W[s_P Y/\bar{I} - 1]/(s_P - s_W), \qquad (3A.1)$$

and so

$$K_W/Y = s_W[s_P K/\bar{I} - K/Y]/(s_P - s_W). \qquad (3A.2)$$

From (3.21), the second of Pasinetti's added equations,

$$P_W/Y = rK_W/Y.$$

Thus with (3A.2) and equation (3.18) for P_C/Y it follows that

$$P/Y = P_C/Y + P_W/Y = [\bar{I}/Y - s_W + rs_W(s_P K/\bar{I} - K/Y)]/(s_P - s_W). \quad (3A.3)$$

Now from (3.9) and (3.11) an expression for P_C/K can be determined, which when it is substituted into

$$P/K = P_C/K + P_W/K = P_C/K + r\, K_W/K$$

along with (3A.1) produces

$$P/K = [\bar{I}/K - s_W Y/K + r\, s_W(s_P Y/\bar{I} - 1)]/(s_P - s_W).$$

The third equation added by Pasinetti, (3.22), can now be used to obtain (3.23).

2. To obtain equation (3.33) write (3.32) as

$$(\bar{v} + \Delta v)(\bar{K} + \Delta K) = (\bar{p}_s + \Delta p_s)(\bar{N} + \Delta N),$$

and expand to obtain

$$\bar{v}\bar{K} + (\bar{v} + \Delta v)\Delta K + \bar{K}\Delta v = \bar{p}_s\bar{N} + (\bar{p}_s + \Delta p_s)\Delta N + \bar{N}\Delta p_s.$$

Initially $\bar{v}\bar{K} = \bar{p}_s\bar{N}$ from (3.32). Thus, writing $p_s = \bar{p}_s + \Delta p_s$ and $v = \bar{v} + \Delta v$, G may be obtained as

$$G = \bar{N}\Delta p_s = v\Delta K + \bar{K}\Delta v - p_s\Delta N.$$

3. See preface to Boulding (1962).
4. In fact, the analysis here is simplified slightly by assuming that the supply schedule is vertical at Y_f/n; Haache (1979, pp.210–12) assumed the supply schedule to be somewhat more elastic in the region of Y_f/n. Kaldor (1961, p.198) preferred a supply schedule which did not turn up so sharply at full employment.
5. The author was told by Boulding that he avoided where possible the cross-Atlantic debate on growth and distribution.

Appendix: Wood's Theory of Company Behaviour

This appendix summarizes the main features of Wood's microeconomic theory. It was noted in Section 3.3 that this theory produced a distribution result similar to the neo-Pasinetti equation. In it the management of a firm seeks to maximize long-run sales revenue subject to constraints imposed by the growth of demand, the growth of capacity and the availability of finance for investment. The constraints are summarized in mathematical relations called the 'opportunity frontier' and the 'financial frontier'. (As Wood, 1975, p.81 noted, the forms of the two frontiers are not independent.) Consider first the opportunity frontier.

Managers of a single enterprise have open to them a set of possible strategies, where a strategy is defined (*ibid.*, p.63) to consist of the range of factors which management controls, and which specifically includes prices and outputs for each of the firm's products, the firm's selling policies and its investment decisions. A strategy must be feasible in that the investment to be undertaken must provide sufficient capacity to meet the growth of demand for the firm's products, should the strategy be implemented. Associated with each strategy are particular values for the average profit margin on sales, the growth rate of total sales revenue, and the expenditure on investment. Managers would prefer to operate with a strategy which provides the firm with the highest possible profit margin, the greatest growth rate of sales and the smallest expenditure on investment. However, these three extremes cannot simultaneously be attained, and firms make trade-offs. Management must compromise on the rate at which they wish sales to grow and on the profit margin they earn, given a fixed level of expenditure on investment. Also managers must be prepared to contemplate increases in investment expenditures, for these increases permit higher attainable values for the profit margin and the growth rate of sales. With greater investment expenditures managers are effectively purchasing a larger possible collection of values for profit margins and sales growth. It is within this collection of profit margins and sales growth rates that managers decide their trade-off between a high rate of sales growth and a large profit margin.

The trade-off between the rate of sales growth and the level of the profit margin arises because the firm is locked in a competitive struggle with other companies to increase its share of total demand.

To do this when investment expenditure is fixed, management puts in place a more aggressive selling policy. The components of this policy – such as advertising and promotion, product innovation and quality improvement – cause unit costs to increase, but, because prices cannot in general rise in proportion to unit costs without affecting demand, it follows that a greater volume of sales can only be realized at the expense of the average profit margin.

Investment expenditure has a dual role in Wood's theory. One role is as the means of providing extra capacity when demand increases independently. This is just a version of the accelerator theory (*ibid.*, p.70). Its other role is as 'a weapon in the competitive struggle to attract demand at the expense of other firms' (*ibid.*, p.68). Wood saw this second role as important because of its effects on the firm's selling policy and cost-effectiveness. Selling policy is enhanced because

additional expenditure on the modification and replacement of production and sales facilities enables greater changes to be made in the product mix, which increases the degree to which the firm can improve its demand and profit margin trade-off by replacing its existing products with other products for which demand is growing more rapidly or which can be sold at a higher profit margin. (*Ibid.*, p.67).

Unit operating costs can usually be reduced by using more capital-intensive production techniques, and by replacing old equipment. At the same time the introduction of new capital is likely to be more cost-efficient in raising product quality and varying product mix. Further, investment in stocks of inputs and outputs reduce 'the risks of lost sales due to interruptions in production or unexpected surges in demand' (*ibid.*, p.68).

Wood formalized these trade-offs in the mathematical relation

$$\pi \leq \mu(g,k)$$

where π denotes the profit margin (being the proportion of profits in sales revenue), g denotes the proportional growth of sales over last period, and k is the ratio of investment to the increase in sales revenue (which is the marginal capital–output ratio, but which Wood called the investment coefficient). This is the opportunity frontier. It specifies the maximum profit margin which can be attained given values for the growth rate of sales and the investment coefficient. The opportunity frontier has the following properties: (1) $D_1\mu(g,k) < 0$; (2) $D_2\mu(g,k) > 0$. The first of these is just the demand–profit margin trade-off, for (1) may be interpreted as stating that, given a value for the investment coefficient, k, then on the opportunity frontier an increase in the growth rate of sales, g, can only be realized if there is a decrease in the profit margin, π. The second inequality ensures that, given a particular growth rate for sales, a higher profit margin is attainable when the investment coefficient is increased.

The finance frontier relates the minimum level of profits needed to provide finance for any particular level of investment. A firm will choose a strategy generating a level of profits which allows the firm to finance its investment plans. Wood assembled a relation describing the finance frontier by considering three ratios:

1. The financial assets ratio, f, being the ratio of a firm's acquisitions of financial assets to its investment expenditure;
2. The ratio of external finance (that is, new borrowings and share issues) to investment, denoted i; and
3. The gross retention ratio, s_c, which is the ratio of retained earnings (and depreciation provisions) to profits.

In particular, Wood introduced the idea that firms determine a minimum value for f and a maximum value for i. Together these extreme values determine the minimum amount of internal finance needed to fund any level of expenditure on investment. If the firm plans investment expenditure I, then, to overcome short-run fluctuations in profits which would otherwise restrict investment spending, a firm will choose to hold the minimum required proportion of its assets in liquid form. This minimum proportion is fI, making the minimum outlay on the firm's capital account $(1+f)I$. Firms are prepared to obtain finance for investment expenditure I from external sources (either by borrowing or with new share issues) up to some maximum level which is given by iI. This maximum is determined by the risks associated with borrowing and by the reluctance of shareholders to accept new issues. Of the total outlay $(1+f-i)I$ must then be funded from retained profits, $s_c P$. That is

$$s_c P \geq (1+f-i)I,$$

which is the relation describing the finance frontier. This may be rewritten as

$$\pi \geq \frac{(1+f-i)I}{s_c} gk$$

The original sales revenue-maximizing problem facing managers can now be written as

$$\max g$$

subject to

$$\pi \leq \mu(g,k)$$

$$\pi \geq \frac{(1+f-i)I}{s_c} gk.$$

A necessary condition for the maximization of the growth rate of sales is that the firm should simultaneously be operating on both frontiers. An economic interpretation of this condition is that:

No growth-maximising firm will choose a strategy inside the opportunity frontier ... because one of the constraints on its expansion is the availability of finance which, at any given growth rate, could be increased by raising the profit margin. Likewise, no growth-maximising firm will choose a strategy inside the finance frontier . . . because one of the constraints on its expansion is demand which, given any particular investment coefficient, could be increased by reducing the profit margin. That is to say, the desire to maximise growth in the face of competition from other firms (ie, to keep the profit margin as low as possible) drives the firm to acquire only the minimum necessary value of financial assets and to make use of the maximum possible amount of external finance. (*Ibid.*, p.85)

The finance frontier may be generalized to account for the entire company sector. This requires changes in the definitions of the entities which appear in the finance frontier relation. These changes are mainly concerned with the change from consideration of one firm's sales volume to the entire company sector value added (*ibid.*, pp.106–7). However, the opportunity frontier cannot be generalized to the macroeconomy. For a single firm the opportunity frontier is determined by its ability to compete effectively for a larger share of demand. Whether an individual firm competes effectively, contracts or ceases operation is of little concern at the macro level. The competitive struggle drives firms on to their financial frontiers. Thus, in equilibrium, the actual profit margin of the corporate sector will be the minimum margin determined on financial grounds,

$$\pi = \frac{(1+f-i)}{s_c} gk.$$

In Kaldor's terms we have an equation which determines the level of profits given investment expenditure

$$s_c P = (1+f-i)I.$$

Throughout Wood's theory his use of the word 'competition' refers to all forms of non-price competition as well as price competition. His view is that the aggregated company sector contains many firms and that each firm is struggling to grow at the expense of at least some of the other firms in the sector. This theory can accommodate collusion between some firms within product markets, but should the company sector consist of a single huge monopoly, the closed version of the theory described here would be indeterminate. For in this latter case there would be no financing requirements at the microeconomic level constraining the size of profit margins. That is, the finance frontier would not be binding (*ibid.*, pp.109–10).

4. Short-run Kaldorian Theories of Distribution

A number of authors have proposed theories of distribution, based on Kaldor's 1955–6 model, which relax the assumption of full employment of labour. As was demonstrated in the previous chapter, Kaldor focused on full employment. Writing in 1963, Samuelson (p.343) succinctly summarized the dissatisfaction of many authors with this emphasis: 'As an American I find it a little ironic that, just in the decade when our problems of unemployment have seemingly become chronic, Nicholas Kaldor has been reverting to a theory of full employment.' Kaldor's theory is similarly inapplicable to the recent experiences of many nations, including those he variously described as Anglo-Saxon or Commonwealth. Riach (1969, p.550, n25) pointed out that 'Australian experience supports Samuelson's position' – a remark which is even truer in 1992 than in 1969. Samuelson's remarks of course overlook the illumination of the distributive process provided by Kaldor's concentration on full employment. Subsequently, our understanding of short-run processes has been enriched by scholars working with modified versions of Kaldor's model. Indeed, neoclassical scholars eagerly seized on the notion that a model, Keynesian – only in its outcomes – in the sense of the *General Theory*, might be constructed by adding marginal productivity and perfect competition to the basic Kaldorian system. In this way Kaldor's work has evolved to illuminate the thinking of those who would integrate neoclassical and post-Keynesian theories. Some interesting results may be deduced from the attempts at synthesis reported in Sections 4.1 and 4.2.

In the final two sections different approaches are taken to the construction of short-run extensions of the basic model. Harcourt (Section 4.3) introduced a pricing rule which leads to a negative output multiplier. King and Regan's addition to the basic system of an endogenous link between investment and consumption is analysed in the final section. There are parallels between the latter extension and Kaldor's own view, discussed in Section 3.5, that firms may eventually operate where increases in output induce further investment.

4.1 Sen's marginal productivity theory

Sen (1963, pp.60–63) proposed a Keynesian model which allowed for the possibility of unemployment. In this model one commodity is produced and is used both in consumption and investment. Output Q is produced according to the production process

$$Q = F(K,L), \qquad (4.1)$$

where F is homogeneous of degree one, K is the stock of the good used in production, and L denotes employment of labour. Additions to the capital stock do not become productive during the current period, so in the short term K is fixed at the value

$$K = \overline{K}.$$

The money wage rate is determined from the marginal product of labour via

$$w = p \, D_2 \, F(\overline{K}, L), \qquad (4.2)$$

where D_2 denotes the partial derivative of F with respect to L. That is, $D_2F(\overline{K},L)$ is the marginal product of labour. Sen assumed the actual price level p is predicted by employers with perfect foresight. Aggregate income is now

$$pQ = P + wL. \qquad (4.3)$$

The equilibrium condition $S = I$ is written as

$$pI = s_PP + s_WwL, \qquad (4.4)$$

where (as already noted in Section 3.2) Sen assumed that workers save at the same rate from distributed profits as from wages and salaries. Investment is exogenously specified in Sen's model:

$$I = \bar{I}. \tag{4.5}$$

With money wages externally determined and set at $w = \bar{w}$ the endogenous variables may be determined from equations (4.1)–(4.5). In particular, from (4.3) and (4.4), the equilibrium level of employment L_e may be written as

$$L_e = (s_P Q - \bar{I})/\{(s_P - s_W)\bar{w}/p\} \tag{4.6}$$

and, from the marginal productivity condition for perfect competition, (3.54),

$$L_e = (s_P Q - \bar{I})/[(s_P - s_W)D_2 F(\bar{K}, L)]. \tag{4.7}$$

The share of profits in income is

$$
\begin{aligned}
P/pQ &= 1 - (\bar{w}/p)(L_e/Q) && \text{(from (4.3))} \\
&= 1 - (s_P Q - \bar{I})/(s_P - s_W)Q && \text{(from (4.6))} \\
&= (\bar{I}/Q - s_W)/(s_P - s_W),
\end{aligned}
$$

which is precisely Kaldor's distribution equation. Not that this should surprise, as the last result has been derived without reference to the marginal productivity theory of (4.2). If the level of employment L_e in (4.7), obtained using the neoclassical addition, is less than the available labour supply, equilibrium occurs with unemployment.

Determination of the real wage rate in accordance with the marginal product of labour allows the existence in Sen's model of solutions described by Samuelson and Modigliani (1966, Section 5) as 'dual' to those obtained by Pasinetti (see Section 3.2). Thus in Sen's model capitalists may be eliminated, or at least become irrelevant, in that even in conditions of unemployment it is only the savings of wage earners which react to increases in investment expenditure. An extreme case of this duality is given by taking the short-run production function

$$F(\bar{K}, L) = L/\alpha, \tag{4.8}$$

where the parameter α might be a function of the level of the capital stock. One choice is $\alpha = (\bar{K})^{-1}$. Alternatively, the chosen production function might be thought of as a short-run version of the Leontief or fixed coefficients technology,

$$min \left(\frac{L}{\alpha}, \frac{\overline{K}}{\beta}\right),$$

when there is excess capacity. In such cases it is not surprising that the condition for equilibrium in the commodity market and the decision to reward labour with its marginal product, according to (4.2), may be combined to deduce the duality condition $p\overline{I} = s_W Y = s_W pQ$. From (4.3) and (4.4),

$$
\begin{aligned}
\overline{I} &= s_P Q + (s_W - s_P)(\overline{w}/p)L & \text{(4.9)}\\
&= s_P Q + (s_W - s_P)D_2 F(\overline{K},L)L & \text{(from (4.2))}\\
&= s_P Q + (s_W - s_P)L/\alpha & \text{(from (4.8))}\\
&= s_P Q + (s_W - s_P)Q & \text{(from (4.8))}\\
&= s_W Q.
\end{aligned}
$$

Therefore in this example only dual solutions exist.

In general, stability of the solution with labour usage L_e will follow if it can be shown that

$$\frac{\partial(w/p)}{\partial L} > 0 \text{ at } L = L_e. \tag{4.10}$$

For in this case, a fall (respectively, an increase) in employment will make the real wage rate less (respectively, greater) than the marginal product of labour, and when it is assumed that employers are profit maximizers, it follows that a disturbance away from L_e will set off an adjustment mechanism that will return the economy to equilibrium. We will first investigate diagrammatically the validity of (4.10) and then rigorously obtain the same result.

Figure 4.1 shows the marginal and average product curves for a total product curve corresponding to a production function initially displaying increasing returns to the variable factor labour, then ultimately diminishing returns. These curves are labelled MM and AA. Equation (4.9) can be reorganized to provide the equation of a demand schedule of the type discussed in Section 3.5:

$$\frac{w}{p} = \frac{s_P}{(s_P - s_W)}\frac{Q}{L} - \frac{1}{(s_P - s_W)}\frac{\overline{I}}{L}. \tag{4.11}$$

Using Kaldor's savings assumption that $s_P > s_W$, the graphs of the

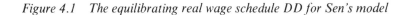

Figure 4.1   The equilibrating real wage schedule DD for Sen's model

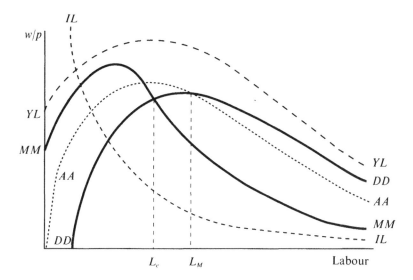

two terms on the right-hand side of (4.11) are sketched separately in
Figure 4.1 (and are denoted by *YL* and *IL*). The (vertical) difference
of these two components is the *DD* schedule showing the real wage
rate which induces equilibrium in the commodity market for a
particular employment level. The intersection of the marginal product curve *MM* for the textbook production function and the *DD*
schedule gives the equilibrium level of employment L_e. This intersection satisfies the stability condition (4.10) because it is to the left of
L_M, which is the employment level corresponding to the maximum
value that the real wage can assume along the schedule *DD*. Clearly,
other technologies would generate different versions of Figure 4.1.
Below we consider a version of Figure 4.1 corresponding to a production function with constant average and marginal costs. Before
considering this other case, a proof of (4.10) is provided.
   Differentiation of the demand equation (4.11) gives

$$\frac{\partial(w/p)}{\partial L} = \{D_2F(\bar{K},L)/L - (Q/L^2)\}s_P/(s_P - s_W) + (\bar{I}/L^2)\,[1/(s_P - s_W)].$$

$$(4.12)$$

This partial derivative will be zero for the employment level L_M satisfying

$$Q/L_M = D_2 F(\overline{K}, L_M) + (\overline{I}/L_M)(1/s_P). \tag{4.13}$$

Thus the extreme value of w/p along the DD schedule occurs at a value of L where the average product exceeds the marginal product. If the real wage w/p is determined by the marginal product of labour, then (4.11) can be rearranged to show that L_e must satisfy

$$Q/L_e = [(s_P - s_W)/s_P]D_2 F(\overline{K}, L_e) + (\overline{I}/L_e)(1/s_P). \tag{4.14}$$

The values determined for L_M and L_e can only coincide when s_W is zero. Finally, to ensure that the value of the average product in (4.14) occurs when L_e is less than L_M, it must be shown that L_M represents a maximum of the DD schedule. That is, we require

$$\frac{\partial^2 (w/p)}{\partial L_M^2} = \frac{s_P}{(s_P - s_W)L_M} D_2^2 F(\overline{K}, L_M) < 0.$$

Provided L_M represents a point of diminishing returns to labour the desired result follows whenever $s_P > s_W$.

Kaldor used an average direct cost function which was constant for a large range of output levels, and increasing thereafter. A production function giving such an average *variable* cost curve has average and marginal products as shown in Figure 4.2. There is an equilibrium employment level, L_e located in the region where marginal product is constant. Now from (4.12)

$$\frac{\partial (w/p)}{\partial L_e} = (1/L_e)\{D_2 F(\overline{K}, L_e) - Q/L_e\} s_P/(s_P - s_W) + (\overline{I}/L_e^2)/(s_P - s_W).$$

As marginal and average products are equal at L_e, in this case the first term on the right is zero, and it follows that the stability condition is satisfied. That is

$$\frac{\partial (w/p)}{\partial L_e} > 0,$$

and, as before, disturbances away from L_e will cause profit-maximizing employers to readjust their production plans so that L_e is

Figure 4.2   The equilibrating real wage schedule DD for Kaldor's
representative firm

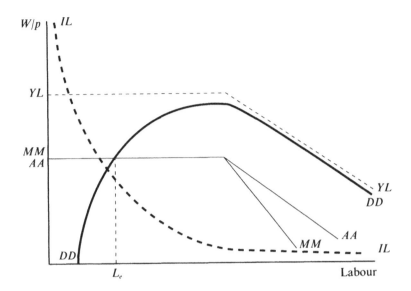

attained once again. Provided that L_e is less than the full employment level, we have a stable unemployment equilibrium similar to
the solution E_1 of Figure 3.2. Some interesting features of Sen's
model are demonstrated in Figure 4.3.

Figure 4.3 is constructed from the previous diagram. Three DD
curves are shown. They were generated from IL schedules corresponding to different levels of investment. There is no value of the
marginal product which will produce a solution of the model when
the equilibrating real wage is given by D_1D_1. However, there is a
solution when either the curves D_2D_2 or D_3D_3 describe the demand
schedule. For D_2D_2 the required level of employment exceeds L_f, and
the stability condition (4.10) is not satisfied. Even when the real
wage is determined by the schedule D_3D_3, a slight increase in investment activity implies over-full employment. In this case the stability
condition holds. Although not shown, it is possible that there will be
a stable equilibrium at full employment for a DD schedule lying
between D_2D_2 and D_3D_3.

The possibilities represented by D_1D_1 and D_2D_2 and the doubtful

Figure 4.3   Location of solutions to Sen's model for Kaldor's representative firm

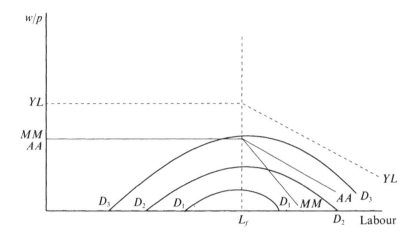

prospect of eliminating entrepreneurs with the technology of (4.8) appear to suggest that the integration of perfect competition with post-Keynesian analysis may not be so useful. In the next section we examine another attempt to integrate marginalism with Kaldor's 1955–6 model.

4.2   Riach's marginal productivity model

Riach (1969, p.543) saw Kaldor's model of distribution as a 'tautological relationship' between the share of each income group and the ratio of investment to income. Tautological, but with theoretical importance attached to the causal links between the components of the identity. This sets Riach apart from Odagiri, who thought that the Kaldorian approach had no theoretical content at all (see Section 3.3). As we have seen, Kaldor thought that at full employment the investment component of aggregate demand determined the distribution of income. Following Dunlop, Riach wanted to promote the reverse causality, from the distribution of income to aggregate demand:

[The] consumption function for the whole community must be affected by the relative distribution of income between wage and salary earners and other groups in the community. It might be thought that, since wages and salaries on balance go to individuals with lower incomes and presumably with higher marginal propensities to consume, an increase in labour's share in the depression would be a factor tending to increase the level of income. (Dunlop, 1950, pp.189–90)

In Riach's model are combined elements of the formal models of Kaldor, Cartter and the marginal productivity school. Like Kaldor, Riach modelled the effects of aggregate demand on the distribution of income, emphasizing the roles of savings and investment. Further, also in common with Cartter, he assumed that the savings properties from each type of income are positive and different (although Riach (1969, p.554) may have seen this as a difference attaching to classes rather than types of income). Second, as with Cartter and the *General Theory*, he relaxed the restriction of full employment and investigated the interdependence between the distribution and the level of income. Cartter's model is indeterminate, so to close the system Riach incorporated a short-run production function and allowed labour to be employed up to the level equating its marginal product with the real wage.

The equations of Riach's model are written here as:

$$Q = F(\overline{K},L) \tag{4.15}$$

$$\overline{w} = p\, D_2 F(\overline{K},L) \tag{4.16}$$

$$L < L_f \tag{4.17}$$

$$pQ = Y = W + P \tag{4.18}$$

$$S_R = sQ - a\sigma \tag{4.19}$$

$$I = b - g\sigma \tag{4.20}$$

$$\sigma = d - eQ \tag{4.21}$$

where σ denotes the wage share of national income, L_f is full employment, F is a production function of other than Cobb–Douglas form, a, b, d, e, g and s are positive constants, with d and e being chosen to ensure that $0 < \sigma < 1$ over the region in which (4.21) is valid. $D_2 F(\overline{K},L)$ again denotes the marginal product of labour. Riach chose a short-run production function for which the wage share is not constant; that is:

$$Q \neq \alpha L^k,$$

where α and k are positive constants. Thus Riach was able to ensure that, when short-run profit is maximized, the wage share σ falls as output increases, and (4.21) is valid.

This system of equations not only adds to the basic system, but also introduces an unusual form for the savings function. Its relationship to Kaldor's preferred form can be seen as follows:

$$\begin{aligned} S &= s_W W + s_P P \\ &= s_W W + s_P (Y - W) \\ &= (s_W - s_P)W + s_P Y \end{aligned}$$

and

$$S = Y[s_P + (s_W - s_P)\sigma] \qquad \text{(as } \sigma = W/Y\text{)}. \qquad (4.22)$$

This savings function is homogeneous of degree one in Y, a property shared with the form used by Cartter (1959, p.156). In fact, Cartter's equation for the aggregate savings propensity differs only from the one obtained from (4.22) in the appearance of a term for distribution of a portion of profit to shareholders. To reach the apparently non-homogeneous version of Riach's equation requires a little further manipulation. Cancel price from S and Y in (4.22), so that

$$S_R = Q[s_P - (s_P - s_W)\sigma]$$

$$= s_P Q - (s_P - s_W)Q\sigma.$$

Now if s in (4.19) is chosen to be s_P and a is set at $-(s_P - s_W)Q$, and (4.19) is interpreted as an equation for real saving, S_R, Kaldor's savings function can be converted to Riach's form. The choice for a violates Riach's belief that a is constant, unless Q is fixed, at say the full-employment-constrained maximum. Cartter (1959, pp.156–7) and Riach (1969, p.552) each assumed that $s_P > s_W$, so the sign for a required by Riach in (4.19) is appropriate. This real savings function is shown below to confound his approach. If, on the other hand,

Riach intended equation (4.19) to explain *nominal* savings, then in the Kaldorian framework it appears from (4.22) that *a* should be equated with $-(s_P - s_W)Y$, implying that nominal income is fixed by his assumption that *a* is constant.

Investment in this model is sensitive to changes in the distribution of income.

> As we are operating in the short run with a fixed capital stock a shift in the distribution of income from profits to wages will mean a decrease in the rate of profit on capital, therefore if expectations about the future rate of profit are to some extent based upon the current rate of profit there will be a fall in investment, and thus we obtain a negative relationship between σ and investment (*Ibid.*, p.555)

Riach suggested that his investment function should be compared with one proposed by Cartter (1959, pp.156–7), in which

$$I = \beta(1 - \sigma)Y,$$

where β, the investment–profit coefficient, is assumed to be constant. In this equation investment, like savings, becomes responsive to the distribution of income, and Riach was able to activate the reverse of the Kaldorian causal linkage. His model may be used then to study the interaction between the distribution and the level of income in the short run. From the savings and investment equations (4.19) and (4.20) equilibrium in the commodity market occurs when

$$sQ - a\sigma = b - g\sigma,$$

and

$$Q = \{b + \sigma(a - g)\}/s. \tag{4.23}$$

This is a positively sloped function of σ when $a > g$. Substitution of (4.21) into (4.23), along with some manipulation, gives

$$\sigma = (ds - be)/\{s + (a - g)e\}. \tag{4.24}$$

Some questions arise concerning the interpretation of this result in the context of the three theories from which Riach borrowed. First, compare Riach's model with Cartter's system,

$$S = Y[s_W\sigma + s_P(1 - \sigma)],$$

$$I = \beta(1 - \sigma)Y.$$

For these equations equilibrium in the commodity market occurs when

$$Y[s_W\sigma + (s_P - \beta)(1 - \sigma)] = 0. \qquad (4.25)$$

This condition is satisfied when income is zero, or when the term within the square brackets is zero. When the wage share, in addition to the savings propensities, is constant the coefficient of Y in (4.25) is constant. In this case the I and S schedules are straight lines passing through the origin, and it follows that (4.25) is satisfied when the schedules are coincident. There exist multiple equilibria, and any level of income can be sustained up to full employment. If planned savings exceed planned investment then Cartter's model produces the prediction that the economy will contract until $Y = 0$. When investment plans amount to more than intended savings, the economy will expand, presumably up to the full employment constraint. In Riach's version of this model, the wage share is considered to be flexible, and a unique solution is obtained. The equilibrium wage share in (4.25) is influenced by savings behaviour via the coefficients s and a of (4.19), investment behaviour via the appearance in the equation of b and g from (4.20), and the production technology through the influence of d and e from (4.21).

But exactly what do d, e, s, a, b and g represent in terms of the Kaldorian paradigm? Comparison of Riach's investment equation with the assumption that I is set exogenously at $\bar{I}$ suggests that

$$b = \bar{I}. \qquad (4.26)$$

Riach used b primarily to represent that part of investment which is independent of fluctuations in labour's share, and which might be set by 'animal spirits'. The term $g\sigma$ in the investment equation (4.20) represents a departure from the basic Kaldorian model where total investment is exogenous, or even from Kaldor's position that I/Y is determined independently of the savings propensities. Riach referenced Kaldor's representative firm (see Section 3.5), but he did not attempt to incorporate into his model Kaldor's notion of induced or endogenous investment. Above, the parameters a and s were related to entities which appear in Kaldor's savings function, although a lost the status of a constant in the interpretation. It is not so easy, however, to interpret d and e in terms of the aggregate production function F.

When profits are maximized, $\sigma = D_2 F(\bar{K},L)L/Q$ and from (4.21)

$$(L/Q)D_2 F(\bar{K},L) = d - eQ,$$

or

$$\frac{L}{Q}\frac{\partial Q}{\partial L} = d - eQ. \qquad (4.27)$$

This partial differential equation has the integral

$$(1/d)\log\{C_1^{-1} Q/(d - eQ)\} = \log(L/C_2),$$

when $d > eQ$ (that is, when $\sigma > 0$), and where C_1 and C_2 will in general be functions of $\bar{K}$. Simplification gives

$$d - eQ = QL^{-d}(C_2^d/C_1)$$

and

$$Q = d\{e + L^{-d}C_2^d/C_1)\}^{-1} \qquad (4.28)$$

A more familiar functional form in the neoclassical literature is the CES (constant elasticity of substitution) production function

$$F(K,L) = \{\alpha_1 K^{-\gamma} + \alpha_2 L^{-\gamma}\}^{-1/\gamma}, \qquad (4.29)$$

which has similarities with Riach's technology. These may be seen by neglecting the index '$1/\gamma$' in (4.29) and also thinking of e in (4.28) as a constant determined by $\bar{K}$ in the short run. Omission of $1/\gamma$ means that the neoclassical production function does not display constant returns to scale for $\gamma \neq 1$. For the rest of this section the production function is assumed to be of the form (4.28) with

$$F(K,L) = d\{\alpha_1 K^{-d} + \alpha_2 L^{-d}\}^{-1}. \qquad (4.30)$$

The elasticity of substitution between capital and labour is given by

$$\rho = 1/(1 + d). \tag{4.31}$$

When K is fixed at $\overline{K}$, it follows that, for (4.28) and (4.30) to be equal,

$$e = \alpha_1 \overline{K}^{-d} \text{ and } C_2^d/C_1 = \alpha_2. \tag{4.32}$$

Now solve the system consisting of Riach's investment and wage-share equations,

$$I = b - g\sigma \tag{4.20}$$

$$\sigma = d - eQ, \tag{4.21}$$

and the modified savings equation,

$$S_R = sQ - a'\sigma Q, \tag{4.33}$$

This functional form was obtained from Kaldor's savings functions, where it is required that

$$s = s_P \tag{4.34}$$
$$a' = s_P - s_W.$$

The coefficients b, d and e in Riach's investment and wage-share equations are taken as being determined by (4.26), (4.31) and (4.32). The model now has the solution

$$Q = (b - g\sigma)/(s - a'\sigma).$$

When Q is eliminated using (4.21), the following quadratic condition for σ is obtained:

$$a'\sigma^2 + (eg - a'd - s)\sigma + (ds - be) = 0.$$

There are at most two positive solutions for σ, satisfying

$$2a'\sigma = - (a'd + s - eg) \pm \{(a'd + s - eg)^2 - 4(ds - be)a'\}^{1/2}.$$

When $a'd + s > eg$, only one positive solution for σ will be obtained when

$$ds < be; \tag{4.35}$$

while when $ds > be$ there might be no solutions, a unique solution or multiple solutions.

Condition (4.35) is preferable, as this guarantees both the existence and uniqueness of a positive σ satisfying the quadratic equation. When (4.26), (4.31), (4.32) and (4.34) are substituted into (4.35), the condition becomes

$$[(1 - \rho)/\rho]s_P < \alpha_1 \overline{I}/\overline{K^d}. \tag{4.36}$$

Even if an appropriate value for s_P is chosen it will not be easy to check this inequality, as a detailed estimation of (4.30) must be undertaken to obtain plausible values for ρ and α_1. Errors introduced in estimating α_1 and ρ from an aggregate data set, along with the objections noted in Chapter 2 to the validity of aggregate production functions in macroeconomic analysis, would make many economists hesitate before accepting the announcement that (4.36) had been observed to hold.

Riach's model, while augmenting the work of Cartter, does not fit convincingly into the framework of Kaldor's 1955–6 model. Riach has identified the importance of a mechanism from distribution to demand, by introducing an endogenous component of investment. The models proposed in Chapters 5 and 7 incorporate a different endogenous determination of investment. In the next section we consider an extension of the basic Kaldorian system to incorporate a price rule based on investment plans.

4.3 Harcourt's price rule

In a digression from his main theme Harcourt (1972, pp.210–13) proposed a short-run model with a Kaldorian savings function designed to illustrate a process described by Robinson, in which an increase in the investment rate raises gross income and the profit share. The growth of the profit share was theorized to occur as prices rose relative to the nominal wage, so that the initial stimulus to investment set off a mechanism which generated the required saving.

The model constructed by Harcourt may demonstrate a non-Keynesian response from income to an autonomous increase in investment. The modified version of Riach's model also has the potential for a negative multiplier response to the same stimulus.[1] This anomalous behaviour is demonstrated in Harcourt's model, and the role of the type of the production function is investigated.

The equations of the model are

$$Q = F(\overline{K},L) = L/\alpha \qquad (4.37)$$

$$pQ = P + wL \qquad (4.38)$$

$$pI = s_P P + s_W wL \qquad (4.39)$$

$$I = \overline{I} \qquad (4.40)$$

$$w = \overline{w} \qquad (4.41)$$

$$p = \lambda I \qquad (4.42)$$

These are the equations solved by Sen, with the exception that, instead of the real wage (and hence the price level) being determined by the marginal product of labour, here price is set by businessmen according to their confidence, their intuition about acceptable profit margins and, in the long run, their desire to set margins so that investment plans may be financed internally. The production function specified by Harcourt is the special case shown in Section 4.1 to have dual solutions only in the sense of Samuelson and Modigliani. Money profits in this model are given by

$$P = pQ - w L,$$

and from the commodity market equilibrium condition (4.39),

$$p \overline{I} = s_P pQ - (s_P - s_W)\overline{w}L . \qquad (4.43)$$

With (4.42) and (4.37) this becomes

$$\lambda \overline{I^2} = s_P \lambda \overline{I}Q - (s_P - s_W)\overline{w}L = \{s_P \lambda \overline{I} - (s_P - s_W)\overline{w}\alpha\}Q;$$

and the equilibrium level of real income is given by

$$Q_e = \lambda \overline{P} / \{ s_P \lambda \overline{I} - (s_P - s_W) \overline{w} \alpha \}. \tag{4.44}$$

To see that the income-investment multiplier might be negative, we could differentiate (4.44) and then proceed to search for the conditions which make the multiplier negative. Instead, we first parallel the steps above in the derivation of (4.44) to obtain an expression for the elasticity of income with respect to investment. In finite difference form the national income identity (4.38) is

$$p\Delta Q + Q\Delta p = \Delta P + \overline{w}\Delta L.$$

Divide this equation by pQ. Then in terms of the proportional changes in each of the variables, denoted by prime superscripts,

$$p' + Q' = B_P P' + B_W L',$$

where B_P and B_W are the shares of profits and wages in national income. From the form of the production function (4.37), $L' = Q'$, and from the price rule (4.42), $p' = I'$, so that

$$Q'(1 - B_W) = B_P P' - I'.$$

For convenience take $s_W = 0$, so that from the equilibrium condition, (4.39) $P = pI/s_P$, $P' = p' + I' = 2I'$ and

$$Q' = - \frac{(1 - 2B_P)}{(1 - B_W)} I'.$$

Obviously the elasticity, and hence the multiplier, is negative only if $2B_P < 1$, that is, if $B_W = (1 - B_P) > 1/2.$[2] To understand this result, first recall that s_W was assumed to be 0. In this case real aggregate consumption is given by

$$C = \frac{\overline{w}}{p} L + (1 - s_P) \frac{P}{p},$$

and real aggregate demand is

$$D = \frac{\overline{w}}{p} L + (1 - s_P) \frac{P}{p} + \overline{I},$$

$$= \frac{\bar{w}}{p} L + \frac{\bar{I}}{s_P}.$$

Demand declines when the expansion of investment induces a greater contraction in that part of consumption accounted for by real wages. This can only occur if the impact of price on the real wage outweighs any tendency to expand production (and therefore employment) to meet the expanded investment demand. When initially consumption by wage earners is a large component of demand, as is the case when $B_W > 1/2$, there will be a significant contraction of real demand caused by the reduction of the real wage.

With the production function (4.37), Sen's model does not suffer from the defect of an unexpected sign for the income multiplier. For this production function it was shown in Section 4.1 that

$$\bar{I} = s_W Y.$$

This is the Samuelson and Modigliani dual condition. Clearly, the income-investment multiplier is positive for $s_W > 0$. However, with investment being financed by workers' savings alone, Sen's theory is not responsive to the savings behaviour of businessmen and corporations. There is a rather severe trade-off between negative multiplier effects in Harcourt's model and loss of the Cambridge distribution result in the Sen approach when a fixed coefficients technology is used.

Should Harcourt's mark-up rule be abandoned? Before taking this decision, a number of other influences in the models might be considered. An obvious sensitivity is the influence of the type of technology. Harcourt's preferred function is consistent with a fixed-coefficients technology without substitution possibilities. Technologies permitting substitution between factors may not induce a negative multiplier, depending on the particular functional form. Cobb–Douglas production functions displaying diminishing returns to labour produce positive multiplier responses, but a CES technology or the production function (4.30) underlying Riach's model will have values of income for which the multiplier is negative.[3] Alternatively, the negative multiplier might be the outcome of the form of the price rule. For example, it might be assumed that the mark-up depends on the investment–income coefficient, rather than the level of investment expenditure. This first possibility does not prevent the multiplier being negative. Two theories of the formation of price are examined in the extensions of the neo-Pasinetti model reported in Chapters 5 and 7. Harcourt's price theory might be more applicable in the context of the 'golden age' environment. This prospect is examined by incorporating the price equation $p = \lambda I$ into the neo-Pasinetti model.

If it is assumed that the investment–income coefficient is fixed, as Kaldor preferred, a proportional increase in investment induces an equiproportional increase in real output, Q. But from Harcourt's rule price will increase in proportion. Thus price and output grow together. That is,

$$\frac{\Delta Q}{Q} = \frac{\Delta I_R}{I_R} = \frac{\Delta p}{p}.$$

When the golden age rate of growth of investment is the natural rate of growth, prices are compelled to grow at this same rate. Note that, if the physical stock of capital, M, is growing at the constant rate g, $I_R = gM$ and

$$\Delta I_R = g\Delta M = gI_R.$$

Hence it follows that

$$\frac{\Delta p}{p} = \frac{\Delta I_R}{I_R} = \frac{\Delta M}{M}.$$

Therefore Harcourt's pricing rule produces the long-run implication that prices and capital grow at the same rate. This parallels the result of Section 3.3, which was required to ensure that, within Kaldor's framework, Tobin's q held to a steady state value.

The possibility that the investment multiplier will be negative arises in this situation also. To see this, first obtain an expression for aggregate real savings. When average cost a is constant,

$$P = (p - a)Q,$$

and aggregate nominal savings in the neo-Pasinetti model are given by

$$S = s_h\{W + (1-s_c)P\} + s_c P - c(q - i)I,$$

$$= s_h\, Y + s_c\, (1 - s_h)(p - a)Q - c\,(q - i)I,$$

where c is used to denote the propensity of households to consume capital gains. Consequently, aggregate real savings are given by

$$S_R = \{s_h + s_c\,(1 - s_h)(1 - a/p)\}Q - c\,(q - i)I_R. \qquad (4.45)$$

An expansion of real investment has two effects on the level of real savings. First, there is an increase in real savings due to the expansion of activity required to manufacture new investment goods, and also real savings are increased because the price level rises. The second effect tends to reduce aggregate savings. When investment activity increases, greater capital gains can be had, so long as the market valuation of planned investment exceeds the amount of investment financed by new share issues (that is, $q > i$). In this model capital gains are taken out in expanded consumption or in the purchase of securities. Provided all capital gains are not ploughed back into share purchases (that is, $c > 0$) there will be a reduction in aggregate real savings. From equation (4.45) the effect on real savings of an increase in planned real investment ΔI_R is

$$\Delta S_R = \{s_h + s_c\,(1 - s_h)(1 - a/p)\}\Delta Q + Q s_c\,(1 - s_h)a\,\Delta p/p^2 - c(q - i)\Delta I_R.$$

But real output and price grow at the same rate as real investment, so that

$$\Delta S_R = \{s_h + s_c\,(1 - s_h)\}\Delta Q - c(q - i)\Delta I_R.$$

From the requirement that the increased investment is just met by the increase in savings, it follows that

$$\Delta Q = \frac{1 + c(q - i)}{s_h + s_c(1 - s_h)}\,\Delta I_R.$$

When s_h and s_c are positive and less than one, the denominator of the multiplier is also positive and less than one. Hence the multiplier will have an unconventional sign when

$$ci > 1 + cq.$$

There are a number of special cases which we can informatively explore. First when $i = 0$, that is when corporations finance all investment from internal sources, the multiplier is always positive (assuming that c is positive). When firms finance new investment solely from new issues, that is $i = 1$, then the multiplier will potentially be negative whenever Tobin's q is less than one. For example, with $c = 1.5$ and $q = 0.3$ the inequality above is satisfied when $i = 1$. This is a peculiar, unrealistic long-run state. Household consumption out of capital gains exceeds the actual gain by 50 per cent, implying high household hopes for large dividends in the future or implying household confidence in the future bullishness of share markets. By contrast, confidence in corporations is at such a low ebb that share prices reflect only 30 per cent of the value of the existing capital stock. The activities of speculators and corporate raiders may be the bridge between the deterioration in the market value of the capital stock and the high propensity for households to consume out of capital gains. Presumably, corporate raiders are prepared to purchase very large parcels of securities because they see the benefits of seizing control of under-valued assets. This might give households in aggregate the confidence to maintain a high propensity to consume out of capital gains, because they believe that households' future dividend streams are secure and will continue to grow. This scenario represents a short-term phenomenon and is very unlikely to persist into the long run. If a more realistic value for i is allowed, say $i = 0.2$, and assuming that households do not indulge in excessive spending from capital gains, by setting $c = 0.9$, the investment multiplier will be negative only if q is unrealistically lower than $-0.82/0.9 = -0.9$. If it is assumed that households scrupulously save capital gains, setting $c = -0.1$, and if i remains at 0.2, the inequality is satisfied when the securities market is booming with $q > 1.02/0.1 = 10.2$. This again seems an unlikely long-run equilibrium situation.

In later chapters, other theories of price are assessed. We turn now to a type of short-run model proposed by Goodwin and later integrated into the basic Kaldorian system by King and Regan.

4.4   Goodwin's aggregate demand analysis

In this section we consider a post-Keynesian model which does not include the Kaldorian savings hypothesis, but which uses a mark-up of price over the costs of labour and intermediate inputs. Nevertheless, its main implications are reproduced in a Kaldorian model proposed by King and Regan. Goodwin (1983) analysed the model described by the system:

$$Q = min\ (R/a,\ L/a_1), \tag{4.46}$$

where Q = total output,
     R = the level of intermediate usage of the one commodity produced in this economy, and
a and a_1 = the technological coefficients;

$$Y = p(1 - a)Q - F_d, \tag{4.47}$$

$$W = wa_1Q + F_w, \tag{4.48}$$

where F_d = depreciation and
     F_w = fixed wages and salaries;

$$P = Y - W, \tag{4.49}$$

$$Q = (a + wa_1/p)Q + A, \tag{4.50}$$

where A = 'the sum of all unsystematic real demands' (*ibid.*, p.306); and

$$p = (1 + \lambda)(pa + wa_1), \tag{4.51}$$

where the constant mark-up λ 'may be roughly calculated to cover fixed charges and desired profit . . . at an expected output' (*ibid.*, p.307). In this economy, production occurs via the two-input fixed-coefficient technology of (4.46), with prices determined by producers as in (4.51). Equation (4.50) is the commodity market equilibrium condition. In this form supply responds passively to changes in demand. The equation may be rearranged to

$$p(1 - a)Q = pA + wa_1Q, \tag{4.52}$$

so that

$$Y = pA + wa_1Q - F_d.$$

It follows that Goodwin's unsystematic real demands consist of aggregate demand net of replacement investment, and the usage of the output-dependent component of wage income. From (4.48) and (4.52) the share of wages and salaries in this model is given by

$$\frac{W}{Y} = \frac{wa_1Q + F_w}{p(1 - a)Q - F_d} = \frac{wa_1Q + F_w}{pA + wa_1Q - F_d}. \qquad (4.53)$$

At full employment the numerator in the expressions in (4.53) for the wage share is fixed when the unit wage and overhead labour costs are constant. However, the denominator increases owing to the direct impact of the growth in unsystematic real demand and owing to the subsequent pressure on price. The wage share is therefore predicted to fall. When there is unused labour and the spare capital capacity with which this labour might operate, both the numerator and the denominator grow, suggesting the possibility that the change in the wage share may not be as great as at full employment. This result is sensitive to the introduction of at least one of overhead salaries or depreciation. For, when it is assumed that $F_w = F_d = 0$, then

$$\frac{W}{Y} = \frac{w}{p} \frac{a_1}{1 - a}, \qquad (4.54)$$

which is independent of total output, so that the wage share is only affected by the real wage. It is directly proportional to the real wage, with the constant of proportionality being determined by the technology. This special case can be taken a little further. If (4.51) is used to eliminate p, the wage share may be written as

$$\frac{W}{Y} = \frac{[1/(1 + \lambda)] - a}{1 - a}.$$

Thus the share of wages and salaries in net income is inversely related to the mark-up, and is independent of increases in unit wage costs, wa_1.

King and Regan (1988, pp.56–60 and 85–6) outlined a Kaldorian model which captures the impact of rising wage incomes on consumption and investment, and replicates Goodwin's results on the volatility of income shares. They used the equations

$$Y = P + W,$$

$$I = s_P P + s_W W, \tag{4.55}$$

$$I = f(C), \tag{4.56}$$

where C denotes aggregate consumption. The investment function (4.56) was thought to be 'Keynesian in spirit' in that it assumed 'investment is positively related to the level of consumption (so that the construction of breweries, for example, is encouraged by increased consumption of beer)' (*ibid.*, p.59).

In (4.56) investment is not related to *changes* in consumption, as is implied by King and Regan. Provided consumption of beer continues – no matter at what level – there will be investment in breweries. Fluctuations occur in expenditure on breweries as beer consumption level fluctuates. But this expenditure is choked off only when beer is no longer drunk. At the aggregate level investment expenditure is predicted by (4.56) to continue so long as there is consumption, no matter at which part of the business cycle the economy is operating. During a boom, for example, there may be *over-investment*, leading eventually to a downturn:

In expansion, rapidly rising demand for investment goods (overinvestment) causes a rapid rise in the cost of these goods to investors. The prices of consumer goods rise more slowly, squeezing profit margins in that sector, and as a result, the increase of total profits proceeds more slowly. Because investment is determined by the increase in profits, less increase in profits causes less investment. Less investment causes less income which causes less consumption, and so forth until the depression is well under way. (Hunt and Sherman, 1975, pp.443–4)

The King and Regan investment equation also raises an issue related to *under-consumption*. A redistribution from wages to profits reduces overall consumption as the propensity to consume from profits is lower (certainly among the one-income class receiving only profits) than from wages and salaries. But with (4.56) investor demand cannot take up the shortfall in aggregate demand. This is odd. Consumption is the larger part of demand and, even though it may decline, investment expenditure continues, keeping wages higher in the capital goods sector relative to those in the consumption goods sector. Also the prices of investment goods will tend to be relatively higher. Consumption goods industries therefore face increased costs of investment programmes, but receive greater revenues from workers who are employed by capital producers. At best these effects might cancel out, suggesting that the investment demand during downturns can only be from capital producers acquiring more of the plant and equipment required for the production of capital goods. That is, capital producers are acting to keep the widow's cruse full. An alternative to (4.56), closer in spirit to the accelerator theory, would be $I = f(\Delta C)$. Nevertheless, the theory of King and Regan is retained for this discussion.

When the savings propensities are positive and unequal, the system of equations devised by King and Regan may be solved to obtain

$$\frac{W}{Y} = \frac{s_P - f(C)/Y}{s_P - s_W}.$$

The sensitivity of the wage share to variations in income is measured by

$$\frac{\partial W/Y}{\partial Y} = -\frac{1}{Y}\left\{\frac{\partial f(C)}{\partial Y} - \frac{f(C)}{Y}\right\}/(s_P - s_W). \qquad (4.57)$$

The sensitivity of the wage share to variations in the wage bill is given by

$$\frac{\partial W/Y}{\partial W} = -\frac{1}{Y}\left\{\frac{\partial f(C)}{\partial W} - \frac{f(C)}{Y}\frac{\partial Y}{\partial W}\right\}/(s_P - s_W). \qquad (4.58)$$

When the capitalists' savings propensity exceeds that of workers it is clear from (4.57) that increases in income Y will induce increases (respectively, decreases or no change) in the wage share if the marginal propensity to invest is less than (respectively, greater than or equal to) the average propensity to invest, $f(C)/Y$. If we write

$$I = I_0 + iC,$$

and

$$C = C_0 + cY,$$

with the latter function also being Keynesian in spirit, then the difference between the marginal and average propensities to invest is $-(I_0 + iC_0)/Y$. In this case the sensitivity of the wage share to variations in output depends on the levels of the autonomous components of investment and consumption, the level of income and the sensitivity of investment to consumption.

Now consider the effect on the wage share of changes in the income of all labour, wL. When the economy under study is closed and there is no government, aggregate investment is given by

$$f(C) = Y - C.$$

Suppose, assuming excess capacity, that Q is given by the short-run production function

$$Q = min\left(\frac{L}{\alpha}, \frac{\overline{K}}{\beta}\right) = L/\alpha \qquad (4.59)$$

Suppose too that w is set at $\overline{w}$, then

$$\begin{aligned} f(C) &= Y - (1 - s_W)W - (1 - s_P)P \\ &= s_P Y - (s_P - s_W)W \\ &= \{s_P(-1 + p\overline{w}\alpha) + s_W\}W, \end{aligned}$$

and if there is no impact on prices

$$\frac{\partial f(C)}{\partial W} = s_P(-1 + p/\overline{w}\alpha) + s_W = \frac{f(C)}{Y}\frac{\partial Y}{\partial W}.$$

It now follows from (4.58) that

$$\frac{\partial W/Y}{\partial W} = 0,$$

and the wage share will be completely insensitive to changes in unit wage costs.

In general

$$f(C) = s_P Y - (s_P - s_W)W,$$

and so (4.58) can be rearranged to

$$\frac{\partial W/Y}{\partial W} = -\frac{(s_P - s_W)}{Y}\left\{\frac{W}{Y}\frac{\partial Y}{\partial W} - 1\right\}.$$

The sensitivity of W/Y to changes in the wage bill now depends on the responsiveness of income Y to such a change. Clearly, Y will respond to changed consumption spending arising from a change in the wage bill. But changes in Y will also be induced as capitalists modify investment plans in response to the change in consumption. Where there is spare capacity, it seems likely that these plans are, at best, unresponsive to increases in the wage bill, and the effect on the wage share is likely to be muted. This outcome is similar to the result deduced from Goodwin's model.

When a production function is specified it can be seen that the responsiveness of the wage share depends on the parameters specifying the technology. For example, in the short run, when Q is given by

$$Q = \alpha L^k \overline{K}^l$$

then

$$\frac{\partial Q}{\partial W} = \alpha k\, L^{k-1}\overline{K}^l/w = k\frac{Q}{W},$$

and

$$\frac{\partial(W/Y)}{\partial W} = -\frac{kp - 1}{Y}\frac{W}{p}\frac{\partial p}{\partial W}\frac{1}{Y}.$$

The sensitivity of the wage share may be positive so long as kp is less than one. This last relation allows scope for the interaction of both supply and demand in the determination of changes in the wage share.

In this chapter some extensions of Kaldor's 1955–6 theory to the short run have been surveyed. These were attempts to incorporate neoclassical marginal productivity theories of employment and pricing (Sen in Section 4.1 and Riach in Section 4.2), price formation by a mark-up on investment expenditure (Harcourt, Section 4.3) and the endogenous determination of investment as a function of the wage share (Riach) or of consumption (King and Regan, above). Doubts were expressed about each theory. There were problems of existence, uniqueness and the properties of solutions to Sen's model; difficulties in reconciling Riach's model with Kaldor's savings function and determining the number of solutions; the possibility of negative multiplier effects discovered by Harcourt; and doubts about the functional form of the investment equation used by King and Regan. The work of building a short-run version begun in Section 3.3 is continued in the following chapters, where theories of the mark-up and investment are introduced. The determination of investment proposed in the next chapter departs from the efforts of Riach and of King and Regan.

Notes

1. In the version of the model presented in Section 4.2, real income is given by

$$Q = (b - g\sigma)/(s - a'\sigma), \tag{4A.1}$$

where b corresponds to the portion of investment which is independent of fluctuations in the wage share, σ. In terms of finite changes:

$$(s - a'\sigma)\Delta Q = (a'Q - g)\Delta\sigma.$$

When there is a unique solution for σ (given by the solution with the positive root in the equation preceding (4.35))

$$\Delta\sigma = 2e\,\Delta b\,\{(a'd + s - eg)^2 - 4(ds - be)a'\}^{-1/2},$$

which for convenience is written as

$$\Delta\sigma = A\Delta b.$$

Hence the investment multiplier is given by

$$\frac{\Delta Q}{\Delta b} = \frac{A(a'Q - g)}{(s - a'\sigma)} = A(a'Q - g)\frac{Q}{I}.$$

The multiplier will be positive only if $a'Q > g$.

2. The condition given by Harcourt is

$$2\frac{\bar{I}}{Q} < s_P.$$

This may be obtained by noting that

$$\frac{P}{pQ} < \frac{1}{2}.$$

With $s_W = 0$

$$\frac{P}{pQ} = \frac{1}{s_P} \frac{\bar{I}}{Q}.$$

With the rule

$$p = \lambda \bar{I}$$

the derivation leading to (4.44) in the text now yields

$$2\lambda\bar{I} = s_P\lambda Q + \{s_P\lambda\bar{I} - \bar{w}\alpha\}\frac{\partial Q}{\partial I},$$

and the multiplier is given by

$$\frac{\partial Q}{\partial I} = (2\lambda\bar{I}/Q - s_P\lambda)Q^2/\lambda\bar{I}^2.$$

It is possible that $\bar{I}/Q$ may have values for which one of the numerator or denominator is negative and the other positive.

3. In the case of the Cobb–Douglas technology,

$$Q = \alpha L^\delta \bar{K}^\gamma$$

and when the real wage is determined by the marginal product of labour,

$$\begin{align}
\bar{I} &= s_P Q + (s_W - s_P)(\bar{w}/p)L \\
&= s_P Q + (s_W - s_P)D_2 F(\bar{K},L)L \tag{4A.2} \\
&= s_P Q + (s_W - s_P)\delta Q \\
&= [s_P(1 - \delta) + s_W\delta]Q.
\end{align}$$

The multiplier is given by the inverse of the term contained in square brackets in the last equality.

Consider the production function (4.30) implicit in Riach's analysis,

$$Q = F(\bar{K},L) = d(\alpha_1\bar{K}^{-d} + \alpha_2 L^{-d})^{-1}.$$

Here

$$LD_2 F(\bar{K},L) = \alpha_2 Q^2 L^{-d},$$

so that (4A.2) gives

$$\bar{I} = [s_P - (s_P - s_W)\alpha_2 QL^{-d}]Q.$$

When $s_W = 0$

$$\begin{align}
\bar{I} &= s_P[1 - \alpha_2 QL^{-d}]Q \\
&= s_P[1 - D_2 F(\bar{K},L)/(Q/L)]Q \\
&= s_P[1 - MP_L/AP_L]Q
\end{align}$$

where MP_L and AP_L denote the marginal and average products of labour. The multiplier will be negative when

$$MP_L > AP_L.$$

5. Financial Markets, Corporate Decision Making and Distribution

The neo-Pasinetti model discussed in Section 3.3 consists of corporations owned by shareholders, and controlled by managers and directors who finance investment plans from retained profits, or from the sale of new securities to households. The household sector receives income in the forms of wages, dividends and capital gains, and whose only savings avenue is the purchase of corporate securities. In this system it was shown that the share of profit is given by

$$\frac{P}{Y} = \frac{(1 - i)}{s_c} \frac{I}{Y} \tag{5.1}$$

Except for the occurrence of the propensity $(1 - i)$ of firms to finance investment from sources other than new issues, this result is Pasinetti's Cambridge equation for distribution. This model shifted attention from the savings behaviour of hereditary or enduring classes of capitalists and workers to the propensities of households and corporate management. With this theory Kaldor also overcame the criticism of Pasinetti's original model that there were solutions other than the Cambridge equation.

The extension of the neo-Pasinetti environment to the short run, begun in Section 3.3, is continued in this chapter. It was earlier noted that Kaldor had taken the valuation ratio to be the measure of the relative value of paper to physical assets. He assumed it to have settled at the long-run value, which assures equilibrium in the securities market. This constancy is acceptable in a golden age, but not for short-run analyses. Allowing the share market indicator to vary suggests the possibility of investment being responsive to changes in conditions in share markets. These are influenced by corporate decision making on share issues (among other things) and households' desires to realize capital gains. This approach to investment is a departure from the proposals of Riach and of King and Regan discussed in the previous chapter. The theoretical approach taken in Section 5.1 draws on the work of Brainard and Tobin which links a component of investment to variations of Tobin's q around its long-run value. The substitution of Tobin's q for the valuation ratio in the neo-Pasinetti model does not affect the distribution result.

Another addition made in this chapter is a mark-up theory of price, (Section 5.2) which draws on Harcourt's theory of the mark-up and Kaldor's belief in the existence of a minimum margin which cannot be eliminated by competition among firms. The closeness of the rule adopted here to Harcourt's work provides a link to Eichner's research on the mark-up and the megacorp (see Section 5.2). The additions provide two-way linkages between prices and quantities in the commodity market and the securities market. The implications of the newly-activated mechanisms on distribution are taken up in Section 5.3. While Tobin's q is allowed to vary in the model built here, it is not determined endogenously, but its growth rate is set exogenously to a non-zero value. The endogenous determination of q is held over until Chapter 7.

5.1 Speculation, enterprise and investment

Brainard and Tobin (1968, p.357) introduced the idea that 'the market value of equities, relative to the replacement cost of the physical assets they represent, is the major determinant of new investment'. Accordingly, investment will be stimulated when the market value of capital is greater than the cost of producing it, and discouraged when its valuation is less than its replacement cost. Other theories have been proposed which might have been considered as alternatives for this purpose. For example, Marris (1963, 1964) has argued the case of a trade-off in the utility functions of management between firm growth and the valuation ratio. The different emphasis of the research of Tobin and Brainard is adopted, partly because q has been shown to have strong links to measures of market power. This becomes important when a price equation based on the structure/conduct/performance literature is introduced in Chapter 6.

There are two broad issues to consider in devising an investment theory based on Tobin's q: for individual firms, how does q affect investment expenditure; and do macroeconomic studies support the endogenous determination of investment as a function of q? The first question is considered in this section while the second is held over until the next chapter. There is a theoretical case to be made, along with some empirical justification, for adding the equation

$$\frac{I}{K} = \frac{I_0}{K} + \alpha(q - 1), \tag{5.2}$$

in which a portion of the rate of accumulation, I/K, is determined by fluctuations of average q around its long-run value, unity. Investment is thought to be an increasing function of q, implying that the parameter α is positive. In a Keynesian formulation the autonomous component I_0 of investment may be associated with 'animal spirits' and 'spontaneous optimism' (Tobin and Brainard, 1990, p.545). The endogenous component, to do with share market frenzy or ennui, is not the greater, for 'it is by no means always the case that speculation predominates over enterprise' (*ibid.*). This is one manifestation of the differences between shareholders and corporate managers, who are far from united in the aim of maximizing the firm's net worth. Managers propose investment strategies and in response shareholders might dispose of the firm's paper securities. Equally, management is not led passively along by securities markets. Animal and entrepreneurial spirits motivate corporate management to procure funds for expansion from other sources too. 'At the same time . . . corporate CEOs are very concerned (some would say obsessed) with the market value of their shares. Especially in these days of takeovers, they have to be. Consequently, one might expect financial markets to influence managerial decisions' (*ibid.*, p.544).

At the level of individual firms it is marginal q which matters for investment. In maximizing net worth, management will only undertake an investment project if shareholders appraise the project as producing future earnings which will exceed the cost: that is, if the increment in market valuation exceeds the marginal increase in the replacement cost of capital. When marginal q is 1 the addition to future earnings is just sufficient to justify the cost of an investment project. An investment programme with marginal q less than 1 implies capital losses for existing shareholders, while a marginal q greater than 1 stimulates the additional expenditure. However, average q may be widely different from 1 when marginal q is unity. Tobin and Brainard (1990, p.545) acknowledge that marginal and average qs may differ, and they have variously mentioned several possibilities:

1. firms losing market share to foreign competitors (*ibid.*, pp.545–6);
2. a firm with monopoly power, or other sources of diminishing returns to scale, has average q greater than marginal q, the difference being due to the market valuation of the firm's rents or monopoly profits (Tobin and Brainard, 1977, p.243);
3. technological progress might lead to the introduction of new capital goods having marginal qs very much greater than the average qs generated by existing capital (*ibid.*);
4. changing input prices may cause adjustment of the marginal qs for capital goods which use input-saving technologies. Tobin and Brainard quote oil price shocks as making 'attractively profitable on the margin investments embodying energy-saving technologies' (*ibid.*);
5. differential risks associated with new classes of investment in parts of the economy not normally associated with a firm's activities may cause marginal qs to exceed average qs. This might occur because the degree of risk to shareholders is diversified without the need for them to bear the transactions costs of diversifying their portfolios. Equally some managers might drive marginal q below average q by indulging in unusually risky activities, causing shareholders to lose confidence (*ibid.*); and
6. obligatory investments, such as those prescribed in anti-pollution legislation, having associated with them large implicit profit rates, may raise marginal q above average q (Tobin, in a comment on Clark, 1979, p.124).

Lindenberg and Ross (1981) investigated the strength of the effect of monopoly power on average q values for a sample of 246 US firms over the 18-year period 1960–77. They reasoned that, if marginal q is greater than 1, then the firm would have an incentive to invest. Further, if all investment projects with marginal q greater than 1 were undertaken, over time the marginal value of q should tend towards unity. But at any time they believed perfectly competitive firms should have average q equal to 1, while for firms having increasingly greater degrees of monopoly power q should increase to higher values. Unregulated monopolists able to bar entry were thought to earn monopoly rents which exceeded normal returns on capital, so that, when capitalized by the share market, the market value of such firms was likely to exceed the replacement cost of their capital. That is, for those firms able to realize monopoly rents, average q would be persistently greater than unity. There are two reasons, not associated with market power, which may make the average q of a competitive firm differ from 1. First, firms may possess factors of production which are not assessed as part of the firm's replacement cost, but the effects on profit performance are included in market valuations. For example, because of its location a brewery might have access to a source of water which has superior chemical properties for use in beer-making compared with other water supplies. Second, a firm may be in decline. In such a case the capital stock is likely to be obsolescent and not worth replacing, so average q will be less than 1. After adjusting for firm effects and for the influences of industry-level and economy-wide qs on each firm's average q, Lindenberg and Ross found that industry q ratios of about 1.5 were often associated with firms marketing differentiated products or having strong patent protection. Also firms operating in regulated industries tended to have q values 'below the upper ranges of the distribution' (*ibid.*, p.24). The distribution of the Lindenberg and Ross q ratios changed little over time. Apparently some of the unusually large values of q declined over the period. For all firms the mean and median changed little, while the standard deviation narrowed.

In a study for US firms, using data for 1976, it was found that a variable measuring the degree of unionization in manufacturing firms had a (significant) coefficient greater than 1 in a non-linear regression with q. At the sample mean of the unionization variable, Salinger (1984, p.167) estimated 'that workers capture 77 per cent of the monopoly rents in a typical firm'. A cross-term between the unionization variable, an index of industry concentration, and a variable modelling scale economies, was significant at the 5 per cent level. Also the coefficients of variables modelling advertising and research and development were 'almost significant' at the same level. This suggested 'that the combination of concentration and entry barriers allows firms to raise price above cost and that the primary beneficiaries of the monopoly power are the workers' (*ibid.*, p.167).

The lack of clear significance for some of the regression coefficients, along with some other problems discussed on pages 167–9 of his article, cast some doubt over Salinger's conclusion.[1] Nevertheless, in an empirical framework, the paper raises seriously the idea that q values may be depressed, along with profits, when unions successfully negotiate unwarranted increases in real wage rates. More recent work confirms the tentative conclusions drawn by Salinger: 'labour can extract rents which depend on how much damage it could do by temporarily stopping the firm from producing. Production interruptions are more costly for . . . those [firms] earning high profits than for other firms' (Katz and Summers, 1989, p.241). It appears likely that some sectors of US manufacturing have been willing to share industry rents with workers, without the coercion of unions (*ibid.*, p.240). Conyon and Machin (1991) report instrumental variables regressions on UK data for 1983–6 which confirm that unionization depresses profit margins. It has been argued by Bronars and Deere (1991) that the threat of unionization distorts managers' choices of financial instruments. If threatened by the possibility of unionization, one strategy is to reduce the proportion of firms' profits available to unions by using long-term debt to finance business activities. This diverts cash flows to shareholders and away from workers. Non-unionized firms were estimated to increase their debt 'by $[US]1 million, for a given level of equity, in response to a one-point increase in the industry unionization rate' (*ibid.*, p.253).

Wernerfelt and Montgomery (1988) have investigated another firm-level influence on q values. They found that firms who have their assets focused within a small number of industries tend to have higher average qs. Admittedly, this effect is small, but it emerges with statistical significance. An explanation for this is that firms experience efficiency losses in transferring assets and competencies out of the market for which they were initially acquired. As noted above, Tobin and Brainard thought diversification of risk by management implies marginal qs above average q. However, the results of Wernerfelt and Montgomery are consistent with the view that they have observed average qs which have decreased owing to diversification. That is, the marginal qs associated with diversification were less than the average qs for the previously more narrowly focused firms. Lower marginal qs may be the result of the effect identified by Tobin and Brainard and the efficiency loss of diversifying assets and expertise. It is of course a huge step to accept that average qs have been decreasing, even amongst diversified firms. Schmalensee (1985) draws on management literature to support the related claim that widely diversified firms fail to obtain maximum profits. The data set of Lindenberg and Ross, which was used by Wernerfelt and Montgomery, produced q values which were approximately 50 per cent above the long-run value of 1 over the 18-year period 1960-77.

The importance of marginal q and its difference from average q at the microeconomic level did not deter Tobin and Brainard (1977, p.243) from persisting with an average q theory of investment at the aggregate level: 'Nevertheless, the forces of continuity in the economy are strong. Especially for short-run variations of aggregate demand, we can expect that the same factors which raise or lower q on the margin likewise raise or lower q on average.' That is, Tobin and Brainard view the occurrence of opposing movements in average and marginal qs as temporary phenomena. This is as well, for obviously marginal q is generally unknown both *ex ante* and *ex post*. In Section 6.1, where the econometric evidence on Tobin's theory of investment is discussed, there emerges a significant short-run dependence of investment on average q. As pointed out by Tobin and Brainard (*ibid.*, p.244) investment would not be related to q if instantaneous arbitrage could keep market values and replacement costs in line.[2] This does not happen and q deviates from its normal value.

When q settles at a value greater than 1, equation (5.2) predicts that investment will be stimulated. Securities are valued more highly than the replacement cost of the capital stock they represent, creating conditions in which, in aggregate, firms can raise funds with new share issues. By contrast, when q is less than 1, capital is valued at less than its replacement cost, and attempts to raise funds in securities markets are likely further to deflate investor confidence, providing an impetus for q to fall to an even lower value. Sustained reductions in q are in the interests neither of managers (who fear takeovers) nor of long-term shareholders (whose capital gains will be depressed).[3] Thus it is not unreasonable to expect that investment activity will be diminished to some extent when securities markets are bearish.

In Section 3.3, the condition $v = 1$ was shown to be equivalent to the long-run requirement that capital gains are equated with the level of retained profits. When q replaces v in the neo-Pasinetti model, capital gains are given by

$$G = (q - i)I + qM\Delta p$$
$$= (1 - i)I + M\Delta p$$

assuming q is fixed at its long-run value. From the neo-Pasinetti result, $s_c P = (1 - i)I$, and so

$$G = s_c P + M\Delta p.$$

That is, when q is used instead of v in the model, the condition $q = 1$ implies that capital gains absorb retained profits *plus* the securities-market revaluation of existing capital. Further, when q is greater than 1, it is possible that capital gains exceed retained profits. This might happen in an economy able continually to acquire significant technological advances, or which owns vast reserves of strategic natural resources, or has access to a labour force enriched with special business, technical or entrepreneurial skills, or has important sectors of the economy protected by patents or high entry costs. Such conditions seem unlikely to persist in aggregate into a distant golden age. Conversely, when q is less than 1 in the long run and capital gains are less than long-run retained profits, an economy may have special geographical or human factors limiting the success of business and industrial activity. For example, industry may be on a long-run expansion path involving retention of profits to finance investment, despite persistent under-valuation of assets in securities markets. Von Furstenberg *et al.* (1980, p.402) suggests that firms with low (marginal) qs may continue to use retained earnings for long periods to finance more investment than is efficient. Such firms may be dependent on the 'civic responsibility' of already committed local lending institutions, be protected by quotas, tariffs or price support, or be part of government-supported utilities. As a golden-age outcome, q being less than unity seems unattractive, compared with the prospect, when $q = 1$, of households sharing in all of profits, whether distributed or retained, and also sharing in security-market fluctuations.

With the investment equation (5.2) the solution obtained for the profit share in the neo-Pasinetti model becomes

$$P/Y = (1 - i)\frac{[I_0 + \alpha(q - 1)K]}{s_c Y}, \qquad (5.3)$$

which relates the distribution of income to fluctuations in q. While i and s_c, the propensities of corporations to raise new investment funds through new share issues and to retain profits respectively, are held fixed, only changes in y and k can counter the influences of changes in q on the profit share. It is possible, however, that managers will increase the proportion of investment funds raised in securities markets when q is high. Presumably the proportion will be reduced when q is close to 1, and will be zero once q becomes less than 1. That is, there is the possibility of a positive correlation between i and q, at least for q values greater than 1. Of course, it is equally feasible that managers might adjust their policies on retention ratios as conditions in securities markets change. Allowing i to vary directly with q may mean that in (5.3) the influence of fluctuations in q on the distribution of income is modified by the inverse effects of variations in $(1 - i)$.

When i and s_c are variable they will cause variations in the distribution of income directly. Benzie (1988, p.76) presented a table in which dividends as a proportion of total income are shown as relatively stable over the period 1980–83, varying only between 0.076 and 0.082. Total income in that article consisted of the gross trading profits of UK industrial and commercial companies (ICCs) plus rents, non-trading incomes and income from abroad. The mean for the period 1980–83 of 0.08 is indistinguishable from the mean value, 0.078, of the ratio for the 13-year period 1973–85. These means are considerably lower than the values reported by Benzie for 1970 and 1971 (about 0.17) and for 1986 (0.12). Nevertheless, it appears that the UK dividends–income ratio might be stylized as remaining stable over the period 1973–84, to the extent that it was maintained at a low value, often less than 0.1. In the world of the extended neo-Pasinetti model, where there are no dividend taxes, one type of security, and no liquidity cushions or bank finance, the stability observed in the UK data corresponds with the corporate savings propensity, s_c, being relatively steady at a value around 0.9. It was noted earlier that Kaldor took s_c to be the proportion of gross savings (including capital consumption allowances) out of gross profits. For 1966, he concluded that, calculated on this basis, s_c was around 0.7 for the UK and the US. Values for s_c closer to Kaldor's benchmark may be inferred from Benzie's data for 1970 and 1971.

Benzie identified a number of influences which could have constrained the values of the ratio over the period 1973–84, relative to its values in 1970, 1971 and 1986. There were two reforms of the UK corporate tax system in 1973 and 1984. Also, during the latter half of the 1970s, dividend payments were restricted as part of the government anti-inflation measures in force until 1979. For the four years, 1975–8, dividends on ordinary shares were, in real terms, just half their aggregate values for 1970 and 1971, while other dividend and interest payments were fairly constant. Nominal interest rates doubled over the years 1973 and 1974 and remained both 'relatively high and relatively volatile' until 1984 (*ibid.*, p.78), providing a partial explanation for the collapse of the UK debenture market. Between 1972 and 1974 there was also rapid growth of inflation which squeezed current-cost profits and induced very large increases in taxation payments on income by ICCs. In real terms the total income of ICCs was also depressed throughout the mid- and late 1970s, only returning to its 1973 value in 1978, and, with the exception of 1979, this value was held until 1983. It might be inferred that, faced with declining profits, constrained income and a collapse of the market for long-term debt, ICCs were compelled to seek new, higher levels of equity finance to maintain investment expenditures. An incentive favouring equity was provided in the UK in 1973 by the introduction of the dividend imputation system. After 1974, new equity became a relatively more important source of external funds amongst sources which were severely constricted during the mid-1970s. If firms had been induced to seek greater volumes of new equity finance after 1973 this should have caused a sustained increase in dividend payments. In fact dividend payments fell in nominal terms between 1972 and 1974 (*ibid.*, p.79). It was not until 1984–6 that ICCs were generally able to exploit the tax bias available on equity funds. Consistent with this, dividends grew significantly more quickly than income in 1985 and 1986.

Among US corporations there was a trend towards declining profits and retained earnings over the 1970s. Companies tended to reduce investment expenditures and to be more reliant on external financing:

In the 1970s, as retained earnings became scarce, equity issues increased, but only when the stock market was moving out of a slump. This happened during 1971 and 1972, after the stock market trough of 1970, and again in 1976 and 1977, after the stock market trough in the recession of 1974. (Campbell, 1982, p.324)

Unlike the British counterpart, the US market for long-term debt did not disintegrate. 'On the whole, during the 1970s, corporations used more internal than external funds; they used more debt than equity; more long-term debt than short-term debt; and most debt was privately rather than publicly distributed' (*ibid.*, p.305). Dougherty (1980, p.128, n) noted that the increase in the use of all external funds over the 1970s observed by the Federal Reserve Bulletin 'proved to be a temporary phenomenon and was undoubtedly caused by the acceleration in inflation'. Campbell's primary concern was with the distortion of corporate profits during the 1970s and the consequent over-statement of tax liabilities. Based on Federal Reserve Bulletin data, he reported (p.321) that both retained earnings and corporate profits, adjusted for inflationary distortions, declined as shares of gross national product (GNP). When s_c is calculated using the Federal Reserve Board data according to Kaldor's definition in terms of gross profits, the resulting series shows little variation from year to year. For the years 1968–79, s_c is above 0.7 but less than 0.8, while for 1980–82 the ratio is less than 0.7. Mains (1980, p.685) reported that: 'Despite the weakness in after-tax operating profits [in the US], dividend payments of non-financial firms continued upwards'. If the increase in dividends was caused by the shift from internal finance towards external equity financing during the 1970s, then the fall in s_c after 1979 might be interpreted as evidence of some variation in the propensity, i, of management to seek securities financing. Obviously i is responsive to wider macroeconomic and business cycle influences.

The propensity to seek finance from financial markets may take values in the range $-1 < i < 1$. When i is positive, corporations are net suppliers of securities to households, while when i is negative, corporations are overall expending greater sums on the repurchase of previously issued securities than the sums raised from new issues. Mayer (1988, p.1174) estimated values of i for five nations as weighted averages of observations for each of the 16 years 1970–85. For the UK and the US, the calculated values were negative. Kaldor (1966, p.312) proposed that i may depend *ex post* on the difference between retentions and investment expenditures. Shortfalls only emerge at the close of accounting periods, and in the intervals leading to these realizations the differences are financed from cash reserves. Alternatively, when retentions are found to be greater than actual investment expenditure, firms use the increment to their cash reserves to redeem securities in the following period.

Clearly, as income streams change from period to period the proportion of planned investment financed externally must change, if investment plans are to be realized. Although short-run variability of i is evident from year to year, for example in the data of Benzie, i will here be considered to be constant. An empirical rationalization for this assumption is possible. On the basis of data for the five major economies, Mayer (1987, p.viii) concluded that nowhere 'has new equity finance contributed substantially to the financing of physical investment'. Barroux (1988, p.1189) put the similar view that the issuing of stocks by a firm is not 'the normal way of funding its investment'. Rather, new issues are 'restricted to very special moments in the life of the firm: the creation, a major development, a change in basic activities, a privatisation' (*ibid.*). Using data sets for the UK for 1970–85, and for 1949–77, Mayer (1988, pp.1170–71 and 1987, pp.ix–x) provided estimates of i in the range 0.04 to 0.08. For the fast-growing, high-technology electrical engineering and electronics sector, his estimate was 0.15. Even so, equity finance did not represent the main source of investment funds for this industry. In the other four countries (the US, Japan, Germany and France) investigated in Mayer (1988), the estimates of i varied between -0.03 and 0.05.

Thus, in recent times, it seems the mean values of i for advanced economies have, in general, been small. Variations in i around such small mean values can explain only a small component of actual changes in economy-wide distributions of income as described by the neo-Pasinetti model. Next, a full-cost mark-up pricing theory related to the one proposed by Harcourt is introduced. In Section 5.3 price and investment equations are added to the neo-Pasinetti model.

5.2 Mark-up pricing

Kaldor postulated a role for the degree of monopoly in determining the minimum mark-up of price over average cost. Profit margins, in Kaldor's view, were inflexible downwards in the short run, and in the long run flexible in this direction when the intensity of market competition increased. This idea of relating the degree of price competitiveness between firms to the margin is derived from Kalecki

(1950, pp.204–8) and Robinson and Eatwell (1973, p.154). Kaldor (1961, pp.197–9) analysed an economy having a representative firm with productive capacity in excess of the level required to employ the available labour force (Section 3.5 above). Average cost was assumed constant up to a point close to full employment, and increasing thereafter. The mark-up of price over average cost was upwardly flexible, bounded below (at least in the short run) by a minimum which depended on the extent to which markets were not competitive, and was set at the same value for all output levels up to full employment. Beyond full employment of labour the profit margin increased steeply for small additions to supply. With this theory of flexible profit margins determined by demand, Kaldor was able to prove that his 1955 and 1961 models of distribution produced stable solutions at full employment.

There is a large literature on full-cost pricing policies whereby oligopolistic producers set prices as a fixed mark-up over long-run average costs, with little or no regard for demand considerations. A review of the relevant literature is given in Section 6.2. For the representative firm operating in a closed economy write unit price, p, as

$$p = (1 + m)a,$$

where m is the margin of price over a measure of unit average cost a. For simplicity this measure of costs is taken to be prime or direct costs (*ibid.*, pp.197–9). Further, firms are assumed to be vertically integrated, so that average and marginal prime costs consist only of labour costs. Although this assumption simplifies the notion of prime cost, this measure should not be confused with variable cost. For example, prime cost does not include the value of supervisory labour, as this component of the labour input is not used directly in producing output. However, it is likely that the value of supervisory labour varies to some extent with output. More importantly, prime cost does not encompass profit or the return to the owners of firms. As pointed out by Sylos-Labini (1979a, p.156) the originators of the full-cost pricing literature, Hall and Hitch, took prime cost as the base from which to determine the mark-up. Below we incorporate a variant of the fixed mark-up pricing policy into the neo-Pasinetti model. One variation on the fixed mark-up model is the 'normal' or 'target return' procedure. Given expected long-run costs and the

normal (capacity) output level, the mark-up is determined *ex ante* to generate a target or desired rate of return on capital. The return achieved depends on the actual level of production.
Eichner's 1973 model represents another strand of the mark-up pricing literature. For Eichner mark-ups are set so that firms may finance long-term investment plans from retained profits. Dorward (1987, p.102) describes such an investment-oriented model as

> based on a long-run theory of full cost pricing, in which the industry price leader has to trade off the short-term gain of a higher mark-up against the longer term costs of consumers switching to substitutes and an increased probability of new entry.

Oligopolistic firms with price-setting power increase the amount of the margin to generate the cash flow required to finance increases in investment expenditure. Thus Eichner, like Kaldor, saw the mark-up as upwardly flexible. However, reductions in planned investment expenditure ought to lead to downward pressure on the value of the margin. But Eichner (1973, p.1193) put the view that reduction of the margin is unlikely. That is, also like Kaldor, Eichner saw the mark-up as inflexible downward. It might be expected that there are long-term effects on pricing arising from government intervention (say, through anti-trust legislation) and from the threat of new entry. Contractions in investment, for whatever reason, in one period are hardly likely to reduce, or reverse in the next period, the effects of new entry (presumably, by inducing exits from the industry) or undo any harmful effects of government intervention (*ibid.*). Thus price leaders receive little incentive from these sources to reduce prices. Further, because firms are most likely to be operating along the inelastic portion of their short-run demand curves, there is little likelihood that consumers will switch to substitutes (*ibid.*, p.1191).
In Kaldor's work (1961, p.200) on flexible mark-ups, investment is induced at levels of activity where revenue is at least as great as *total* costs, with total costs including a 'normal' rate of return on capital. For Kaldor investment demand was determined in the long run by the rate of growth of output, while in the short term investment varied with changes in output, which in turn reflected changes in the unemployment level.
The solutions of the neo-Pasinetti model for the distribution of income and Tobin's q obtained in Section 3.3 are

$$P/Y = \frac{(1 - i)}{s_c} \frac{I}{Y} \qquad (5.4)$$

$$q = \frac{(Y/I - 1)s_h}{(1 - s_h)(1 + p'/M')}, \qquad (5.5)$$

where p' and M' denote the rates of growth of price p and physical capital M. With price determined as a constant mark-up m over average direct cost a, which in our vertically integrated representative firm consists of labour costs, aggregate revenue is given by $R = pQ = (1 + m)aQ$, where Q is the quantity of output. Profit is then given by $P = maQ$ and the profit share is

$$\frac{P}{Y} = \frac{P}{pQ} = \frac{m}{(1 + m)}. \qquad (5.6)$$

Now when the investment–income coefficient (I/Y) is fixed, and when the household propensity to acquire securities (s_h) and the fraction of corporate investment funded from new share issues (i) are both constant, it is clear that the neo-Pasinetti solution for the profit share will not, in general, be consistent with the solution (5.6) obtained from the fixed mark-up assumption. Only when I/Y is set at the value

$$\frac{I}{Y} = \frac{s_c}{(1 - i)} \frac{m}{(1 + m)}$$

will the two solutions for the distribution of income be identical.

To look at this another way, recall from Section 3.3 that the solution for q was obtained using the assumption that q is constant. Provided that s_h is fixed, and p and M grow at the same rate, it follows from (5.5) that the investment–income coefficient will be constant. Equation (5.4) then implies that the long-run, golden age profit share is also constant. Therefore the neo-Pasinetti model contains the implication of a (constant) profit share determined endogenously by the corporate retention rate, and by the ratio of investment to national income. However, if firms adopt a fixed mark-up pricing strategy then P/Y is already determined. In other words the system is over-determined, which provides the opportunity to redraw the list of endogenous variables. For example, one of national income, investment, the growth rate of one of these variables, or even the corporate retention rate may be explained within the model. Clearly, we might also specify a short-run scenario in which q need no longer be required to be constant. The mark-up pricing rule introduced by Harcourt (see Section 4.3) is incorporated into the neo-Pasinetti framework. The extension of the neo-Pasinetti model preferred here is one in which the idea that prices are set in relation to investment plans is combined with Kaldor's notion of a minimum level for the mark-up (m_m):

$$p = \left(1 + m_m + \beta(1 - i)\frac{I}{K}\right)a. \tag{5.7}$$

With this rule the mark-up of price over cost ($m = m_m + \beta(1 - i)I/K$) consists of a component allowing for market power, including a normal return on capital, and another component which sees the proportion $(1 - i)$ of investment as a cost to be financed from revenue. The use of the investment rate in the mark-up ensures that, like m_m, the second term is dimensionless in the sense that the result of multiplication by the current value of average direct cost yields a unit price. The proportional change in price following an increase in investment activity may be written as

$$\frac{\Delta p}{p} = \frac{\beta(1 - i)\Delta(I/K)}{1 + m_m + \beta(1 - i)I/K},$$

$$= \frac{\beta(1 - i)I/K}{1 + m}\frac{\Delta(I/K)}{I/K}, \tag{5.8}$$

$$= \frac{m - m_m}{1 + m}\frac{\Delta(I/K)}{I/K},$$

$$= \left[\frac{P}{Y} - \frac{m_m}{1 + m}\right]\left(\frac{\Delta I_R}{I_R} - \frac{\Delta M}{M}\right). \tag{5.9}$$

The growth in prices is now seen to be proportional to the rate of growth in investment, with the factor of proportionality depending on the actual distribution of income to profits, relative to its minimum share. In the short run equation (5.9) may be rearranged to

$$\frac{P}{Y} = \frac{I_R}{p}\frac{\Delta p}{\Delta I_R} + \frac{m_m}{1 + m}. \tag{5.10}$$

The profit share is now seen to depend on the inverse of the price elasticity of investment demand, and on the relative size of the minimum level of the mark-up. When price is set independently of investment, that is when $\beta = 0$, the elasticity is zero and profit is assigned its minimum share,

$$\frac{P}{Y} = \frac{m_m}{1 + m_m}.$$

Consider the combination of the pricing rule (5.7) and the investment equation (5.2),

$$\frac{I}{K} = \frac{I_0}{K} + \alpha(q - 1).$$

With these linkages management is modelled as having influence over the levels of autonomous investment and the pricing decision. For the moment assume there is no induced component of investment, that is, $\alpha = 0$. In this case

$$p = (1 + m_m + \beta(1 - i)I_0/K)a,$$

and corporations are modelled as setting the exact level of expenditure on plant and equipment. A distinction should be drawn between the planning of either real or nominal investment. If management sets real investment $I^R = I_0^R$ then

$$p = (1 + m_m + \beta(1 - i)I_0^R/M)a,$$

where M denotes the real capital stock, which is fixed in the short run. Once investment plans are set, and costs and the determinants of the minimum margin known, corporations are able to make a precise announcement of the unique price level which will prevail. If, however, investment plans are decided independently of price as a nominal outlay, then I is set at level I_0, and

$$p = (1 + m_m + \beta(1 - i)I_0/pM)a.$$

Some manipulation generates the quadratic

$$p^2 - \gamma p - \delta = 0,$$

where $\gamma = (1 + m_m)a$ and $\delta = \dfrac{\beta I_0(1 - i)a}{M}$. This quadratic has a unique economically sensible solution for all values of γ and δ (even when α is non zero). In this model there does not seem a sensible rationale for separating the pricing and investment decisions. But if the model were expanded to include a government sector, then it might be assumed that price is regulated by legislation, while investment spending remains the prerogative of corporations. Without extending the model in detail to accommodate government activity, it could be that, if an economically sensible solution is to be obtained, care in assigning responsibility and setting the price must be exercised. A paper by Weitzman (1974) on monopoly under uncertainty has spawned a number of contributions on the desirability of regulating price or quantity. Chen (1990) has shown that, compared with many of these schemes, none is necessarily better than allowing the monopolist to set price freely. He also concluded that, when the monopolist can be subsidized to account for society's interests, it may be better to allow the producer to set quantity rather than price. This strand of the literature differs in many respects from the post-Keynesian analysis pursued here. But the extensions of the neo-Pasinetti model proposed here and in Chapter 7 might be adapted to analyse comparable questions for the oligopolists of the post-Keynesian world.

Return to the investment equation

$$\frac{I}{K} = \frac{I_0}{K} + \alpha(q - 1),$$

where a component of activity, $\alpha(q - 1)$, depends on the securities market assessment of corporate assets and management strategies including, presumably, planned autonomous investment expenditure (in nominal terms) and the effect of these plans on price, because now

$$p = \left\{1 + m_m + \beta\frac{I_0}{K} + \beta\alpha(1 - i)(q - 1)\right\}a.$$

That is, there is now a mechanism through which households have an influence on investment expenditures and the overall price level. Corporations are no longer able to exercise absolute control over these macroeconomic indicators. Management can attempt to predict the state of the securities market and build these expectations into their nominal investment plans. By varying the corporate savings rate, dividend payments might be raised or lowered in the neo-Pasinetti model to influence the attitudes of households. An increase in either autonomous investment expenditure or in Tobin's q (assumed exogenous) induces an inflationary response. The multipliers are

$$\frac{\partial p}{\partial I_0} = \frac{\beta ap}{A} > 0 \text{ and } \frac{\partial p}{\partial q} = \frac{\beta \alpha aKp(1 - i)}{A} > 0,$$

where $A = pK + \beta I_0 a$. The second term in this divisor is contributed by the variation of $K = pM$ to changes in either I_0 or q. Revaluation of the replacement cost of capital, which here is simply p, serves to dampen the overall effect on price. When price is not sensitive to investment, $\beta = 0$, and both multipliers are also zero. In this case price is insulated from investment decisions as well as activity in securities markets. When investment is not responsive to changes in q, $\alpha = 0$, and only the price–investment multiplier is non-zero. Now corporate investment decisions affect p, but the response of financial markets to investment strategies cannot feed through to price.

In the next section, the investment and price equations are combined with the neo-Pasinetti model. It will have been noticed that the mark-up equation introduced here is a generalization of Harcourt's formulation, $p = \lambda I$, where λ was taken as a constant. In Section 4.3, it was shown that in each of Kaldor's distribution models this rule was associated with a negative investment multiplier. This problem is re-examined in the next section, using the generalization in equation (5.7), along with the impact of the new equations on distribution.

5.3 An extension of the neo-Pasinetti model

In this section the mark-up and investment theories discussed in the previous sections are added to the neo-Pasinetti model and the implications for distribution are explored. To do this, the original specification is recast in terms of Tobin's q, rather than the valuation ratio, v. First the equations of the entire system are assembled. The augmented system of equations corresponding to the model analysed in Section 3.3 is:

$$s_h\{W + (1 - s_c)P\} = (1 - s_h)G + iI \qquad (5.11)$$

$$s_cP + s_h\{W + (1 - s_c)P\} = (1 - s_h)G + I, \qquad (5.12)$$

where G denotes the capital gain realized when households dispose of paper assets. The definition of Tobin's q may be used to obtain an expression for this gain. Here a slightly different procedure from that in Section 3.3 is used to obtain G. Tobin's q is defined to be the market value of paper titles to items of capital, p_sN, relative to the replacement cost, pM, of the stock of physical items. That is,

$$q = \frac{p_sN}{pM}, \qquad (5.13)$$

where p_s is the price of a security, and N is the number of securities in circulation. The entities in the equation for the capital gain are represented in terms of growth rates defined by

$$p = \bar{p}(1 + p') \qquad\qquad p_s = \bar{p}_s(1 + p'_s)$$

$$M = \bar{M}(1 + M') \qquad\qquad N = \bar{N}(1 + N') \qquad (5.14)$$

$$q = \bar{q}(1 + q').$$

A bar over a variable denotes its value immediately before the short-run period commences, a prime superscript denotes the growth rate of the period, and a variable unencumbered by superscripts denotes the value at the close of the short-run interval under investigation. With this notation the capital gain, G, is given

$$G = \bar{N}\Delta p_s, = N\bar{p}_sp'_s = \bar{q}\bar{K}q' + q\bar{M}(pM' + \bar{p}p') - p_s\bar{N}N' \qquad (5.15)$$

where Δp_s, indicates the change in the security price,

$$K = pM, \qquad (5.16)$$

is the replacement cost of capital in this one commodity model, and $\bar{K} = \bar{p}\bar{M}$ denotes the cost just as the period begins.[4] Kaldor's assumption that the proportion i of total investment is funded by issuing new shares may be written in terms of growth rates as

$$iI = p_s \bar{N} N' = \bar{p}_s \bar{N} (1 + p_s') N'. \qquad (5.17)$$

To the collection of ten equations labelled (5.11) to (5.17) which specify the neo-Pasinetti system are added the price and investment theories discussed in the previous two sections:

$$p = (1 + m)a, \qquad (5.18)$$

$$m = m_m + \beta \frac{I}{K}, \qquad (5.19)$$

$$\frac{I}{K} = \frac{I_0}{K} + \alpha(q - 1). \qquad (5.20)$$

The identities

$$Y = P + W, \qquad (5.21)$$

$$W = wL, \qquad (5.22)$$

and

$$Y = pQ \qquad (5.23)$$

are appended. It could be argued that the complete list of equations should include

$$W = aQ,$$

which encapsulates the assumption that the model represents a closed, vertically integrated economy. There is, however, no need to include this equation as it may be deduced from the identities (5.21), (5.22) and the price equation (5.18). The application of Walras's law allows the equation $W = aQ$ to be omitted from the simultaneous system.

   In the original formulation of the model, Kaldor included a restriction of the form,

$$q' = 0,$$

which ensured that only long-run solutions were obtained in which q

had a value consistent with the capital stock growing at the natural rate. Here a short-run perspective is taken and the capital stock (in real terms) is assumed fixed, so it is inappropriate to impose the endogenous requirement that q is also fixed. As will be apparent shortly, allowance is not made here for the endogenous determination of the variation in q. This is held over until Chapter 7, when another theory of the mark-up is considered. Until then q is exogenous, and we study the short-run impact of externally-specified changes in q. Based on a consideration of security market valuations we have seen that the long-run value of q is unity. In the short run, variation of q around this steady state value may produce investment outcomes via (5.20) different from the planned expenditure on plant and equipment. In turn this also implies (via (5.18) and (5.19)) that price expectations may not be realised.

The system to be solved consists of 17 equations in the 28 variables

W aggregate wages	P aggregate profits
Y national income	G capital gains
I aggregate investment	K aggregate capital stock
$\bar{q}, q', q$ Tobin's economy-wide q	a average direct cost
$\bar{p}, p', p$ the price level	m_m minimum mark-up
m mark up of price over a	I_0 autonomous investment
Q real output	L employment of labour
w nominal wage rate	$\bar{p}_s, p'_s, p_s$ price of a security
$\bar{N}, N', N$ number of securities	$M, \bar{M}, M'$ physical capital

Eleven of the variables must be set exogenously if the model is to be solved. For the short run it seems reasonable to choose

$$M \quad I_0 \quad m_m \quad a \quad w \quad q \quad \bar{q} \quad \bar{p} \quad \bar{N} \quad \bar{p}_s \quad \overline{M}$$

as exogenous. Assignment of M to this list corresponds to the usual interpretation of the short run as the period over which changes in the stock of productive capital may be ignored. K, the replacement cost of capital, is endogenously determined, along with the commodity price, p. Additions to the capital stock, say because of the autonomously determined investment expenditure, I_0, are not productive in the short run. Autonomous investment is thought to be decided by management on the basis of their long-range plans, about which nothing is hypothesized. Kaldor (1961, p.198) suggested that the minimum margin m_m could not be eliminated by competition, and so for now m_m is assigned to the exogenous list, but this setting is revised in Chapter 7. There a theory of the mark-up from the structure/conduct/performance literature in industrial economics is used in place of the full-cost rule employed here.

Average direct cost is assigned to the exogenous list as it seems the most likely way in which reductions in a are linked to long-run improvements in technology. Recalling the equation $W = aQ$, the assignment of a to the exogenous list may be seen to imply that unit labour cost is unchanged in the short run. This in turn implies how nominal wage rates and average productivity are handled in this scenario. The economy-wide wage bill is $W = wL$ which is also given as $W = aQ$. Therefore average direct cost may be written as

$$a = w(L/Q).$$

With a fixed exogenously, either the nominal wage rate w and average physical productivity (Q/L) are both constant, or the wage rate and the productivity measure adjust in the same direction. By also placing w on the exogenous list, in this short-run scenario the measure of productivity can only adjust in line with external variations in a and w. For example, with a held constant an increase in w will be matched by an increase in productivity. An attraction of making w exogenous is that the model may then be used to simulate the effects of growth in wages.

Except for the starting values $\bar{q}$, $\bar{p}$, $\bar{N}$ and $\bar{p}_s$, this leaves only the current value of Tobin's q. In the short term variations in shareholders' preferences, fluctuations in enterprise profitability and shifts in macroeconomic monetary policy might all be expected to impinge on Tobin's q. However, none of these factors is explicitly included in this version of the neo-Pasinetti model. For this reason q is assigned to the exogenous list. With q exogenous, the model may be used to simulate the impact of fluctuations in q on income and its distribution.

In Section 3.3 the equations of Kaldor's original neo-Pasinetti model were solved to obtain

$$P = \frac{(1 - i)}{s_c} I \qquad (5.24)$$

Exactly the same result emerges from the system specified here, even when q is changing. Thus in the short term this extension of the model preserves the result that profits are determined independently of households' savings decisions. Also, profits continue to be directly proportional to investment. But now investment is given by

$$I = I_0 + \alpha(q - 1)K, \tag{5.25}$$

so that

$$P = \frac{(1 - i)}{s_c} \{I_0 + \alpha(q - 1)K\}. \tag{5.26}$$

Profits are directly linked to variations in the securities market valuation of capital, autonomous investment expenditure and the money value of capital.

In the short term, q may be subject to wide and rapid fluctuations caused by speculative activity and changes in investors' confidence. Equation (5.26) predicts that these fluctuations will be translated to profits. Lindenberg and Ross (1981, p.23) reported a time series of annual q values for the US which, for the years 1960–73, is around (and generally greater than) 1.5. This implies a positive influence of q on P in (5.26). For their period Lindenberg and Ross recorded values for q up to 2.0. Tobin and Brainard (1977) obtained qs greater than 2.5. *The Economic Report of the President* for 1978 and von Furstenberg (reported by Lindenberg and Ross) have series in which q is less than 1.5. Von Furstenberg's series is in general less than unity for the years 1960–73, implying from (5.26) that investment activity and profits were depressed by share market valuations. After 1973, all but one of the series reported by Lindenberg and Ross were close to or less than unity. The exceptional series was generated by Lindenberg and Ross after allowing for the effects of 'dying' firms which did not replace their capital as it depreciated.

On the evidence of the Lindenberg and Ross series, q has a relatively constant, positive impact on profitability. However, the other time series suggest frequent annual variability of approximately 33 per cent in q. The extent to which changes of this order translate into variations in profits depends on the magnitude of the parameter α, which captures the sensitivity of investment to financial markets, and the nominal value of the stock of capital. Here variations in q affect price, as from (5.18) and (5.19),

$$p = (1 + m)a,$$

$$= (1 + m_m + \beta\frac{I}{K})a,$$

$$= \{1 + m_m + \beta\frac{I_0}{K} + \beta\alpha(q - 1)\}a. \qquad (5.27)$$

When $K = pM$ is replaced in (5.26) using this expression for p, a rather messy nonlinear dependence of profits on q emerges. Solution of the whole system is simplified if β is assumed to be zero, as

$$p = (1 + m_m)a$$

and the dependence of profits on q becomes linear.

The evidence presented by Oulton (1981) suggests the stylized fact that the investment elasticities with respect to q are in the range 0.7 to 0.8 for both the US and Britain. In the unpublished work of Ciccolo on US data, this elasticity for the period 1953–73 is reported as 0.77. When the mark-up is affected by q, that is when $\beta \neq 0$, this induced investment translates into an inflationary bias in the model, depending on the magnitude of β.

In terms of the mark-up, m, the profit share is given by $P/Y = m/(1 + m)$, and so the profit share increases as m drifts upwards in response to an increase in Tobin's q. Now,

$$Y = \frac{(1 + m)}{m}P, \qquad (5.28)$$

and this, together with (5.26) implies that

$$Y = \frac{(1 + m)}{m}\frac{(1 - i)}{s_c}\{I_0 + \alpha(q - 1)K\}. \qquad (5.29)$$

Once again it is easier to proceed by assuming that $\beta = 0$. In this case m is fixed at its minimum value m_m and nominal income Y can be determined from (5.29). Clearly increases in q result in increases in Y, as i is less than 1. Real income may be computed from

$$Q = Y/p.$$

At this stage solutions have been obtained for m, p, I, P, Y and Q. Knowing Q, it is easy to obtain the wage bill $W = aQ$, the level of employment L from $aQ = wL$; and with p, p' may be determined and K found from $K = pM$. It remains to obtain solutions for the growth rates p'_s and N', and for the value of the capital gain, G. From the equilibrium condition for the securities market (5.11),

$$(1 - s_h)G = s_h\{W + (1 - s_c)P\} - iI.$$

All of the entities appearing on the right have been determined in the commodity market, so that G can be evaluated. The growth in the price of securities then follows by rearranging (5.15) to

$$p'_s = G/\overline{p}_s N,$$

and, finally, N' can be determined from (5.17), as

$$N' = iI/\overline{p}_s N(1 + p'_s).$$

When β is non zero the solution method is similar.

Now some critical multipliers are analysed and the comparative statics investigated. From (5.29) the nominal income-q multiplier is given by

$$\frac{\partial Y}{\partial q} = \frac{(1 - i)}{s_c} \frac{1}{m} \left\{ -\frac{I}{m} + (I - I_0) \right\} \frac{\partial m}{\partial q} + \frac{(1 + m)}{m} \frac{(1 - i)}{s_c} \alpha K. \tag{5.30}$$

The first term on the right in (5.30) consists of the total effect on Y of changes in m (induced by variation in q). The negative term is the effect on the distribution of income (given by $P/Y = m/(1 + m)$) when the mark-up is sensitive to investment (that is, when $\beta \neq 0$). When $\beta = 0$ these effects may be ignored and the multiplier depends on the direct sensitivity of investment to the change in q. That is,

$$\frac{\partial Y}{\partial q} = \frac{(1 + m)}{m} \frac{(1 - i)}{s_c} \alpha K,$$

which is positive. An increase in Tobin's q thus induces further investment activity, leading to an overall expansion of income in the short run.[5] To obtain the multiplier for real income differentiate $Q = Y/p$, so that

$$\frac{\partial Q}{\partial q} = \frac{1}{p} \left\{ \frac{\partial Y}{\partial q} - Q \frac{\partial p}{\partial q} \right\}.$$

As for nominal income, when $\beta = 0$ the multiplier

$$\frac{\partial Q}{\partial q} = \frac{a}{m} \frac{(1 - i)}{s_c} \alpha K$$

is positive.[6] When price is responsive to changes in Tobin's q the multiplier is smaller by the effect of price changes on nominal income, together with the influence of the distributional term $(-I/m)$ in (5.30). For the multiplier to be negative, these effects must outweigh the combined impact of the variation in replacement cost and the growth in investment. There is a parallel in the work of Harcourt, where the mark-up rule directly linked price and planned investment, $p = \lambda I$. In both Kaldor's 1955–6 distribution theory and the neo-Pasinetti model, there arose the possibility that the investment multiplier would be negative when the nominal influence of price changes outweighed the real effect of increasing investment. The sign of the multiplier depended critically on the distribution of income. This is particularly apparent in Harcourt's equation on p.97.

$$Q' = -\frac{(1 - 2B_P)}{(1 - B_W)} I',$$

where the prime superscript again denotes the growth rates of the variables, and B_P and B_W denote base-period shares of profits and wages in income. For the pricing and investment mechanisms preferred in this section the possibility of a negative multiplier is considerably reduced. For, as we saw, the direct effect of an increase in investment is reinforced by a price effect, working through replacement cost to compensate for the price mechanism at work both here and in Harcourt's analysis. The present case is better than that which arose for Harcourt. It was the autonomous investment multiplier that had the potential to be negative for him. It is shown below that this is not possible here.

We turn now to the comparative statics of changes in autonomous investment, I_0, the minimum margin, m_m and Tobin's q. It was noted that for the full-cost pricing strategy (5.18) the share of profits in national income is

$$\frac{P}{Y} = \frac{m}{1 + m}. \tag{5.31}$$

Further, to be consistent with the neo-Pasinetti distribution of income, Y had to satisfy

$$Y = \frac{1 + m}{m} \frac{(1 - i)}{s_c} I.$$

Also $Y = P/\pi$, where π denotes the share of profits in national income. Clearly Y changes in the same direction as profits, P, while it is oppositely affected by variations in the distribution of income, π. With this equation the effects of changes in price induced by exogenous shifts in I_0, m_m and q may be investigated. In proportional change form

$$Y' = P' - \pi'. \tag{5.32}$$

When i and s_c are treated as parameters then in proportional change form the neo-Pasinetti equation for profits is

$$P' = I'. \tag{5.33}$$

From $\pi = m/(1 + m)$

$$\pi' = m'/(1 + \bar{m}), \tag{5.34}$$

and from (5.32)

$$Y' = I' - m'/(1 + \bar{m}). \tag{5.35}$$

The occurrence of $\bar{m}$ refers to the initial value for the mark-up. Just which particular value of m is chosen depends on the reference point assumed for the computation of growth rates. As for the other growth rate equations, the occurrence of $\bar{m}$ is thought of as the value of the mark-up at the beginning of the short-run period under consideration, before the effects of any exogenous changes have influenced the model. Equation (5.35) may be transformed further using the behavioural equations (5.19) for the mark-up and (5.20) for investment. In proportional change form these equations are

$$\bar{I}I' = \bar{I}_0 I'_0 + \alpha \bar{q} \bar{K} q' + \alpha \bar{\pi} \bar{K} (\bar{q} - 1)m',$$

$$I' = S_I I'_0 + S_q q' + S_m m',$$

and

$$m' = A\{\bar{m}_m m'_m + \beta \bar{I} I'\} = B_m m'_m + B_I I',$$

where A is a positive constant determined by the initial values of m, K and I and the parameter β, and

$$S_I = \bar{I}_0/\bar{I} \qquad S_q = \alpha \bar{q} \bar{K}/\bar{I} \qquad S_m = \alpha \bar{\pi} \bar{K}(\bar{q} - 1)/\bar{I},$$

$$B_m = A\bar{m}_m \qquad B_I = \beta \bar{I} A.$$

The constants B_m, B_I, S_I and S_m are each less than one.

Suppose that q and m_m are unchanged and I_0 is expanded. For this simulation

$$P' = I' = S_I I'_0 \qquad \text{(from 5.33)}$$

$$\pi' = m'/(1 + \bar{m}) = B_I S_I I'_0/(1 + \bar{m}) \qquad \text{(from 5.34)}$$

and so, proportionately, profits expand more than the profit share when autonomous investment grows. From the equation for Y', (5.35), we obtain the Keynesian multiplier result that income expands, as

$$Y' = I'_0[1 - B_I/(1 + \bar{m})]S_I > 0. \qquad (5.36)$$

Consider next the case where managers not only expand autonomous investment but, once the size of the expansion is decided, endeavour to realize their plans by increasing the minimum margin m_m of price over unit direct cost. Corporations might take this second step because they wish to ensure the growth in revenue required for the increase in investment activity. Now both I'_0 and m'_m are positive, and

$$P' = I' = S_I I'_0$$

$$\pi' = (B_m m'_m + B_I S_I I'_0)/(1 + \bar{m}), \tag{5.37}$$

when it is assumed that q is unchanged. Therefore

$$Y' = I'_0[1 - B_I/(1 + \bar{m})]S_I - m'_m B_m/(1 + \bar{m}).$$

Compared with the previous scenario, the growth of income is here restrained by the influence of the increase in the minimum margin. This negative effect is precisely of the same magnitude as the growth in the profit share attributable to the minimum margin.

As a third application of the comparative statics, consider the situation suggested by the last simulation. Managers announce an increase in the minimum margin of price over average direct cost which is not tied to an increase in autonomous investment. Now recall that q is exogenous, $P' = 0$, and

$$\pi' = B_m m'_m/(1 + \bar{m}),$$

and

$$Y' = -B_m m'_m/(1 + \bar{m}).$$

There is a contraction of nominal income. How does this occur? First an increase in m_m raises the price of the commodity produced in the economy, which in turn raises the replacement cost of the existing capital stock. With q and I_0 fixed, I is unchanged and N is unchanged. Thus it follows from the definition of q that the price of securities p_s also rises as

$$q = p_s N/pM,$$

and so an upward shift of the minimum margin does not harm existing shareholders. The price of securities simply rises with the commodity price. Next, notice that the profit share, given by $P/Y =$

$m/(1 + m)$ also grows. But aggregate investment is constrained in this scenario and so the neo-Pasinetti result

$$\pi = \frac{(1 - i)}{s_c} \frac{I}{Y}$$

implies that the redistribution of income to corporations can only occur if national income falls. Because nominal income is given by $Y = pQ$, it is clear that real output must contract by more than the magnitude of the growth in price if Y is to fall. A contraction of real output occurs because the increase in the margin is not used to fund new investment, but rather is an unproductive withdrawal from the system. Firms might do this to expand the size of the liquidity cushion available to them in later periods. While this does not disadvantage shareholders, it is bad for consumers because the commodity price rises, and there is a redistribution away from wage and salary earners – the group with the greatest propensity to consume. Economy-wide aggregate consumption falls, and output and employment fall.

In Chapter 7 a modified version of the model outlined in this section is used to analyse the impact of industry structure on the distribution of income. Before this study is undertaken, a review of the literature is presented in Chapter 6.

Notes

1. In particular, coefficients which are either insignificantly different from zero, significant for tests as wide as 10 per cent at best, or have unexpected signs, weaken the entire study.
2. Obsolescence and distortionary taxes might keep market values and replacement costs apart. For example, a type of capital widely in use may quickly come to be seen as redundant when an innovative enterprise introduces very different machinery. In this case average qs could fall substantially below unity.
3. For a discussion of the roles of managers and shareholders, see Wood (1975, Chapter 2).
4. After substituting q for v convert (3.33) for G and the algebra preceding (3.36) into relations involving growth rates, using (5.14). A little manipulation then yields the result.
5. To return to the case where $\beta \neq 0$, it follows from (5.27) for the mark-up that

$$\frac{\partial m}{\partial q} = \frac{\beta \alpha K^2}{K^2 + \beta M I_0 a} > 0.$$

Hence, provided the distributional effect of an increase in q does not outweigh the effects on replacement cost and investment, the multiplier will be positive when $\beta \neq 0$.

6. It follows from the previous note that

$$\frac{\partial p}{\partial q} = a\frac{\partial m}{\partial q} > 0.$$

6. Investment, the Mark-up and Tobin's q

A version of the neo-Pasinetti model was augmented in the previous chapter by a theory of investment, and by a full-cost pricing equation. In that version of the model, q was set exogenously, precluding assessment of the effects on q of changing conditions in financial and commodity markets, and inhibiting the simulation of short-run scenarios in which q is endogenous. To arrive at a preferred theory for the endogenous determination of a market valuation ratio, the intention to use the Tobin–Brainard theory of investment, proposed in the previous chapter, is first confirmed. In Section 6.1 there is presented a review of evidence supporting a simple structural equation, in which causality flows from q to aggregate investment.

Next, price theories and econometric studies of them are reviewed in Sub-sections 6.2.1 to 6.2.3. In the first sub-section, econometric evidence on mark-up and competitive theories of price is assessed. It appears that conditions of demand and supply have little influence on price, but a case can be made for price being influenced by market structure and collusion between imperfectly competitive producers. Sub-sections 6.2.2 and 6.2.3 contain reviews of two approaches to imperfect competition. The market concentration approach outlined in the first of these sub-sections has been attacked as being a misinterpretation of the existence of many industries in which activity is dominated by a small number of firms. In addition, empirical findings on the link between profit margins and market structure have been inconclusive, or have been weak in periods of price regulation or inflation. Two of the studies reviewed provide a little support for Kaldor's notion that there is minimum mark-up which cannot be eliminated by competition.

Profit-maximizing oligopoly is introduced in Sub-section 6.2.3, and an approach to the determination of the margin of price over average cost, chosen to replace the mark-up rule used in the analysis of the neo-Pasinetti model in the last chapter. In this theory, the margin varies with a measure of market structure, an index of collusion between producers, and the price elasticity of demand. While in some circumstances this approach preserves the notion of a minimum margin which survives price competition among oligopolists, it does not preserve a role for investment in the determination of price. The version of the neo-Pasinetti model constructed in the next chapter includes such a price rule. In this extension to the model, mathematical techniques often used to build neoclassical models are adopted.

6.1 Estimating the relationship between investment and Tobin's q

In Chapter 5, the neo-Pasinetti model was extended with an equation explaining a component of investment in terms of Tobin's q. There the microeconomic determination of q for individual firms was discussed. Here we investigate the empirical evidence on Tobin's aggregate investment equation. A further discussion of the endogenous determination of q is held over to Sub-section 6.2.4, following a review of some ideas from industry economics.

Chirinko (1987, pp.78–9) identified a number of difficulties which have plagued most econometric studies of the relationship between investment and q:

1. low adjusted R^2's;
2. serially correlated residuals;
3. the importance of lags of both q and the dependent variable in the determination of investment; and
4. the very sluggish adjustment of investment to changes in q implied by many structural theories underlying econometric analyses.

Chirinko concluded that these empirical problems are caused by serious specification errors.[1] Despite these difficulties a small number of studies for the US and Britain have established a strong link between investment spending and Tobin's q.

Econometric analyses usually concentrate on the relationship between q and the investment rate. A reason for this emphasis lies in the observation that the q theory of investment is similar to the flexible accelerator theory. In the accelerator approach, investment is related to the difference between the desired and actual levels of the capital stock. In the q theory, the market value of capital goods, which appears in the numerator of the definition of q, may be viewed as an estimate of the desired capital stock. When q is not unity, the desired capital stock K^*, appropriate to the discount rate r applied by shareholders, will differ from the actual stock, which has marginal efficiency of capital R. For q greater than one, r is less than R, and the desired capital stock will be larger than the actual stock.[2] When the elasticity of the marginal product of capital with respect to the desired capital stock is one, the market value of the existing stock is an exact estimate of the desired stock, and we have

$$K^*r = KR.$$

Because $q = R/r$ (see note 2) this may be rearranged to $K^* = qK$ and

$$K^* - K = (q - 1)K.$$

Suppose now that investment expenditure is undertaken according to the rule

$$I = b\,(K^* - K),$$

where b is the adjustment coefficient, then $I = b\,(K^* - K) = b\,(q - 1)K$ and

$$I/K = b(q - 1),$$

which is a relation between the investment rate and q.

Amongst the early econometric studies of Tobin's q theory were two works undertaken by Ciccolo (1975, 1978). The first of these has been widely cited and compared with later studies. (See, for example, Oulton, 1981, pp.197–9, Tobin, 1974, pp.225–7, von Furstenberg, 1977, p.364 and pp.371–6, Tobin and Brainard, 1977, p.243 and Hall, 1977, pp.88–90.) Ciccolo (1975, pp.40–42) attempted to explain US investment rates solely by q and the inverse of the real stock of gross fixed capital, with adjustment for first-order autocorrelation of the residuals. Von Furstenberg (1977, p.371) pointed out that, as the occurrence of the second independent variable with a negative coefficient accounts merely for the persistent updrift in the ratio of gross fixed investment to the gross capital stock that is due to the growing importance of equipment in total capital compared to longer-lived structures, q is the only variable that can explain short-term fluctuations in the investment rate in such equations.

In Ciccolo's analysis, q was assumed to appear with an unconstrained distributed lag structure. With aggregate fixed investment as the dependent variable, the sum of the lagged coefficients of q is 0.033. When fixed investment was disaggregated into structures and equipment, the sums of the lagged coefficients of q were found to be 0.052 for structures and 0.124 for equipment. Tobin and Brainard (1977, p.243) summarized Ciccolo's regressions as explaining '40 per cent of the 1953–73 quarterly variations of the ratio of gross investment to the capital stock, I/K. The eventual full effect of a 0.10 increase in q is to raise I/K by 0.08.' Hall (1977, p.88) noted that Ciccolo's observed short distributed lag structures for q had means in the range from two to four quarters.

Ciccolo (1978, pp.48–52) presented evidence to support the q theory of investment using the Granger–Sims tests of exogeneity. For Granger, the time series q is said to cause the time series I if the current value of I can be better predicted using past values of the q series. Sims translated this definition of causality into an operational test of exogeneity for, in our case, q with respect to I. Given a regression of I on current, past and future values of q, the future coefficients should be zero if q is exogenous with respect to I. What this means in practice is that the direction of causality is from q to investment, and *not* the reverse, when the sum of the coefficients of the future values of q in the regression are not significantly different from zero. The Granger–Sims test of causality attempts to eliminate spurious serial correlation of economic variables and of regression residuals (*ibid.*, pp.49–51). When successful, the test implies exogeneity of q with respect to investment in the sense that q and the error term in the investment equation can be treated as independently distributed. However, it is a consequence of Granger's definition that this test cannot detect exogeneity, or the order of regression, when variables are only contemporaneously correlated.

Ciccolo tested the order of regression for the relationships between q and the ratio of real fixed investment to the capital stock, I/K, and between q and the ratio of US GNP to the capital stock, Y/K. For q, Ciccolo used the ratio of the valuation placed on non-financial corporations in equity and bond markets to an estimate of the reproduction cost of their physical assets. In the Granger–Sims tests, quarterly observations spanning the years 1953–74 were used. On the strength of F-tests at the 5 per cent significance level, Ciccolo rejected the null hypothesis that either I/K or Y/K were exogenous with respect to q. But at the 15 per cent level the null hypothesis of exogeneity of q with respect to the two ratios could also be rejected. This left 'room for doubt as to whether these relationships are one-sided' (*ibid.*, p.57). That is, there might be some feedback from investment onto future values of q.

This apparent bidirectionality may have been caused by investors' expectations of future returns to capital being influenced by current or past movements in GNP. That is, changes in economic activity, say due to changes in investment plans, would influence future values of q. In this case causation would actually flow from income to q and then on to investment. To test this hypothesis, Ciccolo first regressed the investment rate on its own past performance and on current and past values of Y/K and q. Using the estimated coefficients $\hat{a}_i$ and $\hat{b}_i$ from this regression, Ciccolo endeavoured to eliminate income effects on investment by calculating the investment rate series

$$IK^*(t) = IK(t) - \sum_{i=1} \hat{a}_i IK(t - i) - \sum_{i=0} \hat{b}_i YK(t - i),$$

where IK and YK denote the ratios of investment income to the capital stock. Next, IK^* was tested for exogeneity with respect to q. The null hypothesis was rejected at the 5 per cent level, and Ciccolo dismissed the successive linkages between income, Tobin's q, and then investment as the cause of the apparent bidirectionality.

Nevertheless, it is not difficult to imagine feedback from investment to Tobin's q. For example, suppose that expectations of future values of q play a role in the determination of current investment expenditure. In the event that these expectations are accurate (and a significant part of current q is explicable by its own past performance) then there is a causal relationship flowing from I to the q ratio.[3] At the microeconomic level, managerial theories of the firm such as those evolving from Marris's work imply the existence of a long-run causal linkage of this type. See, for example, Marris and Mueller (1980, pp.41–2) and Odagiri (1981, pp.45–8). In this literature, management endeavours to choose its growth rate to realize a valuation for its shares which will satisfy existing shareholders, and so reduce the threat to management of possible takeovers. In a study for the US over the years 1956–76, von Furstenberg *et al.* (1980, p.431) report a high correlation between industry-level qs and the aggregate q for the non-financial sector. In this study the authors also argue that expectations of q appear to be important in the determination of investment behaviour. It is therefore surprising that Ciccolo's work, which covered the years 1953–74 – a period similar to that studied by von Furstenberg *et al.* – did not report stronger evidence of bidirectionality in the relationship between q and investment.

A non-economic explanation of the apparent feedback in Ciccolo's tests is possible. Wallis observed that, when a seasonally adjusted variable is regressed on a non-seasonal independent variable, a one-sided distributed lag function might appear as a bidirectional relation. This suggested that a distributed lag regression of each of the seasonally unadjusted series for I/K and Y/K on q would provide estimates of the coefficients free from seasonal bias.[4] Application of the Sims test for exogeneity to these regressions produced the conclusion that the null hypothesis of exogeneity of q cannot be rejected.

Ciccolo also conducted another set of tests to ensure the elimination of the effects of seasonality. Investment and q were corrected for trend and mean and then deseasonalized using Fourier techniques. Ordinary least squares regression of I/K on q was then undertaken. A further deseasonalizing of the time series was performed using the ordinary least squares residuals, but this did not produce results very different from the process just described (Ciccolo, 1978, pp.58–9). From this analysis, Ciccolo concluded that there is a mean lag of 3.4 quarters between changes in q and changes in investment. Also Ciccolo was able to estimate the long-run elasticity of real investment with respect to q as 0.77.

The tests for exogeneity of q were repeated using two other investment series: (1) a seasonally unadjusted investment series for non-financial corporations available from US flow-of-funds accounts; and (2) a monthly series on new orders for producers' durable equipment. Ciccolo also employed an alternative measure of q, in which the denominator is the constant value stock of physical assets rather than replacement value. The results of these subsequent tests did not suggest rejection of the hypothesis that q is exogenous. In the investment equation used in Chapters 5 and 7, part of investment expenditure is proportional to the deviation of q from its long-run equilibrium value of 1. To reiterate the point made earlier, the results reported here suggest that, for the period 1953–74 in the US, the disturbance term in the investment equation and q are independent. A more direct message of support for the Brainard and Tobin theory is that 'it is appropriate to treat a regression of investment on current and past values of q as a structural investment equation' (*ibid.*, p.61). In Chapter 5, q was fixed exogenously. In the next chapter, q is postulated to be endogenously determined by variables which proxy market power, collusion or other special attributes of firms. This approach depends on financial markets efficiently capitalizing the above normal rents which accrue to producers. The approach is introduced in Sub-section 6.2.4.

Von Furstenberg (1977, pp.371–88) provided a comparative study of the explanatory power and significance of q, capacity utilization, and the variable modelling fixed investment. For this study von Furstenberg used quarterly US data for non-financial corporations for the period commencing with the first quarter of 1952 and terminating in the final quarter of 1976. Capacity utilization and q were introduced into the regressions with second-degree Almon lag structures. For capacity utilization, the lag structure encompassed four quarters, whereas, for q, the coefficients in the Almon polynomial were constrained to zero for lags of less than one and more than seven quarters. Throughout his ordinary least squares regressions, q combined with the type of fixed investment, q combined with capacity utilization, and q combined with both of these were each found to explain very large parts of the variance in investment rates, although 'serial correlation of the error terms [was] most debilitating' (*ibid.*, p.374). In a comment, Lovell noted that 'the coefficient of q is always significant, even when it is placed in tandem with the lag and accelerator effects of capacity utilization and a host of other variables' (*ibid.*, p.400). By contrast, the coefficient of capacity utilization lost significance in some equations when it was used together with q. Discussants of von Furstenberg's paper felt that the work supported q as a determinant of investment. Tobin pointed out that the coefficient estimates obtained by von Furstenberg were generally in the range of those obtained by Ciccolo.

For Great Britain, Oulton (1981) empirically compared the explanatory and predictive power of q in an equation of the form

$$GI(t)/K(t - 1) = \beta_0 + \sum\beta_i q\ (t - i) + v$$

with plausible alternative variables in similar equations. $GI(t)/K(t-1)$ is the ratio of real gross investment in fixed capital by industrial and commercial companies (net of dwellings and petroleum and natural gas) to their real stock of capital at the end of the previous quarter; $q(t-i)$ is the ratio at period $t-i$ of the market value of these companies to the current replacement cost of their physical assets. The alternative candidates as independent variables were capacity utilization, CU, defined as the ratio of an index of industrial production to its trend; Δy, the difference in the index of industrial production expressed as a percentage of capital; and YD, the redemption yield on company debentures (*ibid.*, pp.196–7). The empirical investigation consisted of lagging each variable by one period and running ordinary least squares estimations involving eight period Almon lags. Correction was required for severe first order correlation in each regression. The data set consisted of quarterly observations for the period from the fourth quarter of 1962 to the second quarter of 1977. This was a shorter period than was used by von Furstenberg and Ciccolo, but there were substantial overlaps.

Similar results emerged from the British and US studies. Oulton found that q alone was able to explain almost all of the variation in investment rates, and the coefficient on this variable remained significant when other variables were introduced. None of the other variables performed as well as q. Capacity utilization had a significant coefficient only once, while the accelerator variable Δy performed better, although its coefficient tended to become insignificant when used in tandem with q. The interest rate YD, which had a correlation coefficient of -0.89 with q, was a good explanator of investment behaviour. The correlation coefficient suggested that most of the variation in q in Oulton's series was due to variations in firms' discount rate on the marginal efficiency of capital (which would affect YD), rather than variations in the rate of return on existing assets.

In Oulton's work the best alternative to q as an explanator of investment rates was a model incorporating the accelerator and capacity utilization. Estimations of this model and the q theory were used to forecast investment rates for 18 quarters. On a number of statistical criteria the q theory appeared to perform better than the accelerator model. Oulton estimated the long-run elasticity of investment with respect to q as 0.70. This compares favourably with the values estimated for this elasticity in the US by Ciccolo (0.77) and von Furstenberg (0.73).

A divergence of Oulton's findings from the conclusions of US studies lies in his result that the redemption yield on 20-year debentures YD was the variable which on its own came closest to the performance of q in explaining British investment. This interest rate was negatively correlated with q, which is not surprising as YD was used by Oulton in the construction of his series for q. The success of both q and YD in separately explaining investment led Oulton (pp. 200–201) to stress the importance of stock market prices and cost of capital variables in the decision-making processes of British industrialists. Von Furstenberg (1977) and other US researchers (for example, Tobin, 1977; Clark, 1979) took an opposing view. Rather, they emphasized the marginal efficiency of capital as an important determinant of investment performance: 'of the factors that influence q, those related to current and prospective earnings – to the marginal efficiency of capital – do affect investment, whereas the rate at which earnings are discounted – the cost of capital – does not' (Tobin, in von Furstenberg, 1977, p.402). Von Furstenberg (1977, pp.361–3, 376–88 and Appendix) highlighted permanent changes in corporate taxation, and the implicit taxation effects of inflation on capital valuation and on investment financing, as important determinants of investment which act through their influence on the marginal efficiency of capital.

These observations suggest that our preferred investment equation might be seriously misspecified or, at least, that it may be as effective in explaining investment schedules in terms of the marginal efficiency of capital in the case of the US as using a cost-of-capital proxy in Britain. This problem, and the further specification difficulty of the persistent significance of lagged qs in most econometric studies, can be resolved within the framework of Tobin's investment theory by appealing to the work of Udea and Yoshikawa (1986).

In their theoretical paper they built a stochastic model of firms' decision making in which there are delays between the placement of orders for investment goods and their delivery, installation and operation. When these delays can be ignored and when the information set of the firm contains only observations of past and present

qs, Udea and Yoshikawa (1986, p.14) proved that current investment depends only on current q; that is, the preferred investment schedule in Chapters 5 and 7 is valid. When delivery delays are significant, however, current investment depends on a distributed lag of the qs, thus explaining the persistent significance of lagged q coefficients in empirical investment equations (*ibid.*, pp.14–16).[5]

Within this framework of delivery delays, it can be demonstrated that, when the time series of profit rates and of discount rates r have distinct stochastic properties, then q will no longer be a sufficient statistic for investment. That is, when delivery delays existed, investment equations containing only lagged and current qs as the explanatory variables would be misspecified. Addition of either profit rate or discount rate variables to the equation would produce significant coefficients.

In summary, Udea and Yoshikawa's work has shown that the econometric importance of lagged qs, discount rates and marginal efficiencies of capital do not contradict Tobin's q theory. Rather, these econometric results would be expected in an imperfect world in which there exist delays between the decision to invest and the eventual operation of new plant and equipment.

Another study for Britain by Poterba and Summers (1983) supported Oulton's finding that q is a powerful explanator of investment. Unlike the other work reported here, this study used annual data. Poterba and Summers estimated the system

$$(I/K)_t = \beta_0 + \beta_1 q_t + \beta_2 q_{t-1} + u_t$$

$$u_t = \rho_1 u_{t-1} + \rho_2 u_{t-2} + \zeta_t.$$

The value of q lagged by one period was always significant in their ordinary least squares, generalized least squares and instrumental variables regressions for the periods 1950–72, 1963–80 and 1950–80. This coefficient was about two-thirds of the value of the coefficient of the current value of q. The reported coefficients of q are larger than those given by Oulton. The authors offered the explanation that with annual data the effect on q of short-term speculative fluctuations in asset valuations by share markets would be reduced. Thus regressions with annual data were thought more likely to capture the long-term relationship between q and investment which truly reflected investors' views of the returns to investment.

Poterba and Summers exploited this line of argument to examine further the econometric relationship between q and investment. Using spectral analysis techniques, they decomposed their data into frequency components to generate three new series for q. For these series they filtered out those components of variation in q which occurred with periods less than one, three and then five years. These refined data were then used to estimate the equation

$$I/K = \alpha + \beta q + \zeta. \qquad (6.1)$$

The regressions produced a stronger relationship between the investment rate and q than had been observed for Britain using either quarterly or annual data. Thus 'the effect of an increase in q which is caused by a permanent change in the corporate environment, for example, a new tax policy, is larger than one caused by a momentary increase in stock market values' (*ibid.*, p.159). This is in line with the conclusions drawn by American research which held that the greatest impact feeding through q to investment comes from changes in the marginal efficiency of capital, rather than from fluctuations in share market discount rates.[6] Depending on the frequencies filtered out of their q data, Poterba and Summers found coefficients for β in equation (6.1) ranging from 1.54 to 2.31. They concluded from their regressions with unfiltered data that 'about 60 per cent of the total investment response to q occurs within a year of the change in [this] ratio' (*ibid.*, p.157).

A recent investigation focused on a dynamic q theory by assuming that firms maximize their real present value subject to an intertemporal investment cost function. The 'empirical results are robust with respect to variations in specification, to the choice of measures for the variables, to data sets, and over time. These are desirable properties which make the ... model a valid representation of investment data' (Sensenbrenner, 1991, p.819). This approach, like a number of others surveyed here, is of the type Tobin and Brainard (1990, p.547) have described as 'more strongly neoclassical than "Tobin's q"'. Nevertheless, for six OECD countries, including Britain and the US, Sensenbrenner has shown that q has a role in explaining investment. The data sets covered different periods, but all spanned the period 1971–81. For the US, this finding has been verified in a review by Berndt (1991) of three comparative studies of investment theories undertaken by Kopcke using quarterly data. On

Berndt's criteria, Tobin's q emerges consistently as a satisfactory means of explaining investment, relative to other theories, in forecasts up to the fourth quarter of 1984.[7]

In the next two sub-sections, theoretical and empirical work on price theories which might be used to extend the neo-Pasinetti model are considered. Following this, in Sub-section 6.2.4, the empirical evidence on the determinants of q is considered.

6.2 The price mechanism

For the price equation of the extended neo-Pasinetti model

$$p = (1 + m_m + \beta\frac{I}{K})a,$$

there are a number of issues to examine. This equation represents a full-cost model in which price is determined as a variable mark-up over average direct cost. As will be seen in the first sub-section, there is no consensus in the literature on whether a full-cost strategy is preferable to other regimes. This is partly due to a problem of identification: many of the equations subjected to econometric testing are consistent with widely different theories of price. In the extended neo-Pasinetti model the variation in the mark-up factor is ascribed to changes in planned investment expenditure, which is a component of final demand. In the econometric literature changes in demand are usually associated with classical theories of supply and demand. It should also be noted that the empirical literature provides no clear guidance on which unit cost measure might be used in reaching the pricing decision. Kaldor chose unit direct cost but, as we will see, other researchers have favoured average variable costs or unit normal costs. Setting aside the econometric uncertainty surrounding the choice of pricing rule and the unit cost measure, there is the issue of whether oligopolistic pricing is associated with a variable mark-up. Some evidence on this variability is presented in Sub-sections 6.2.2 and 6.2.3.

The early literature on the detection of an empirical linkage between industry concentration and the mark-up is examined Sub-Section 6.2.2. In Sub-section 6.2.3, recent work in industry economics on oligopolistic theories of the partial dependence of price-cost margins on industry structure and conduct is examined. In one strand of this research Tobin's q has been interpreted as a measure of firm or industry profitability. The developments surveyed in Sub-section 6.2.4 explore the linkage from measures of structure, con-duct, and other characteristics of production units to q. This linkage is generalized to the macroeconomic context in Chapter 7.

6.2.1 Competing theories of price

In the extended neo-Pasinetti model, price is determined by a full-cost theory as a variable mark-up over average direct cost. Theories of this type are generally thought to be appropriate in industries involved in imperfectly competitive markets. Such an industry might be a monopoly, or consist of a small number of firms which function as an oligopoly, or include one or two firms which provide price leadership to a competitive fringe, or be controlled by an Eichnerian megacorp. However, in the classical theory of competitive markets, price is thought to change in response to variations in demand and supply. The swiftness and completeness of such price adjustments vary from market to market and partially depend on the difficulties associated with price changes. Other factors which tend to amelior-ate price adjustment include variations in optimal inventory levels and the costs of carrying inventories, the desire of management to maintain recent capacity utilization levels, and the extent of unfilled orders. Eckstein and Fromm (1968, p.1163) observed that the theory of short-run profit maximization also predicts that prices change in response to changes in unit labour and material costs when disequilibrium influences are ignored. Thus the classical theory and the full-cost pricing strategies lead to a positive correlation between changes in average costs and changes in price.

Eckstein and Fromm also investigated two non-competitive pric-ing strategies, which set price as

$$p = rK/x^N + ULC^N + UMC^N \qquad (6.2)$$

or

$$p = (1+\lambda)(ULC^N + UMC^N) \qquad (6.3)$$

where r denotes a target rate of return on a firm's capital stock K, ULC^N and UMC^N denote unit labour and material costs when the firm's 'normal' output x^N is produced, and λ denotes the mark-up. For these rules 'price is altered if the cost of producing the standard output changes either because of changes in the prices of the main inputs, or because of technological progress. However, price will not respond to cost changes caused by changing operating rates, nor to changes in demand' (*ibid.*, p.1165). Further, price changes either in response to variations in the target rate of return and the short-run capital output ratio, or whenever the mark-up changes. In an empirical analysis for the US over the period 1954–65, Eckstein and Fromm constructed price and price change equations which included, as explanators, important variables in either or both the classical and full-cost theories. They offered the following summary of their results:

> While the different forms of the equations yield varying results on the relative importance of the competitive mechanism vis-à-vis oligopolistic pricing, there is pretty strong evidence that equations combining both mechanisms are superior to equations using either approach in isolation. Tests for asymmetries in pricing showed some evidence in support of the proposition that prices have a greater tendency to increase than to fall. Only small bits of evidence could be found to distinguish [between the non-competitive pricing strategies]. (*ibid.*, p.1171)

Consider first the clear concluding remark that a combination of classical and oligopolistic pricing performs better in the estimations than either does separately. It seems that this part of their conclusion is consistent with the price determination scheme used in the extended neo-Pasinetti model. To see this we write the price equation $p = (1 + m_m + \beta I)a$ in finite change form,

$$\Delta p = a\Delta m_m + a\beta\Delta I + (1 + m_m + \beta I)\Delta a.$$

Prices change as a consequence of variations in one element of final demand, namely planned investment, average costs a, and the minimum margin m_m. Thus factors central to the classical theory of price, as well as factors highlighted by oligopolistic theories, are important in the determination of price and price changes. Eckstein and Fromm's conclusion on asymmetry is consistent with the downward stickiness of price favoured by both Kaldor and Eichner in the context of mark-up pricing.

At a more detailed level Eckstein and Fromm (*ibid.*, p.1173) also found in their regressions for all US manufacturing that:

1. normal unit labour costs had a very strong impact on quarterly

price changes; by comparison deviations of actual unit labour costs from the normal unit cost had a much smaller effect;
2. changes in unit labour costs, if used without the normal measure in the regressions were insignificant; and
3. two demand variables measuring capacity utilization and the ratio of unfilled orders to sales, along with a third classical theory explanator – actual material prices – were found to be significant.

Conclusions (1) and (3) suggest that in the pricing theory of the extended neo-Pasinetti model a formulation in which average normal cost is marked up may be more appropriate. Other econometric studies (examples of which are discussed below) have found that actual unit cost variables are significant explanators of price, and so a judgement on which cost measure to use is difficult to make. Harcourt and Kenyon (1976, p.109) analysed a similar pricing model to the one proposed here, in that price responded to investment, but the measure of cost was normal cost.

In the summary of their work quoted above, Eckstein and Fromm noted that 'Only small bits of evidence could be found to distinguish' between the non-competitive pricing strategies. The evidence comes from their regressions for price changes in industries manufacturing durables. To understand their results, we must first return to equation (6.2). In finite change form, this target return pricing rule may be written as

$$\Delta p = (K/x^N)\Delta r + r\Delta(K/x^N) + \Delta ULC^N + \Delta UMC^N$$

(6.4)

Quarterly changes in the ratio of capital to normal output (that is, the finite change $\Delta(K/x^N)$ in (6.4)) are small (*ibid.*, p.1169). Accordingly, the role of this ratio in explaining price changes is ignored. For the change in the target rate of return (Δr) a measure of after-tax profit π was proxied in the regression for price changes in durable manufacturing. The coefficient of π was found to be approximately -3 and significantly different from zero at the five per cent level. With the assumptions that $\Delta(K/x^N) \approx 0$ and π proxies r, then (6.4) may be stylized as

$$\Delta p = (K/x^N)\pi + \Delta ULC^N + \Delta UMC^N$$

(6.5)

$$= -3\pi + \Delta ULC^N + \Delta UMC^N \qquad (6.6)$$

The sign of the coefficient of π was consistent with the prior expectation that, because they reflect below-target rates of return, low profit rates induce price increases. For this reason Eckstein and Fromm took the negative coefficient of π as supporting the target return pricing mechanism.

However, the coefficient of π might well be interpreted in terms of λ, the full-cost mark-up factor in (6.3), in which case the evidence on π also supports this pricing strategy. To see this,[8] equations (6.5) and (6.6) are compared with the first difference form of the full-cost mark-up rule (6.3) to obtain

$$\Delta p = -3(x^N/K)(ULC^N + UMC^N)\Delta\lambda + \text{other terms.} \qquad (6.7)$$

Clearly (x^N/K) and the level of short-run unit costs are positive. Thus it may be inferred from (6.7) that the coefficient of $\Delta\lambda$ in a regression for price changes in durable manufacturing (using Eckstein and Fromm's data) would be negative. This sign is consistent with the normal-cost version of the full-cost pricing theory, for, when output levels are below normal or when unit costs are above normal, the effective mark-up λ is lower than required, so that $\Delta\lambda < 0$ and there will be pressure to increase prices.

A study by Ripley and Segal (1973) is closely related to the work of Eckstein and Fromm. They estimated an equation of the form

$$p = \alpha_0 + \alpha_1 ulc + \alpha_2 m + \alpha_3 x$$

where the variables are named with lower-case letters to indicate that they are logarithmic or proportional changes in unit labour costs (ulc), material costs (m) and real output (x). This equation can be derived from a competitive theory of price, a target-return pricing mechanism, a full-cost mark-up model, or the mark-up rule

$$P = \beta_1 ULC + \beta_2 UMC,$$

in which unit labour and material costs are differentially marked up by the factors β_1 and β_2.[9]

In a regression using annual observations on about 400 US manufacturing firms pooled for the years 1959–69, Ripley and Segal obtained the results

$$p = 1.22 + 0.36ulc + 0.17m - 0.20x \quad R^2 = 0.57$$
$$(12.0) \quad (9.9) \qquad (7.3) \qquad (8.0)$$

where t-statistics are given in parentheses (*ibid.*, p.265). The *ulc* term could represent the competitive response to a shift of the manufacturing industry's supply curve or, equally, it could be present because of a mark-up pricing policy. For the cost of materials term the interpretation is different. This measure was constructed using value-added deflators as price indices so that 'one would expect the coefficient on the growth of material costs to be close to zero. However, to account for the possibility that there are pure mark-ups 'on material costs this variable was included in the equation' (*ibid.*, p.266). On this reasoning the finding of a high t-statistic on the coefficient of m suggests that, for each 1 per cent increase in materials costs, price is marked up by 0.17 per cent. One interpretation of the term in the rate of growth of output x is to combine it with materials input growth to obtain an estimate of the growth in unit materials costs. Alternatively (*ibid.*), the output growth term might be interpreted as capturing the price effects of changes in unit fixed costs.

Ripley and Segal also estimated their equation for the periods 1959–61, 1962–5 and 1966–9. In each of these regressions, the t-statistics were again significant at the 1 per cent level and the signs of the coefficients were as for the regression for the entire period 1959–69. The coefficients in the sub-period regressions tended to be of smaller magnitude than those shown above for the whole period, with the exception that the constant for the sub-period 1966–9 was much larger. This was a period of generally greater inflation, and Ripley and Segal suggested that the constant might include the effect of inflationary expectations on price.

Nordhaus and Godley (1972) and Coutts, Godley and Nordhaus (1978) investigated the hypothesis that prices move with variations in the level of unit costs realized when output is following its long-run trend path. Series for 'normal' unit cost variables were obtained by eliminating cyclical fluctuations from unit costs for British manufacturing (excluding food, drink and tobacco) for the years 1953–69. In deriving the cost series, Nordhaus and Godley (1972, pp.855 and 862) assumed that firms use an historical cost pricing technique. With their series for historical normal unit cost they estimated *predicted* price, p_t, using the equation

$p_t = (1963 \text{ mark-up}) \times (\text{Historical normal unit cost})_t.$

The '1963 mark-up' was calculated as the ratio of the total value of output to total historical normal cost for 1963, and historical normal unit cost was the 'sum of the lagged components of cost, where the components [were] estimated unit costs when output equal[led] normal output' (*ibid.*, p.866). The predicted price series mirrored actual prices very closely.

When comparing the predicted and actual price series, the mark-up of price over normal costs was found to have fallen in Britain after 1961. That is, prices were apparently being determined as a *variable* mark-up over historical normal unit cost. Three explanations were offered (*ibid.*, pp.866–9). First, Nordhaus and Godley conceded that prices might actually be determined as full-cost mark-ups, rather than as margins over current costs. Second, they allowed that price competition may 'one way or another' be operating to reduce profitability below previous normal levels. As an example they drew on the import-competing segment of manufacturing. Finally, they suggested that government policies on nationalization and on incomes might have affected profit margins. Nordhaus and Godley were also able to show (pp.869–70) that the difference between their predicted price and the actual price could not be explained by changes in demand variables. The main conclusion of the later study by Coutts, Godley and Nordhaus (1978, p.139) confirmed the result that prices are determined as a mark-up on normal unit cost with temporary changes in demand having no effect. In an analysis of the pricing decision in an oligopolistic economy, Harcourt and Kenyon (1976, p.110) drew support from the works of Coutts, Godley and Nordhaus for the idea that 'price is fixed on the basis of the [trend in unit costs], ignoring short-period variations in unit prime costs which stem exclusively from alterations in rates of capacity utilization as demand changes over the course of the trade cycle'.

In studies of the influence of unit input costs, capacity utilization and price expectations on changes in indices of price for Britain and the US, Solow (1969, p.31) confirmed that demand in particular has a greater influence in the US than in Britain:

My results seem to confirm the common belief that the British price level is moved mainly by labour costs and the prices of imported raw materials. That doesn't mean that it is insensitive to the pressure of demand, but rather that demand pressure operates primarily through the labour market. In the United States, the independent operation of demand pressure in commodity markets is much more clearly visible.

For Britain, variations in unit labour costs had a much greater impact on price than did changes in expected price, which were modelled in an adaptive expectations framework (*ibid.*, Table 3, p.22).

Sylos-Labini (1979b) reported the results of studies in which he fitted data for manufacturing in each of Italy, the US, the United Kingdom, West Germany and Argentina to the equation

$$p' = aw' + br'$$

where $w + r$ is unit direct cost, w is the ratio of hourly money wages to hourly productivity in real terms, and r is the unit cost of raw materials. The prime superscripts on each variable indicate the rate of change. For each nation the time series spanned different periods, but included the years 1955–71.

Only in Argentina were cost changes translated completely into price changes. In each of the other economies adjustment was partial, with the sum of the coefficients of the cost terms in the regressions being greatest for the US and least for Britain. Demand pressures (modelled by including the growth of capacity utilization in the price equation) were found to have no influence on price determination in either Britain or Italy. For the US demand pressure had a statistically significant effect, but this was not of 'crucial importance' (*ibid.*, p.7). Foreign competition tended to reduce the extent to which cost increases were transferred to prices in Italy and Britain. Raw material costs had a greater influence on prices than did labour costs. The reason given for this was that increases in raw material costs generally affected producers in each competing country, while wage rises were domestic phenomena associated with union strength. For Italy, the rate of growth of prices was almost entirely explained by changes in direct costs and the prices of industrial products in international markets (*ibid.*, pp.8–9), whereas in Britain around 80 per cent of the growth of prices was explained by these variables. In Italy, and the US, *increases* in labour costs influenced prices more than reductions in this component of direct costs. This was attributed to the absence of international pressure to translate local reductions in labour costs into price reductions. The version of the extended neo-Pasinetti model considered here is closed, and so these implications of trade on the Sylos-Labini regressions will not be pursued further.

Explicit in the interpretation of Sylos-Labini's regression results is the assumption that underlying the equation

$$p' = aw' + br' \qquad (6.8)$$

were economic agents who determined price as a simple mark-up over direct cost, according to

$$p = \lambda(w + r). \qquad (6.9)$$

Equation (6.8) is consistent with the rule (6.9) when

$$a = S_L(1 + \lambda'/w') \text{ and } b = S_r(1 + \lambda'/r') \qquad (6.10)$$

where S_L and S_r are the shares of labour and raw material costs in total direct costs (*ibid.*, pp.10–11). Equation (6.8) might equally be the outcome of other price determination practices. For example Wilder, Williams and Singh (1977, p.733) and Eckstein and Fromm (1968, pp.1162–3) manipulated the profit-maximizing condition for a competitive firm into the form of equation (6.8). Also Ripley and Segal (1973, p.264) begin with a price formation rule involving differential mark-ups on labour and material costs and generate a functional form of the type (6.8). If in some of the economies in Sylos-Labini's study other price theories are more appropriate, the explanations and policy implications drawn by him may be inappropriate.

It is clear from (6.10) that, when price is marked up, the coefficients in (6.8) depend on changes in the mark-up, λ'. In the extended neo-Pasinetti model, the price equation is of the form of (6.9), where λ is

$$\lambda(m_m, I) = 1 + m_m + \beta\frac{I}{K}, \qquad (6.11)$$

and a in the extended neo-Pasinetti model is interpreted as average direct cost. If the pricing mechanism is accurately described by the extended neo-Pasinetti model, then equations (6.10) and (6.11) imply that the coefficients in the Sylos-Labini regression equation can be expected to depend on changes in investment plans and in the minimum mark-up. But in (6.10) the coefficients are also functions of the growth in the direct inputs. It is therefore possible that the coefficients in the regression equation might be determined as the outcome of complex interactions between the growth rates of the mark-up and direct input costs. Rather than endeavour to extract from Sylos-Labini's empirical work evidence in support of the price theory adopted in the previous chapter, it is much easier to augment his data base (presented in an appendix to the 1979 paper) with investment data and estimate equation (6.11) in the form

$$\lambda_i = \alpha_1 + \alpha_2 I_i + u_i. \tag{6.12}$$

For the years 1947–78, Sylos-Labini drew data for the US from various issues of the *Economic Report of the President*. Data for the same period for manufacturing industry on investment in plant and machinery may be extracted from Table B-51 of the 1979 presidential report. When Sylos-Labini's mark-ups for the US were regressed on investment using ordinary least squares, the following results were obtained:

$$\lambda_i = 1.71 + 0.0033 \, I_i + e_i, \quad R^2 = 0.77,$$
$$(160.71) \quad (10.15)$$

where e_i denotes the error term and the numbers in brackets are t-statistics. Both the intercept and slope have the expected signs and are significantly greater than zero at the 1 per cent level. When the regression equation (6.12) is compared with equation (6.11) for λ it seems that an estimate of m_m might be obtained by subtracting one from the estimate of α_1. Certainly the value $1.71 - 1 = 0.71$ has the expected sign and a plausible magnitude.

It should be obvious, however, that, while the estimated model reflects the pricing developed here, it is crude and misspecified. One cause of the crudity is that a number of variables important in the determination of mark-ups have been omitted. For example, it has been seen already for the US that demand influences are important determinants of price. Here only the investment component of final demand plays a role. In terms of the extended neo-Pasinetti model, omitted variables would have their values fixed exogenously, and their contribution to λ absorbed into a term which changes only with changes in any of these exogenous entities. For the regression equation, some of these exogenous influences may be aggregated by the ordinary least squares method into the estimate for α_1. In this event the value 0.71 will not be a true estimate of the minimum mark-up m_m. Of course omission of variables from the regression model will also bias the estimates obtained for α_2. Another source of misspecification is that the price equation belongs to a simultaneous system including equilibrium conditions for the commodity and securities markets, and an equation for the determination of investment. A correctly specified regression procedure should estimate the entire system simultaneously. Nevertheless, the regression results reported above provide some support for the determination of the mark-up assumed in the extended neo-Pasinetti model.

A number of the studies reviewed in this sub-section have found evidence that, in the US economy in particular, price is sensitive to variations in demand. Hall (1988) has vigorously rejected the notion that most US industry groups observe the neoclassical pricing theory of jointly operating constant returns technologies (see Section 2.1) and behave competitively (setting price equal to marginal cost). In many industries he found that marginal cost is small, but price is much larger. At the one-digit level of classification, the mark-up of price (less materials cost) over marginal cost (net of marginal materials cost) for each industry ranges from 1.9 to 3.8 (*ibid.*, pp.938–40). Having found against pure competition, Hall proposed that 'the most obvious explanation . . . is monopoly power in the product market. Since few American firms are simple monopolies, the finding probably requires an interpretation in terms of theories of oligopoly and product differentiation' (*ibid.*, p.946). A simple theory of this type is incorporated into the post-Keynesian neo-Pasinetti model in the next chapter. In the next sub-section the industry economics literature is surveyed for evidence of variables which determine the mark-up.

6.2.2 Industry structure and the profit margin

No clear conclusion could be drawn from the econometric tests of the alternative theories of competitive and non-competitive price determination considered in the previous sub-section. However, it appeared that the evidence from a number of countries and for a number of time periods was broadly, even if only weakly, consistent with the pricing theory of the extended neo-Pasinetti model. This appears to be true at least in the context of Eckstein and Fromm (1968) and other investigators who have preferred price mechanisms which incorporate the influences both of a mark-up and of demand. The focus in this sub-section is on non-competitive theories of price formation. The aims are to investigate the extent to which prices are formed as a mark-up over cost and how such mark-ups vary, if at all.

A large body of early research on non-competitive pricing used the concept of the concentration ratio to measure the extent to which firms operating in particular markets engage in oligopolistic behaviour. Usually the n-firm concentration ratio was defined as the share of the n largest firms in either an industry's total value of shipments or its employment. Comprehensive surveys of this work are given in Semmler (1984, pp.111–28) and Weiss (1974, pp.204–20). In many US studies of concentration, stimulated by the publication of an article by Bain in 1951, the existence of a few large firms within an industry was taken as *prima facie* evidence of collusion between firms in setting price and output levels. For example, Collins and Preston (1968, p.8) used evidence on the influence of concentration on prices and profits to support the view that

given the cost structure of the firm and the market demand, prices are higher and price–cost margins wider under conditions of monopoly . . . than under conditions of competition. If we define total costs to include normal profit, then we would expect the revenue–cost ratio to have [a] minimum value of unity for competitive firms, and to reach an upper limit, determined by cost and demand conditions, in a single-firm monopoly.

Weiss (1974, p.193) also considered that 'the main lines of oligopoly theory point rather consistently to higher prices in more concentrated industries' and 'high concentration involves a lessening of competition'. The association between firm size or industry concentration and collusion is known as the 'market' or 'differential concentration hypothesis'. Interest in the US in the econometrics of the profitability–concentration relationship was sustained over the 1950s and 1960s by the political appeal of the market concentration hypothesis as a justification for legislative attempts to end supposed collusion between large firms (see Brozen, 1982, pp.306–93). Some of this econometric evidence is reviewed here.

Another rich source of empirical observation on price–cost

margins sprang from a theoretical tradition opposed to the market concentration hypothesis. In 1974, Demsetz expounded the view that industry structure is largely determined by technological efficiency or the extent to which scale economies are possible. He reasoned that price needs to be high enough to cover the unit costs of small, relatively inefficient firms considering operation within a market. But, when this happens, large firms having superior efficiency, and which are already operating in the market, will have established high margins and will be making large accounting profits. Thus efficiency is seen as being responsible for both high concentration and large price–cost margins. Demsetz also argued that government intervention was responsible for collusion between firms. For Demsetz, government protection or subsidization were the only effective barriers to entry and, behind these, firms would feel encouraged to collude. This thesis will be referred to as the 'market efficiency hypothesis'. After Demsetz's attack on the lack of a theoretical foundation for the market concentration hypothesis a number of papers were published on the formal analysis of imperfectly competitive markets.

The line of research emphasized here is the one propounded in Cowling and Waterson (1976) and Cowling (1982). They put forward theoretical linkages between price–cost margins, market structure and collusion in the tradition of the work of Kalecki. In 1938, Kalecki produced a model in which the average value of the Lerner index of competitiveness (that is, the ratio alternatively referred to here as the price–cost margin) is related to the share of profits plus overheads in aggregate turnover, defined as gross national income plus the aggregate cost of raw materials. For a closed economy in which industry is vertically integrated, this means that the share of profits plus overheads and the share of wages in national income are determined by the average value of Lerner's index. Kalecki was interested in a capitalist economy in which industries engaged in imperfect competition, and operated under conditions of excess capacity at output levels where their average cost curves were horizontal. This was the type of representative firm for which Kaldor (1961, p.198) introduced the notion of the minimum margin of profit which competition could not eliminate (see Section 3.5). He called this minimum margin the 'degree of market imperfection' or the 'degree of monopoly'. For Kaldor (*ibid.*) 'the greater the intensity of competition the lower will be this minimum margin of profit'.

A number of studies in the tradition of the market concentration hypothesis have investigated how variations in firm concentration, that is, the percentage of sales, employment or some other indicator of activity controlled by a small number of firms, affect the relative size of the margin of price over a measure of average cost. Collins and Preston (1968) investigated how firm concentration affects the size of the relative price–cost margin,

$$(\text{price} - \text{marginal cost})/\text{price},$$

which they approximated (p.10) by calculating

$$(\text{value of shipments} - \text{cost of materials} - \text{payroll})/ \\ \text{value of shipments}.$$

This study used an n-firm concentration ratio as the indicator of concentration within an industry. The studies by Collins and Preston (1968, 1969) for the years 1958, 1959–60 and 1963, Weiss (1974, pp.227–31) reworking the Collins and Preston 1963 data, Rhoades (1973) for 1963, and Qualls (1972, 1974) for the periods 1936–40, 1947–51, 1950–60 and 1960–65 used four-firm concentration ratios, derived from US census data aggregated to the four-digit industry classification level. Studies for Britain by Phillips (1972), covering the years 1948, 1951 and 1954, and Khalilzadeh-Shirazi (1974) for 1963 used, respectively, three- and five-firm concentration ratios. All of the studies found a positive and statistically significant relationship between the price–cost margin and concentration at the 5 per cent level (at least). The work by Qualls also revealed a linkage between barriers to entry and the price–cost margin. Collins and Preston (1968, Chapter 3) showed that the effect of concentration on their proxy for the Lerner index was greatest for large firms. Also the work of Collins and Preston showed a significant correlation between the price–cost margin and the capital–output ratio. Phillips's investigation revealed no association between measures of collusion and the margin.

Two early studies which parallel Kaldor's interest in a minimum mark-up of price over average direct cost in an oligopoly were undertaken by Schwartzman (1959) and by his student, Bodoff (1975). To measure the effect of monopoly on price, Schwartzman constructed an index as follows, using 1954 data for manufacturing industry in Canada and the US:

1. identify a group of industries operating in each country which may be regarded as competitive. The test for this is that the four leading firms in the industry account for less than 50 per cent of total employment;
2. select another group of industries within which the Canadian operations may be regarded as monopolistic (that is, the four largest firms account for 50 per cent or more of total employment) and the US counterparts may be considered competitive;
3. estimate the ratio of price to average variable cost by computing the ratio of gross value product to total direct cost for the Canadian and US industries in each group. For industries in the competitive group these price–cost ratios are denoted by R_i^{Can} and R_i^{US}. The total number of industries in this group is denoted by m. Within the second group of n concentrated Canadian industries and *u*nconcentrated US activities the price–cost ratios are denoted by R_i^c and R_i^u; and,
4. compute the value of the index

$$\frac{1}{n}\sum_{i=1}^{n}\left(\frac{R_i^c}{R_i^u}\right) - \frac{1}{m}\sum_{i=1}^{m}\left(\frac{R_i^{Can}}{R_i^{US}}\right).$$

Only industries whose product definitions were the same in the two countries were included in this study. In this way, Schwartzman minimized the effect on the index of differences among *industries* in demand and technology. Also regionally segmented industries were excluded from each group. The unweighted average

$$\frac{1}{m}\sum_{i=1}^{m}\left(\frac{R_i^{Can}}{R_i^{US}}\right)$$

appearing as the second term in the index allowed Schwartzman to control for some variations in demand and cost curves associated with differences between the two *nations*. With these precautions most of the variations in the price–cost ratios are attributable to differences in the degree to which markets were monopolized. Hence, if the observed value for the index was greater than zero, and this was a statistically significant result, then the hypothesis that the price–cost ratios were higher in monopolized industries than in competitive industries was confirmed.

One potentially serious source of bias in the index was that the concentrated Canadian industries operated in markets where foreign trade was important. Canadian industries competing with imports may have been part of an international market in which prices were determined outside Canada or were influenced by tariffs. Such industries might have been inappropriately placed in the concentrated category. On the other hand, export industries faced pressure in international markets to keep prices low. To control for the influence of foreign trade, Schwartzman calculated the index using sub-collections of his concentrated–unconcentrated industries which:

(A) operated in purely domestic markets;
(B) consisted of the industries in (A) and also the industries competing with imports;
(C) consisted of the industries in (B) plus the exporting industries; and
(D) consisted of the industries in (A) plus the exporting industries.

The index values were found to be significant except for the sub-collections involving exporters. Statistically significant values for the index were calculated at the 5 per cent level for sub-collection (A), and at the 1 per cent level for sub-collection (B). For sub-group (B) the unweighted average of the ratios of Canadian and US price–cost margins for the competitive industries was 101.9, while the unweighted average of concentrated–unconcentrated pairs was 110.2. Therefore the value for the index in sub-collection (B) was 110.2-101.9 = 8.3.

Schwartzman (p.494) interpreted the value of 8.3 for his index as an estimate of the difference between monopolistic and competitive prices in 1954. To do this it had to be assumed that average variable cost in each industry in each country was the same. In that case the term

$$\frac{R_i^c}{R_i^u} = \frac{\left(\dfrac{P_i^c}{AVC_i^c}\right)}{\left(\dfrac{P_i^u}{AVC_i^u}\right)},$$

for example, simplified to

$$\frac{P_i^c}{P_i^{u^*}}$$

Later Schwartzman (1961) revised the estimate by evaluating instead the expression

$$\frac{1}{n}\sum_{i=1}^{n}(R_i^c - R_i^u) - \frac{1}{m}\sum_{i=1}^{m}(R_i^{Can} - R_i^{US}).$$

With this formula the estimate of the monopoly effect on price for 1954 was calculated as 11.2 per cent of average direct cost.

Subsequent recomputation of Schwartzman's index by Bodoff (1975), using expanded industry groupings for the years 1958, 1963 and 1967, yielded statistically insignificant values, challenging the conclusion that 'the ratio of price to average variable cost is higher in monopolistic than in competitive industries' (Schwartzman, 1959, p.354). The Schwartzman and Bodoff studies may be put into context by looking at the work of Weiss (1975). After reviewing both his own and many other econometric studies for the US, Weiss concluded that for the period 1953–8 concentration had a positive and statistically significant effect on price when account was taken of changes in direct costs (*ibid.*, pp.206–9). This was explained in the following way. In concentrated industries, prices rise because leading firms decide to raise them. Over the years 1950–52, price controls were in operation and there followed an episode of inflation associated with the Korean War. For Weiss it was unlikely that the management of leading firms would have violated the price guidelines of 1950–52. Similarly, the management of leading firms would not raise prices with every change in the market during periods of inflation. Rather, oligopolistic firms would tend to wait until they could invoke price changes, using as justification substantial changes in costs. After the relaxation of price controls and the cessation of inflationary pressure, Weiss reasoned that leading firms in oligopolistic industries would endeavour to re-establish their price–cost margins at higher levels. The year 1954, chosen by Schwartzman for his study, could reasonably be seen as such an opportunity.

Between 1959 and 1963, Weiss found that concentration had an insignificant impact on prices. For the period 1963–8, concentration had a negative but statistically insignificant effect on price changes, whether or not unit cost and demand changes were taken into account. 'Thus it appears that oligopoly had the effect of dampening the inflation of the 1960s' (*ibid.*, p.209). In both the Schwartzman and Bodoff analyses, the concentrated industries were Canadian, while all of the unconcentrated industries were American. If Weiss's conclusion may be extended to the Canadian experience, it appears that Bodoff's analysis was carried out in years when the concentrated Canadian industries were experiencing pressure to reduce price–cost margins. In fact Bodoff (1975, Table 5, p.181) reported that in 1967 the price–cost margins in 25 concentrated Canadian industries were, on average, very much less than the margins for the corresponding competitive US industries, the result being that, in 1967, the Schwartzman index yielded a negative value when calculated for the expanded groups used by Bodoff. For 1958 and 1963, the index returned positive but statistically insignificant values. For these two years (see Bodoff's Tables 7 and 8, p.183) the margins in concentrated Canadian industries were close to the price–cost margins prevailing in competitive US markets. It also appears that from year to year price–cost margins in the concentrated industries decreased, while for the competitive US industries margins grew (*ibid.*, Table 11, p.184).

Weiss's own work (1974) and his assessment of the wider body of research on price determination suggests that oligopolistic industries were influential in deciding price increases from the end of the Korean War to about 1958. Further, he found that this influence did not re-emerge until 1969. Thus Schwartzman's cross-section study was conducted in a year when it could be expected that the positive linkage between concentration and price–cost margins would be very strong. We may also infer that Bodoff used data for three years in which the relationship between concentration and price–cost margins was:

1. positive but possibly weakening in 1958 (as this year occurs at the end of the period detected by Weiss as displaying the strongest positive linkage);
2. at its weakest in 1963; and,
3. negative in 1967.

A criticism of Schwartzman's work is that the manufacturing

industry groups chosen by him were too small and too unrepresenta-
tive to allow generalization of his results to all manufacturing. To
accommodate this criticism, Bodoff revised and expanded the group
consisting of unconcentrated Canadian and unconcentrated US
industries from 27 to 65 representatives, and also worked with a
concentrated–unconcentrated group consisting of 34, rather than
19, industries. As has already been seen, Bodoff's expanded groups
failed to show evidence of the effect of monopoly on price. But
Schwartzman's original sample continued to show in 1967 a strong
positive linkage between concentration and price–cost margins,
although the relationship was weaker than in the original 1954 study
(Bodoff, 1975, p.178). Bodoff used the US government census of
manufactures and comparable Canadian government data on concentration ratios to select suitable industries. The test applied to
assign an industry to one group or the other was that the four-firm
value of shipments was above or below 59 per cent of the industry
total. This choice of the dividing line between the two groups was
thought to be consistent with the 50 per cent share of industry
employment used by Schwartzman. However, Weiss (1974, p.194)
concluded that studies of the concentration–profits relationship
using the US census concentration data are likely to produce 'a bias
in the estimated . . . relationship toward zero'. The underlying cause
of this bias is the misspecification of the economic markets in which
census industries operate, so that markets which 'appear concentrated in the Census are not really concentrated . . ., and some that
do not appear concentrated really are' (*ibid.*). These remarks
obviously apply equally to studies of the linkage between concentration and price–cost margins, and may also apply to Canadian
concentration data. Thus, in choosing expanded industry groupings
on the basis of concentration ratios, Bodoff may have introduced a
larger source of bias into her study than exists in Schwartzman's
results.

More generally, Weiss's 1974 paper contains a thorough review of
British, North American and Japanese econometric work on the
relationship between profitability measures and concentration. This
was augmented with a careful re-examination of the work of Collins
and Preston. Weiss (1974, pp.202–3) formed the conclusion that a
statistically significant, but weak, relationship exists between profitability (and therefore between price–cost margins) and concentration. In the course of his review Weiss found many studies which

established the existence of a relationship, but he also reported a substantial collection of studies which yielded no significant effect of concentration on profits or margins. Dixon (1988, p.6) took the more pessimistic view that 'the hypothesis of a significant positive relationship [is] rejected in most studies'. Coase (in Goldschmid *et al.*, 1974, p.163) summarized the empirical evidence on the market concentration hypothesis as only revealing a weak relationship. Many studies of the profit–concentration relationship have produced low R^2 values, small magnitude slope coefficients, or slopes which were insignificantly different from zero. But further, as is demonstrated in the re-examination of Schwartzman's work by Bodoff, often a significant statistical association discovered by one researcher vanishes in subsequent studies for later time periods using extended samples. Weiss has argued that there are many disturbances tending to bias the measured relationship to zero. Some of these disturbances were thought to have more significant influences during some periods than during others, for example during periods of inflation or price controls. Clarke (1985) reviewed the more recent statistical work. He considered that there is evidence of a modest, positive relationship for the US, while for the UK such a conclusion cannot be reached (*ibid.*, p.117). Over the 20 years to 1984, the UK was subject to a series of increasingly severe downturns and at the same time had to deal with increasing pressure from foreign competitors (*ibid.*, p.114). It was therefore not surprising to Clarke that clear relationships between industry structure and conduct and indicators of profitability or margins had not emerged in the UK.

What does this review of the econometric work on the market concentration hypothesis indicate about the variability and size of mark-ups? It seems that inflationary and price control factors are important in determining the size of the price–cost margin. However, the bias identified by Weiss suggests that margins might be under-estimated, implying also that the contribution of a minimum mark-up similar to Kaldor's might also be discounted. The studies reviewed here do not explicitly model the minimum margin, m_m, used in Chapter 5, and so no definite conclusions can be drawn. It is nevertheless tempting to think that mark-ups near the minimum were being observed in studies undertaken during periods when oligopolists or price leaders were being squeezed. In two such years the Bodoff study found that the price–cost margins in concentrated Canadian industries were insignificantly different from those in more competitive US markets. It is further tempting to claim Bodoff's results as evidence in favour of the minimum mark-up concept, which in Kaldor's view associated the minimum with the competitive outcome. But this really foreshadows later analytical and empirical developments attributable to researchers working in a different tradition. An important part of this literature is reviewed in the next sub-section.

6.2.3   The roles of structure and collusion in determining price

Now we examine a strand of the literature on the formation of price–cost margins having its genealogy running from Kalecki, via Cowling and Waterson (1976), to numerous researchers in industry economics over the 1980s. One theory of price formation is settled on for inclusion in the neo-Pasinetti model in the next chapter.

Kalecki (1954, pp.17–18) identified five factors which cause changes in the margin of price over average prime cost. These were changes in the degree of industry concentration, collusion between firms ('tacit agreement'), advertising, variations in firms' overheads, and the significance of trade union power. Like Kalecki, Cowling (1982) took the view that technical progress would most likely raise the degree of concentration in innovative industries. Shifting horizontal marginal cost curves associated with technical change would not lead to price cuts, as innovative firms would fear reprisals for breaching tacit agreements (*ibid.*, pp.29–30). Also, decreasing marginal cost would cause an innovative industry to operate in a region of more inelastic demand when the demand schedule was linear. For Cowling, technical change had only a secondary role in determining the price–cost margin, having its most significant effect through its impact on concentration. It therefore follows that the influence of technical change on income distribution was seen as indirect. This is in contrast to the central role of technical change in the neoclassical theory of distribution.

Following Cowling and Waterson, a number of similar theories were developed. Among these are Waterson (1980); Cowling (1982); Clarke and Davies (1982); Clarke, Davies and Waterson (1984); Schmalensee (1987) and Harris (1988). The last two authors give comprehensive bibliographies on other similar theoretical developments. The basic approach considers an industry consisting of a fixed number of profit-maximizing firms, each having constant marginal costs and producing a single, homogeneous commodity. Profit in firm i is a function of its output, Q_i, which may be written as

$$\pi_i = p(Q)Q_i - a_i,$$

where $p(Q)$ is the inverse demand schedule facing the industry, Q is total industry production, a_i denotes firm i's costs. Now let $Q'(Q_i)$, $p'(Q)$ and $a'_i(Q_i)$ represent the changes in output caused by an infinitesimal change in the output of firm i. To assume that the marginal changes in total output, price and cost always exist is to make the assumption that Q, p and a_i are differentiable functions, and that the derivative of each firm's profit function, π'_i, exists. The neoclassical approach would entail assuming for each firm the existence of a production function, whose partial derivatives (the marginal products of the factors) could always be found. The assumption that the inverse demand curve is differentiable precludes kinks or breaks in this schedule. When profit is maximized its first derivative is zero and so

$$p + Q_i p'(Q)Q'(Q_i) - a'_i = 0,$$

$Q'(Q_i)$ represents the marginal change in total output with respect to an infinitesimal increment in the output of firm i. This may be rearranged to give an expression for the Lerner index:

$$(p - a'_i)/p = Q'(Q_i)(Q_i/Q)/\eta, \tag{6.13}$$

where η is the modulus of the industry elasticity of demand,

$$\eta = -Q'(p)p/Q = -[1/p'(Q)]p/Q.$$

Now write

$$Q'(Q_i) = 1 + \tilde{Q}'(Q_i) = 1 + \lambda_i$$

where $\tilde{Q} = Q - Q_i$, $\tilde{Q}'(Q_i)$ denotes the marginal change in the output of all firms, other than i, to a unit increase in i's output, and λ_i is given by

$$\lambda_i = \sum_{j \neq i} \frac{dQ_j}{dQ_i}.$$

If s_i denotes firm i's share in total industry output (that is Q_i/Q) then (6.13) becomes

$$(p - a_i')/p = s_i(1 + \lambda_i)/\eta. \tag{6.14}$$

For each firm within an industry the Cowling and Waterson theory predicts that the mark-up of price over marginal cost depends on firm size (s_i), the extent of collusion (λ_i) and the inverse of the industry elasticity of demand ($1/\eta$). Exactly what the appropriate sign and value are for λ_i is the subject of a number of theories of oligopoly. For example, in Cournovian equilibrium, λ_i is thought to be 0 as firms take their rivals' output as given. That is, each firm does not expect a response from rivals to an increase in its own activity. In this case the firm does *not* resort to the neoclassical perfectly competitive outcome with price equal to marginal cost, for when $\lambda_i = 0$,

$$(p - a_i')/p = s_i/\eta. \tag{6.15}$$

In this model $p = a_i'$ only if either $s_i = 0$ (corresponding to the firm's exit from the industry) or when the demand schedule is perfectly elastic. With both of these situations excluded then, as for Kaldor's representative firm, there is a minimum margin of profit which is not eliminated by competition. This minimum margin is given by s_i/η. In (6.15) concentration (via the influence of the firm's share of output) determines the price–cost margin even though the equation was deduced on the assumption that firms do not collude.

Another theory suggested by Bertrand takes rivals' prices as given, rather than their output levels. For a model involving more than one firm producing a homogeneous commodity, the Bertrand conjecture implies that firms will attempt what they hope will be unnoticed, marginal reductions in price. But if all firms engage in this practice a price-cutting war erupts and is only stopped when the competitive price is reached. In this case λ_i is -1, as the expectation by one firm of no price response from its rivals is equivalent to the realization that rivals will most likely reduce output to accommodate an expansion of production by one firm. Thus from (6.14)

$$(p - a_i')/p = 0.$$

Following Cowling (1982, p.34, n5) the oligopolists' decision variable will here be taken as output rather than price, and so $\lambda_i > 0$ for each firm. This has been assumed because the instability associated with price competition seems unrealistic amongst oligopolists, and because the implication that prices settle at the purely competitive level is inconsistent with Kaldor's notion of the existence of a non-zero minimum value for the margin of price over unit cost. Of course it is possible that this minimum value might be the result of a Bertrand price adjustment mechanism which, coupled with output adjustment, stops short of the competitive price. This seems a complicated analytical situation. Fortunately, a straightforward theoretical explanation is available.

Clarke and Davies (1982) proposed the idea that each firm expects their *proportionate* expansion of output to be matched by rivals. This assumption may be expressed as

$$\Delta Q_i / Q_i = \Delta Q / Q,$$

and is equivalent to the expectation that rivals try to retain their market shares. In differential form the Clarke–Davies hypothesis may be written as

$$\lambda_i = Q'(Q_i) - 1 = Q/Q_i - 1 = (1 - s_i)/s_i$$

From (6.14) this implies that

$$(p - a'_i)/p = 1/\eta. \tag{6.16}$$

That is, firms jointly maximize profits, with each realizing the monopoly price–cost margin. Collusion of this type relates rivals' responses to their size. Small, inefficient firms must impose on themselves the most stringent restrictions of output (Schmalensee, 1987, p.405). This is inconsistent with Stigler (1964), where small firms raising output above agreed levels are less likely to be detected. That is, the expectation of retaliation is directly related to size. In a paper devoted to the examination of accounting rates of return, Schmalensee postulated a relationship of the form

$$\lambda_i = \lambda + \gamma[s_i - 1/N],$$

where λ is the mean value of the λ_is over the N firms in an industry, and γ is a constant. This relationship is not likely to produce very strong signals in least squares regressions or, where it does, interpretation of the coefficients is difficult. Evidence from such empirical studies on Schmalensee's relationship must therefore be regarded with care. To see this we review Schmalensee's treatment of the Clarke–Davies hypothesis in our context.

Suppose that firms only expect rivals to succeed imperfectly in preserving their output shares; that is, let

$$\lambda_i = \alpha(1 - s_i)/s_i$$

where α is positively correlated with concentration, and is taken to be constant (Schmalensee, 1987, p.405). With this rule (6.14) may be transformed to

$$(p - a_i')/p = \{\alpha + (1 - \alpha)s_i\}/\eta, \qquad \text{(C–D)}$$

where the notation (C–D) alludes to the version of (6.14) obtained using the Clarke and Davies hypothesis. Compare this with the equation for the firm's Lerner index obtained under the assumption that $\lambda_i = \lambda$ for all firms:

$$(p - a_i')/p = (1 + \lambda)s_i/\eta. \qquad (\lambda = C)$$

In these two cases there exist relations of the form

$$Y_i = \beta_1 + \beta_2 X_i \qquad \text{(R)}$$

between the firms' price–cost margin (Y_i) and the firms' shares of industry output (X_i). For the model ($\lambda = C$) (that is, the case where $\lambda =$ constant for all firms) ordinary least squares will produce the estimates

$$\beta_1 = 0$$
$$\beta_2 = (1 + \lambda)/\eta$$

for the generic linear equation (R). For the (C–D) equation the estimates will be

$$\beta_1 = \alpha/\eta$$

$$\beta_2 = (1-\alpha)/\eta.$$

Thus these two models yield the obvious results, that is, estimation using a linear regression equation (R) produces estimates of the constant and coefficient of s_i in the (C–D) and ($\lambda = C$) models. It should be noted that in the (C–D) model the intercept will become larger (and eventually significantly different from zero for a given finite η) as rivals are expected to be more successful in preserving market share. Also the (C–D) specification has associated with it a smaller slope coefficient. That is, Clarke and Davies predict price–cost margins to be less sensitive to market share than the specification where λ is constant.

When the notional estimation procedure is repeated for Schmalensee's formulation of the collusion rule, the outcomes are more difficult to interpret. In this case

$$\frac{p - a'_i}{p} = \frac{\{(1 + \lambda - \gamma/N)s_i + \gamma s_{ij}^2\}}{\eta}. \tag{S}$$

The price–cost margin is a non-linear function of firm size, and also varies with the number of firms. If formulation (S) is estimated using the regression model (R) then

$$\beta_1 = \frac{\gamma\left\{H^2 - \sum_{i=1}^{N} s_i^3\right\}}{(NH-1)\eta}$$

$$\beta_2 = (1+\lambda)/\eta + \frac{\gamma\left\{N^2 \sum_{i=1}^{N} s_i^3 - 2NH + 1\right\}}{N(NH-1)\eta},$$

where $H = \sum s_i^2$ is the Herfindahl index. The intercept is now inversely related to the number of firms in the industry and has a complicated relationship to concentration. If the s_i are lognormally distributed, then the expected value of $\sum s_i^3$ is NH^3 (*ibid.*, p.406) and

$$\beta_1 = -\gamma H^2/\eta.$$

That is, if γ is positive and non-negatively correlated with concentration, the intercept in an ordinary least squares regression is negatively correlated with the Herfindahl index of concentration. To simplify the analysis of the slope coefficient in the (S) formulation, consider first the Herfindahl index,

$$H = \sum_{i=1}^{N} s_i^2$$

If σ^2 is the variance in firm size across an industry and $E(Q_i)$ is the average firm size, then the coefficient of variation of firm size is given by,

$$v = \sigma/E(Q_i),$$

and, as $\sigma^2 = E(Q_i - E(Q_i))^2$, it follows that

$$H = (v^2 + 1)/N.$$

When all firms are of equal size $v^2 = 0$ and $H = 1/N$. If there are very many small firms in an industry, with none of them dominating production, then both v and H approach 0 as N grows. Thus H assumes the limiting value 0 in an industry made up of atomistic producers. At the other extreme, for a monopoly $N = 1$, $v = 0$ and $H = 1$. To see what the relationship is between the slope coefficient and concentration, substitute $H = (v^2 + 1)/N$ into the expression for β_2 given above:

$$\beta_2 = \frac{(1 + \lambda)}{\eta} + \frac{\gamma\left\{N^2\sum_{i=1}^{N}s_i^3 - 2v^2 - 1\right\}}{Nv^2\eta}.$$

As H approaches 1, that is as the market becomes monopolized, v^2 approaches 0, N gets closer to 1, and of course $\sum_{i=1}^{N}s_i^3$ tends to 1.

Consequently, β_2 increases as concentration increases, provided $\gamma > 0$. When $\gamma = 0$, β_2 is related to λ, the average collusive practice between firms, and to the reciprocal of the demand elasticity. Also β_1 is zero, and so this case is similar to the ($\lambda = C$) model. But in the case of N equal-sized firms, $H = 1/N$ and then the β_2 estimated for the (S) formulation is indeterminate. Ordinary least squares (OLS) estimates of β_2 for an industry consisting of a (large) number of equal-sized firms and behaving according to Schmalensee's model will therefore be very unreliable. A corollary of this result is that there is no analogue of the (C–D) specification in the (S) formulation. (This follows because the only zero of the numerator in the second term of the expression for β_2 is given by $H = 1/N$, which is also a zero of the expression for β_1.) The correlations between the regression coefficients and concentration in the (S) specification grow as γ becomes larger. However, both γ and η may vary considerably between industries, so it is unlikely that the correlations predicted by Schmalensee's model will be particularly strong (*ibid.*, p.406).

Now let us turn to the industry-wide price–cost margin. The output-weighted average of all firms' optimal price–cost margins gives a measure of the industry-wide Lerner index. To see this multiply (6.14) by s_i and sum over all firms to obtain

$$\sum s_i \left[\frac{(p - a_i')}{p} \right] = \frac{\sum s_i^2 (1 + \lambda_i)}{\eta}. \qquad (6.17)$$

This simplifies to

$$\frac{(p - a')}{p} = \frac{\{\sum s_i^2 + \sum (s_i^2 \lambda_i)\}}{\eta},$$

where a' is the output share-weighted average of all firms' marginal costs. Now $\sum s_i^2 = H$, the Herfindahl index of concentration, so that, if μ is defined to be

$$\mu = \frac{\sum (s_i^2 \lambda_i)}{\sum s_i^2}, \qquad (6.18)$$

then the industry-wide Lerner index or price–cost margin is given by

$$\frac{(p - a')}{p} = \frac{H(1 + \mu)}{\eta}. \qquad (6.19)$$

There are a number of features of this equation to note. First the industry-wide price–cost margin is predicted to depend on the Herfindahl index and not the m-firm concentration ratio,

$$\sum_{i=1}^{m} s_i.$$

The ratio μ defined in (6.19) is a weighted average of the λ_i, incorporating each firm's expectations of reactions from its rivals to variations in its output. Provided the λ_i are positive then μ is bounded below by 0 and above by 1. The Clarke and Davies proposal that

$$\lambda_i = \frac{\alpha(1 - s_i)}{s_i}$$

converts μ to

$$\mu = \frac{\alpha(H - 1)}{H},$$

and (6.19) expands into

$$\frac{(p - a')}{p} = \frac{\{H(1 - \alpha) + \alpha\}}{\eta}. \tag{6.20}$$

With the Clarke and Davies rule α is given by

$$\alpha = Q'(Q_i)Q_i/Q.$$

That is, α is firm i's expectation of the elasticity of rivals' output with respect to their own production level. Clarke and Davies assumed that α is constant across all firms in the industry. Notice in (6.20) that as α varies between 0 and 1 the industry price–cost margin moves from the Cournot solution through to the joint-maximizing equilibrium value. Only when $H = 0$, $\alpha = 0$ and $\eta \neq 0$ will price be equated with marginal cost for the industry.

When $\alpha = 0$, that is when firms behave competitively,

$$\frac{(p - a')}{p} = \frac{H}{\eta}. \tag{6.21}$$

This equation provides a lower bound (H/η) for the price–cost margin when industry structure and demand conditions are fixed. As the industry becomes more concentrated, this lower bound departs further from the perfectly competitive neoclassical paradigm, arriving at the monopoly outcome when $H = 1$. The lower bound is close to the notion of a minimum margin of profit which Kaldor envisaged competition did not eliminate. In Chapter 7, the Clarke and Davies theory is incorporated into the neo-Pasinetti model in place of the mark-up rule of Chapter 5,

$$m = m_m + \beta\frac{I}{K},$$

where m_m denotes the minimum margin and β is a positive parameter. The idea of a minimum margin survives this replacement. For the minimum margin will make a contribution of the form

$$m_m = \delta H, \tag{6.22}$$

where δ is taken to be a positive parameter and H is the Herfindahl index of concentration. The parallel with Kaldor's concept of the minimum margin is not complete. For example, so far in this theory of oligopoly α might just as easily be negative, giving the competitive outcome in Bertrand price competition.

Where (6.22) is valid with $\alpha = 0$, the parameter δ is a function of the price elasticity of demand. Collectively, the firms in an industry may exert a long-term influence to reduce the elasticity by advertising. Cowling (1982, pp.13–15) and Waterson (1984, p.201) report some econometric evidence for Britain and the US. Waterson concluded:

Unfortunately it would be hazardous to come to any firm conclusion as to the influence of advertising on the price elasticity of demand. Though a large number of studies have looked at the effect of advertising on the demand for products or brands, most suffer from problems of simultaneous equations bias . . . this bias is likely to be in the direction of exaggerating the effects of advertising on industry demand. Even more importantly . . . the overwhelming majority of such studies estimate functions which do not allow advertising effectively to influence the price elasticity of demand.

Sawyer (1985, p.122) concluded that 'the empirical evidence has not been able to [decide] the role of advertising. The linkages between advertising, concentration and profitability are many and probably not very strong.' Both Cowling and Waterson quoted a US study which suggested that advertising is associated with lower price, the mechanism at work being a positive linkage operating from industry advertising to demand, with price falling either because of falling unit costs associated with production economies or because demand becomes more elastic. Cowling's suggestion (1982, pp.29–30) that decreasing marginal cost causes an innovative industry to operate in a region of more inelastic demand also provides another mechanism causing the parameter δ to grow.

Early studies, such as those by Collins and Preston, and most of the papers reviewed by Weiss (1974) and Semmler (1984) used an *m*-firm concentration ratio when estimating the profitability–concentration relationship. There is no support for this in the theory of Cowling and Waterson – rather, they predict that the correct measure is the Herfindahl index. In their 1976 article, Cowling and Waterson compare the performance of the two indices in explaining price–cost margins. Like Kalecki, their approach was to attempt to explain intra-industry differences over time in the share of profits plus overheads in revenue. An equation for this share may be obtained from (6.17) by noting that $s_i = Q_i/Q$ and then proceeding as above to (6.19), but with the left-hand side of the equation written as

$$\frac{\{\sum pQ - \sum a_i'Q_i\}}{pQ}.$$

The denominator is simply industry revenue, R. If the profit of the *i*th firm is given by

$$\pi_i = pQ_i - a_i'Q_i - F_i,$$

where F_i is fixed or overhead cost, then the numerator is simply aggregate profit plus aggregate industry overheads, as

$$\sum pQ_i - \sum a_i'Q_i = \sum(\pi_i + F_i) = \pi + F.$$

Thus (6.19) may be rewritten as

$$\frac{(\pi + F)}{R} = \frac{H(1 + \mu)}{\eta}. \tag{6.23}$$

Now let L_{jt} denote the profits plus overheads share for industry j at time *t*. If it is assumed that demand elasticities and collusive practices do not change over time, then from (6.23)

$$\frac{L_{jt}}{L_{j(t-s)}} = \frac{H_{jt}}{H_{j(t-s)}} . \tag{6.24}$$

Year *t* in Cowling and Waterson's study was 1963 and year *t − s* was 1958. Log-linear equations were estimated in which the 1963–1958 ratios of the Herfindahl indices and the four-firm concentration measures were separately used as explanators for the ratios of the profits plus overheads shares of 94 British industries. The coefficient of the ratio of the Herfindahl indices was found to be positive and significant at the 1 per cent level, while the coefficient of the ratio of the four-firm concentration measures was also positive, but only significant at the 5 per cent level. When a variable modelling the impact of trade union activity and a dummy taking the value one for durable goods and zero otherwise were included as explanatory variables, both concentration measures had slightly larger coefficients, but their significance levels remained unchanged. When the sample was separated into durable goods and non-durable goods industries, the coefficients of the two measures retained their significance levels for the durable goods sample, but failed significance tests at the 5 per cent level for the other sub-collection.

While Cowling and Waterson provided an analytical structure explaining in an oligopolistic framework the relationship between a measure of concentration and price–cost margins, the measure they highlighted did not perform conclusively better than the *m*-firm concentration ratio used widely in the traditional literature. Subsequently, Hart and Morgan (1977) found that the concentration ratio did not have a significant impact on profitability (measured as the ratio of profit to value added) in a comparable sample of industries for the years 1963 and 1968. Drawing on the work of Sleuwaegen and Dehandschutter (1988), Dixon (1988, pp.9–11) concluded that the two measures of concentration are linearly correlated for four-firm concentration ratios in the range 0 to 0.5, and beyond that range the relationship is non-linear and not very strong. This observation may help to explain the divergent econometric results obtained using *m*-firm concentration ratios. Dixon reasserted that the concentration ratios used in most studies of the profitability–concentration relationship must be regarded as proxies for *H*.[10] But at high values the concentration ratio is only a poor proxy for the Herfindahl index, and 'thus the quantitative relationship between profitability and the concentration ratio is likely to differ markedly depending upon whether we are looking at industries with low or high levels of concentration' (*ibid.*, p.11).

An implication of Cowling and Waterson's theory is that in their regressions the coefficient of the ratio of the Herfindahl indices for the two time periods should be one. The closest this coefficient comes to unity is 0.56. The authors suggested that this occurred because 'either price adjustment is falling below that implied by Cournot's assumption that μ is zero or alternately that costs are rising with increased concentration' (Cowling and Waterson, 1976, p.273). Other possibilities are that either demand elasticities or collusive arrangements had changed between 1958 and 1963 to reduce the coefficient of H_{j63}/H_{j58} in (6.24). Some support for these latter possibilities, at least in the US, may be found in the work of Schmalensee (1987, pp.415–21).

This sub-section and the last have been devoted to an investigation of the relationship between price–cost margins, industry structure and conduct. We have noted the comparison between one case of the Clarke and Davies theory and Kaldor's minimum margin. In Chapter 7, the Clarke and Davies theory is used to model the microeconomic determination of price in the neo-Pasinetti model. It might perhaps be more in the spirit of Kaldor's philosophy to use a different theory of imperfect competition. The choice made here seems a relatively simple approach. By doing this, a link is established between the economy-wide price–cost margin and indicators of industrial organization and behaviour. But we can go further and explain the preferred measure of financial market valuations in the neo-Pasinetti model, Tobin's q, as a function of the relative price–cost margin by appealing to the work of Lindenberg and Ross (1981). This and other theories of the determination of q are reviewed in the following sub-section.

6.2.4   What determines the value of q?

Most studies of the structure/conduct/performance relationship have used accounting rates of return or other profitability measures to construct series for the dependent performance variable. (See, for example, the reviews by Schmalensee, 1987, and Weiss, 1974.) The use of accounting data has been widely criticized. Smirlock, Gilligan and Marshall (1984, p.1051) objected to accounting profit rates as proxies for the economic or monopoly rents earned by firms. For Harris (1984, p.166) studies using accounting profitability data were invalid because the data and the models tested did not allow for differences across firms in investor risk or for the capitalized value of earnings from future investment. Hirschey (1985, pp.91–2) drew attention to the accounting practice of treating assets in the form of advertising and research and development as current expenses. This both produces a positive bias in accounting profit rates and leaves out of capital measures a component comprising intangible assets. The criticisms of Harris and Hirschey were supported by Wernerfelt and Montgomery (1988, p.247) who pointed out that the treatment of systematic risk, capitalized returns, tax laws and accounting procedures for dealing with intangible assets are probably more variable across industries than between firms in the same sector.

Rather earlier than these criticisms were published, Lindenberg and Ross (1981) proposed the use of financial data on the valuation of securities to measure firm profitability. They suggested the comparison of financial market valuations with accounting data on resource usage as an alternative to traditional indicators of firm performance. In their study they used the ratio of the firm's market value to its replacement cost, that is, Tobin's q. Thomadakis (1977) and Hirschey (1985) have alternatively used the difference between capitalized and book values divided by sales.

For a firm facing homothetic production possibilities and a constant elasticity of demand, Lindenberg and Ross (1981, p.8) established a link between Tobin's q and the Lerner index or price–cost margin which they summarized in the proposition:

Let S denote the ratio of average to marginal cost, that is, the [inverse of the] elasticity of the cost function. A firm has decreasing costs if $S > 1$ and increasing costs if $S < 1$. A firm engaged in positive (gross) investment has a Lerner's index

$$L = (P - MC)/P \leq 1 - 1/Sq$$

where q is 'Tobin's q' [and MC is marginal cost]. Equivalent statements of this result are $(P - AC)/AC \leq q - 1$ and $q \geq (1/S)[1/(1 - L)]$, and with constant returns to scale ($S = 1$) we have the simple result that $L \leq 1 - (1/q)$ and $q \geq 1/(1 - L)$.

With identical marginal and average costs the last part of the proposition gives an upper bound on the price–cost margin which is a function of q alone. Otherwise the bound is a function also of the effect of scale (that is, of S). For the 18 years 1960 to 1977, Lindenberg and Ross constructed q series for each of 246 US firms, which they used to test the hypothesis that over the sample period each firm's q was strictly greater than

$$\frac{1}{S} \cdot \frac{1}{1-L}.$$

For the majority of firms this was found to be true. Further their statistical tests indicated that the null hypothesis of equality between a firm's q and the firm's value for the expression above was rejected with a frequency much greater than chance, suggesting that their proposition indeed provided a realistic lower bound for firms' q ratios.

To study the structure/conduct/performance relationship, Lindenberg and Ross regressed their 1972 qs on the four-firm concentration ratios for the industry of each firm in the sample, and also jointly on the 1972 concentration ratios together with the price–cost margins. Further they pooled the information on firms and, for the 18 years of their sample, regressed firms' qs on their price–cost margins. The price–cost margin was a significant explanator of q at the 1 per cent level, having large positive coefficients in the regressions; by contrast the coefficients of the concentration ratio were not significantly different from zero, but were positive. Apparently the q measure of performance or profitability was not significantly explained by this indicator of market concentration. However the price–cost margin made a statistically significant contribution to the explanation of q. This suggests a direction in which the theory of Chapter 5 might be extended to include the endogenous determination of q. It will be recalled that there q was set exogenously.

When marginal cost is constant it follows from the proposition of Lindenberg and Ross that there is an upper bound for the price–cost margin, L_i, in terms of q_i, or there is a lower bound for q_i in terms of the margin. One extension of these results is to posit a functional relationship of the form

$$q_i = f(L_i, z_i)$$

or

$$L_i = g(q_i, w_i),$$

where z_i and w_i are vectors of other variables influencing q_i and L_i. The view taken here is that the functional forms f and g are composite relationships which hide the fundamental influence of industry structure on both q_i and on L_i. From equation (6.14) in Sub-section 6.2.3 the price–cost margin for an oligopolistic firm can be written as

$$L_i = \frac{(p - a_i')}{p} = \frac{s_i(1 + \lambda_i)}{\eta}$$

where s_i is the firm's share of industry output, λ_i is the firm's expectations of its rivals' responses to an increase in output, and η is the industry demand elasticity. Thus the linkage from the indicator of structure s_i to the price–cost margin is already apparent. This linkage, taken together with the empirical association between q_i and L_i found by Lindenberg and Ross, suggests that q_i may in part be determined by the firm's output share s_i. The following review of recent empirical work in industry economics provides further support for the existence of a functional linkage from firm-level q to the firm's market share.

Hirschey (1985) studied the effects of three market structure variables on q defined as

$$q = MV(F)/RC(T),$$

where $RC(T)$ is the replacement cost of tangible assets, and the market value of the firm $MV(F)$, is decomposed as

$$MV(F) = MV(T) + MV(I),$$

where $MV(T)$ and $MV(I)$ denote the capitalized values of profits attributable to tangible assets and to intangibles (that is, human capital, research and development, and advertising). If it is assumed that

$$MV(T) = RC(T) + e_1,$$

where e_1 denotes an error term, then q may be written as

$$q = 1 + MV(I)/MV(T) + e.$$

It appears then that the market valuation of intangible assets has a direct influence on q. To test this theory, Hirschey estimated the linear equation

$$q_i = b_0 + b_1M_i + b_2R_i + b_3A_i + b_4G_i + b_5B_i + u_i \,,$$

where M_i is either market share s_i, the four-firm concentration ratio c_i, or the relative market share, s_i/c_i, R_i and A_i denote the intensity or share in sales of expenditure on research and development and on advertising, G_i denotes firm growth, and B_i the share-price beta measure of risk.

First Hirschey regressed q against each of the three market structure variables together with the growth and risk variables for a 390-firm sample extracted from the 1977 *Fortune* 500 companies. He found 'a significant positive link between market share and [q]' (*ibid.*, p.95), but only small and statistically insignificant positive effects of concentration and relative market share on q. This lack of impact of the concentration ratio on q supports the finding of Lindenberg and Ross for this market structure variable. The statistical linkage between market share and q is consistent with our posited functional relationship between q and market share.

Next Hirschey included in the regressions the variables modelling the influence of intangible assets. These regressions produced R^2 values greater by a factor of 100 than those of the initial regressions. Also the coefficients on the research and development and the advertising variables had high t-values, suggesting that equations omitting the influences of intangible assets may be misspecified. In the initial regressions the growth and risk variables were found to be significant explanators of q at better than the 1 per cent level. But, for the regressions involving the intangibles, the risk variable was not significant at the 10 per cent level. This was not the only difference. Hirschey was also confronted with evidence of a significant, negative correlation between q and the four-firm concentration ratio.[11] Even more importantly in our context, the association between q and market share disappeared. These results suggested that 'market value seems much more closely related to research and development, advertising intensity, and growth than to variables reflecting the size distribution of firms' (*ibid.*, p.96).

In an earlier study using the same data, Hirschey (1982) obtained similar results: with q measured as the ratio of market valuation to book value of assets, concentration was not related to q and the coefficient of the four-firm concentration ratio tended to be negative. The coefficients of variables modelling intangible assets were around 3 and were significant at the 1 per cent level. These results should, however, be assimilated with caution. First, there is the possibility of collinearity between Hirschey's measure of firm growth in terms of sales and the market share variable. Second, a number of studies provide strong support for treating advertising as an endogenous variable, which is determined in part by market structure.[12] The occurrence of a significantly non-zero, but negative, coefficient for concentration in Hirschey's work may simply be a consequence of misspecification of his model. Whatever the relevance of this criticism, it remains true that Hirschey's results do not seem to translate easily to other economies and other time periods. For example, Cowling (1982, p.14) reproduces his own study of 88 companies in the British food industry in which the coefficients of both the market structure and advertising variables are of the expected sign, have the same magnitudes and are significant explanators of variations in the price–cost margin. As for Hirschey, the inclusion of advertising in the regression produced a very high value for R^2. Cowling was careful to point out that the causality of the relationship between advertising and profitability might be in the opposite direction to that assumed in the mathematical formulation of his regression equation, as 'the vast bulk of advertising simply does not provide the sort of information that would lead to greater price sensitivity' (*ibid.*).

Smirlock, Gilligan and Marshall (1984) took up the idea of Lindenberg and Ross that the share market provides a superior valuation of firm rents to the various accounting measures. Using data for the period 1961–9 for 132 US firms, they estimated the equations

$$q_i = a_0 + a_1 s_i + a_2 c_i + a_3 B_i + u_i$$

$$q_i = b_0 + b_1 c_i + b_2 g_i + b_3 B_i + u_i$$

$$q_i = d_0 + d_1 s_i + d_2 c_i + d_3 g_i + d_4 B_i + u_i$$

where c_i denotes the four-firm concentration ratio, g_i denotes the growth in market shares over the period 1960–69. A composite variable B_i represents Shepherd's (1972) binary indices of the height of barriers to entry for the industry to which firm i belongs. In the regressions involving the market structure variables separately both a_1 and b_1 were significant and positive. The third equation was estimated in an attempt to distinguish between the market collusion and efficiency hypotheses. In doing this, Smirlock, Gilligan and Marshall took up the suggestion of Weiss (1974, pp.225–6) that the appropriate test of the two doctrines is one which simultaneously accounts for both indicators of market structure. It was found that d_1 was positive and significant, while d_2 was not significantly different from zero 'at any conventional level' (Smirlock, Gilligan and Marshall, 1984, p.1056). This outcome provides support for the market efficiency hypothesis. The paper by Schmalensee (1987) endeavours in the same spirit to differentiate between the market hypotheses or detect the existence of behaviour consistent with both hypotheses. Econometrically this attempt failed. Sub-section 6.2.3 contains a discussion of some reasons for the failure of Schmalensee's hybrid hypothesis.

These authors also tested whether there is a critical value for the concentration ratio below which firms are unable to collude. This idea was put forward by Bain, and was investigated in many of the papers reviewed by Weiss (1974). The papers by Schwartzman and Bodoff analysed in Sub-section 6.2.2 used the notion of a critical value for the concentration ratio to divide industries into two classes – competitive and collusive. Instead of c_i in the third equation, Smirlock, Gilligan and Marshall used a variable c_i^* taking value 1 when the four-firm concentration ratio for firm i's industry was at least 90 per cent. For this regression the coefficients of c_i^* and s_i were both positive and significant at the 1 per cent level. Without the market share variable the value of the critical concentration ratio which produced a significant coefficient was 80 per cent. Barriers to entry fail to be significant at the 5 per cent level in any of the regressions. Interestingly, the growth of the market share has a strongly positive and significant coefficient in all the regressions. 'One possible interpretation of this is that [g_i] is the basis for investors' expectations about which firms are most efficient and will therefore increase their market share over time' (Smirlock, Gilligan and Marshall, 1984, p.1056). This seems to suggest that a dynamic theory of q should include the rate of change of market shares. In the static theory developed in Chapters 5 and 7 this implication is ignored. But in Chapter 7 a macro-equation for q is developed which

192   *Income Distribution in a Corporate Economy*

picks up the influence in the microeconomic context of market shares on firms' *q*s.

Notes

1. Without success Chirinko attempted to eliminate these specification errors by incorporating into the investment-*q* framework the endogenous determination of a firm's choice between debt financing and direct acquisition of fixed capital.
2. On certain assumptions Tobin's *q* may be written in terms of the marginal efficiency of capital *R*, and the discount rate on earnings *r*, as

$$q = \frac{R}{r}. \qquad (6A.1)$$

To see this recall the definition of *q* as

$$q = \frac{p_s N}{pM}. \qquad (6A.2)$$

The market value of all securities is the discounted value of the flow of returns from owning a unit of capital. That is,

$$p_s N = \sum_{t=1}^{n} \frac{RpM}{(1+r)^t}, \qquad (6A.3)$$

where shareholders are assumed to expect the same earnings stream as do the corporate managers who operate the capital stock. This assumption underlies Tobin's (1969, p.328) original analysis. Multiplication of (6A.3) by $(1+r)^{-1}$ gives

$$\frac{p_s N}{1+r} = \sum_{t=1}^{n} \frac{RpM}{(1+r)^{t+1}}. \qquad (6A.4)$$

Subtract (6A.4) from (6A.3) to obtain

$$p_s N = \left(1 - \frac{1}{(1+r)^n}\right)\frac{RpM}{r}. \qquad (6A.5)$$

Suppose now that the equity is held in perpetuity, as would be the case for a consol. The period *n* becomes arbitrarily long, and equation (6A.5) for the market value of securities reduces to

$$p_s N = \frac{RpM}{r}. \qquad (6A.6)$$

Thus,

$$\frac{R}{r} = \frac{p_x N}{pM} = q.$$

This relation holds exactly for financial instruments with infinite life. When the instrument exists for only a finite period, the inverse relation between q and the rate of return on paper assets is only approximate.

3. A formal explanation of why this implies a causal relationship flowing from I to q may be obtained by referring to the interpretation of Granger and Sims offered by Williams, Goodhart and Gowland (1976, p.418). If I causes q, a regression of q on past, current and future values of I should exhibit significant coefficients for past and current values, but insignificant coefficients for future values of I. This is just Granger's original concept of causality. But equally, if q causes I, a regression of I on past, current and future values of q should have significant coefficients for the future values of q. This is the test relevant to the example given in the text.

4. Estimates obtained in this way are inefficient, but the inefficiency may be eliminated by accounting for heteroskedasticity in the errors. See Ciccolo (1978, p.58).

5. The further assumption that q is a moving average of some white noise process is required to prove this result. See Udea and Yoshikawa (1986, p.15).

6. This result should be compared with the findings of Oulton. Udea and Yoshikawa have reported that for Japan the profit rate is likely to be a more important determinant of investment than the discount rate. This is consistent with the results given in the text for the US. The explanation may be to do with the more permanent nature of changes in profit rates, compared with the volatility of share markets. Alternatively there may be international and/or temporal differences in the operation of share markets, or in variables which impinge on the marginal efficiency.

7. A number of studies distinguished between the performance of Tobin's q in explaining investment in structures and in equipment. See, for example, Berndt (1991, p.272), and Clark (1979), including the comments of Greenspan (*ibid.*, pp.114–17).

8. Regression coefficients for λ and $\Delta\lambda$ were not reported by Eckstein and Fromm. So to obtain an indication of the strength of the full-cost mechanism one may proceed as follows. In finite change form the full-cost rule (6.3) is

$$\Delta p = (1+\lambda)(\Delta ULC^N + \Delta UMC^N) + (ULC^N + UMC^N)\Delta\lambda .$$

Together with equation (6.5) for the price change inferred from the target return rule, this gives

$$(ULC^N + UMC^N)\Delta\lambda + \lambda(\Delta ULC^N + \Delta UMC^N) = (K/x^N)\pi.$$

This equation provides an expression for π in terms of λ and $\Delta\lambda$ so that (6.6) may be rewritten as (6.7) in the text.

9. The derivations for the first three pricing mechanisms may be gleaned from Eckstein and Fromm (1968, pp.1162–6). For the fourth price regime the derivation is given in Ripley and Segal (1973, p.264).

10. This presupposes that the Cowling and Waterson model accurately represents reality, which is far from clear. An alternative theory devised by Saving (1970) predicts that a concentration ratio is the appropriate measure. The model in this case is of an industry in which there is a dominant firm or group of firms and a fringe of followers.

11. Other researchers have obtained a negative coefficient for the concentration ratio. Waterson (1988, p.4) noted that the negative effects of concentration, found by Kwoka and Ravenscroft and others, was due to 'rather complex forms of intra-industry rivalry between firms'. Schmalensee (1987, p.420) interpreted the many negative coefficients he obtained as being consistent with the null hypothesis that none of his models was able to explain differences in rates of return across industries.

12. The interested reader should consult Waterson (1984, pp.202–9) who reviews cross-sectional studies of simultaneous systems involving intangible assets.

7. Industry Structure, Conduct and a Keynesian Theory of Distribution

Here the neo-Pasinetti macroeconomic theory of profits is linked with a theory of non-competitive firm behaviour. The resulting model may be used to study the effects of changes in macroeconomic aggregates, industry structure and collusive agreements on income distribution and other macro-indicators. In this chapter the effect of a change in the variable modelling industry structure is simulated. The beginning point for this work is the extension of the neo-Pasinetti macro-model proposed in Section 5.3. There two additions were made to Kaldor's original equilibrium conditions for the commodity and securities markets. One was a mark-up theory of commodity pricing. The other allowed for the endogenous determination of a component of investment as a function of Tobin's q, the securities market valuation of capital relative to its replacement cost.

Two further theoretical additions are made in this chapter. A result on industry structure, conduct and performance due to Clarke and Davies (1982) is used to motivate an explanation of the industry-wide margin of price over marginal cost in terms of the elasticity of demand, the Herfindahl index of industry concentration and an index of the extent to which oligopolists collude to preserve market shares. The theory of Clarke and Davies is in the tradition of models tracing their lineage back to Cowling and Waterson (1976) and, as noted by Cowling (1982, p.6), from that work to the earlier research of Kalecki. Section 7.1 contains a summary of the points of contact between the Clarke and Davies profit-maximizing approach to firm behaviour (see Sub-section 6.2.3) and Kaldor's view (outlined in Section 3.5) of the representative firm.

The second linkage from the behaviour of microeconomic agents to the macro-aggregates is adapted from the work of Lindenberg and Ross (1981). In Section 5.1 it was noted that they interpreted firm-level qs as indicators of the extent to which individual enterprises were able to capture non-competitive rents. A simplified version of the theoretical result of Lindenberg and Ross for firms is proposed in Section 7.2. The resulting firm-level qs are aggregated in a straightforward manner to produce an equation for the economy-wide average q. The various elements of the model are brought together in Section 7.3, where a closure is described. In Section 7.4 the solution of the model is analysed. It is shown that an increase in industry concentration raises price and redistributes income to profits while wages and national income contract. These results are evocative of the insights of Weitzman (1982) and Solow (1986) that 'the unassisted price mechanism may find it hard to extract an imperfectly increasing returns-to-scale economy from an unemployment trap. Small-scale myopic adjustments could be self-frustrating' (Solow, 1986, p.313). The insulation of profits from the effects of such a slump stimulates the securities market in the model of Section 7.4. If the securities market is initially bullish (with q greater than one) the price of a security rises and a capital gain can be realized. This will occur despite the projection of a decline in q.

7.1 Determination of the mark-up

In his macroeconomic modelling, Kaldor (1961, p.197) fixed his gaze upon 'a "developed" economy [operating] under conditions of imperfect competition'. He represented producers with a firm whose output reflected variations in total production, and which accounted for a constant fraction of aggregate employment. A central feature of this theory (*ibid.*, p.198) was that the representative firm 'would not be forced to reduce prices to the bare level of prime costs'. For Kaldor, labour was the bottleneck to production, and over the range of output levels up to a value near full employment, average and marginal direct (or prime costs) were constant. This led Kaldor to posit a reverse L-shaped supply schedule of the type made familiar by Kalecki.

Cowling and Waterson (1976) and a number of other authors have pursued another line of research which also contains elements of Kaleckian thinking. This research presented theories of the formation of industry price–cost margins where profit-maximizing firms expect rivals to react to output changes. Here the approach of Clarke and Davies (1982) is adopted. The profit-maximizing condition for oligopolist i is given by

$$p\left[1 - \frac{1}{\eta}\{s_i(1 - \lambda) + \lambda\}\right] = a_i, \qquad (7.1)$$

where p denotes the price, a_i denotes i's marginal cost, s_i is i's output share, $-\eta$ is the industry-wide elasticity of demand, and λ represents 'the degree of implicit collusion inherent in the market' (*ibid.*, p.279). The parameter λ measures the extent to which firms have scope to improve their market shares, in that each firm j is expected to respond to i's expansion by undertaking the proportional output growth,

$$\frac{\Delta Q_j}{Q_j} = \lambda \frac{\Delta Q_i}{Q_i} \qquad j \neq i.$$

If $\lambda = 1$, then firms collude to preserve their market shares. The case $\lambda = 0$ corresponds to the Cournot model, in which each member of the oligopoly takes the output of rivals to be independent of their own decisions. Clarke and Davies allowed firms some scope to improve their market shares cooperatively by allowing collusive responses for which $0 < \lambda < 1$. Cowling (1982, pp.33–4) used (7.1) to derive the equation

$$\frac{p - a}{p} = \frac{\lambda}{\eta} + \frac{(1 - \lambda)}{\eta} H, \qquad (7.2)$$

for the industry price–cost margin $(p - a)/p$, where H is the Herfindahl index of industry concentration, and where a is the sum of each firm's marginal cost weighted by its output share, Q_i/Q, that is,

$$a = \sum_{i=1}^{n} a_i \frac{Q_i}{Q}.$$

It is possible that λ might be negative or greater than unity. Fine and Murfin (1984, p.87) interpreted the former possibility as corresponding to situations where rivals are prepared to cut output in an attempt to maintain price, while in the latter rivals retaliate very aggressively to variations in output agreements. These possibilities are ignored here. When only one good is produced and one price applies throughout the market, the Herfindahl index is given by

$$H = \sum_{i=1}^{n} \left(\frac{Q_i}{Q}\right)^2.$$

The index has minimum value $1/n$ when the industry consists of n equal-sized firms, and maximum value 1 when the industry is monopolized. The Clarke and Davies theory applies at the industry level, while the mark-up pricing equation of the short-run neo-Pasinetti model developed in Section 5.3 applies to the entire macroeconomy. Here the industry-wide result is extended to the whole economy by making the obvious assumption that the industry described by Clarke and Davies is responsible for the production of all units of the single good 'national income'. Incorporation of this microeconomic structure into the neo-Pasinetti model produces an economy operating under conditions of imperfect competition and, rather like Kaldor's representative firm, having a fixed market share (at least when conditions of demand, concentration and collusion are stable).

Kaldor saw the minimum margin as that portion of the mark-up which is not eliminated by competition. In the Clarke and Davies framework, competitiveness is unconstrained when $\lambda = 0$, and the price–cost margin is given by

$$\frac{p - a}{p} = \frac{H}{\eta}. \tag{7.3}$$

When λ is constrained to lie between 0 and 1, this represents the minimum value of the margin. The minimum value is determinate provided that demand is not perfectly inelastic, and it is not zero when there are not infinitely many atomistic suppliers. There is a correspondence between Kaldor's 1961 notion of a minimum margin and the fraction of the general level of the price–cost margin given by (7.2). But the correspondence is not exact. First, Kaldor divided costs into direct (or prime) and indirect components, while the Clarke and Davies theory used variable and fixed costs. For a closed economy with a vertically integrated industry structure, average and marginal costs are entirely attributable to labour. Further, when no distinction is drawn between the types of labour (say, between supervisory and shop floor) the differences between methods of aggregating costs may be ignored. Second, Clarke and Davies arrived at measures of the margin involving the difference between price and *marginal* cost. This difference is avoided by assuming that firms are operating on the horizontal regions of their short-period supply curves. With these simplifying assumptions, what is the relationship between Kaldor's minimum margin, denoted by m_m, and the minimum value given by the Clarke and Davies theorem? The price p applying across the entire economy is assumed to be formed according to the mark-up rule,

$$p = (1 + m)a.$$

This implies that

$$\frac{p - a}{p} = \frac{m}{1 + m}$$

and so the mark-up over average direct cost, m, may be written as

$$m = \frac{\Omega}{\eta - \Omega}, \qquad (7.4)$$

where $\Omega = H + \lambda(1 - H)$. It follows that m is a monotonic increasing function of λ, and so when the index of collusion is constrained to be between 0 and 1, the margin is minimized when $\lambda = 0$. Therefore, when H and η are given,

$$m_m = \frac{H}{\eta - H},$$

and the mark-up m may be written as

$$m = \frac{\eta - H}{\eta - \Omega} m_m + \frac{\Omega - H}{\eta - \Omega}.$$

In Section 5.2 it was suggested that the mark-up should be written as

$$m = m_m + \beta\frac{I}{K}. \qquad (7.5)$$

That is, the mark-up was thought to respond flexibly to changes in investment plans once its minimum level was established. Both Kaldor (1961, p.200) and Eichner (1973, pp.1184 and 1193) saw the mark-up as being upwardly flexible, but not downwardly so. To the extent that the industry elasticity of demand does not increase, and provided industry structure and conduct evolve towards a more imperfectly competitive environment, the mark-up of (7.4) satisfies the flexibility criteria. By preferring (7.4) to (7.5) prominence is given to the linkages between industry structure and conduct and the mark-up. However, a role for planned investment in the determination of the mark-up is not ruled out entirely. For example, one benefit firms may see in adhering to collusive agreements is that they may have more predictable average profits, which in turn makes more certain the realization of investment plans. Essentially, this is an argument for writing collusion, or the fear of retaliation index, λ, as a function of investment, $\lambda(I)$. In Section 7.3, the choice is made to regard λ and η as being exogenously determined, and implicitly to separate their influences on mark-ups from any effects which investment may have on them.

Another feature of profit-maximizing theories of the mark-up must be considered in the construction of the model in Section 7.3. Recall that the Herfindahl index of concentration is defined in terms of output shares (which equal revenue shares in this one-good model) as

$$H = \sum_{i=1}^{n} s_i^2 = \sum_{i=1}^{n} \left(\frac{Q_i}{Q}\right)^2. \tag{7.6}$$

The necessary condition for profit maximization may be manipulated to derive an expression for H in terms of n, the number of firms, the coefficient of variation in firms' marginal costs, v_a^2 (the ratio of the variance to the mean squared), the elasticity of demand η, and λ, the collusion parameter.[1] The equation

$$H = \frac{1}{n} + \left\{1 - n\frac{\eta - \lambda}{1 - \lambda}\right\}^2 \frac{v_a^2}{n} \tag{7.7}$$

may be substituted into (7.2) for the price–cost margin to eliminate H, but to introduce n and v_a^2 into the determination of the mark-up,

$$\frac{p - a}{p} = \frac{\lambda}{\eta} + \frac{(1 - \lambda)}{n\eta} + \left\{1 - n\frac{\eta - \lambda}{1 - \lambda}\right\}^2 \frac{v_a^2(1 - \lambda)}{n\eta}.$$

In (7.7) the effect of a change in the number of firms depends on the magnitude of the variation in firms' costs. To see this, suppose that the elasticity of demand is unity. Then

$$H = \frac{1}{n} + \frac{(1 - n)^2}{n} v_a^2. \tag{7.8}$$

Suppose that the coefficient of variation v_a^2 is unaffected by a marginal change in the number of firms. If the number of firms increases or decreases by one, then H changes by

$$\Delta H = \left\{ -\frac{1}{n(n + \delta)} + \left(1 - \frac{1}{n(n + \delta)}\right) v_a^2 \right\} \delta,$$

where $\delta = \pm 1$, depending on whether a firm enters or leaves the industry. Thus reduction in the number of firms will increase concentration in the industry only if the coefficient of variation is sufficiently small to ensure that the term in curly brackets is negative. Even if the variation in firms' marginal costs is affected by the change, whether H increases depends on the coefficient of this variation being small.

It might be the case that (7.7) or (7.8) constrain the concentration index to fall when equilibrium is re-established after the sudden exit of a firm. The adjustment process leading to this outcome is not instantaneous. In the situations analysed in Section 7.3, H initially increases. For example, suppose a single firm leaves the industry. At that time, and for as long as the remaining firms do not adjust their price or output decisions, total output is unchanged and each firm's share of output increases. According to definition (7.6), there is an increase in the Herfindahl measure of concentration. Firms might strive to produce a fraction of the forgone quota within the restrictions of the industry's collusive practice, so maintaining output at the level prior to the exit of one firm, increasing at least some shares, and again raising the Herfindahl. For simplicity we ignore this possibility.

In a slump it is possible that the instantaneous increase in H described above will persist. One reason might be that the managers of firms remaining in operation may perceive little likelihood of disposing of additional output, and so each firm's production and total output remain unchanged. Alternatively, each firm may be anxious during a slump to appear to rivals to be observing collusive agreements. The risk to each firm is that an increase in output, consistent with existing collusive practices, may be misunderstood by other oligopolists. They may retaliate with increases in output which result in over-supply. It may be surmised that each firm prefers the maintenance of existing output levels compared with the difficulties of coping with excess supply in depressed markets. Thus heightened uncertainty concerning rivals' reactions may prevent the operation of the mechanisms which induce a reduction in concentration according to (7.7) or (7.8).

Another reason for rejecting the endogenous determination of H via (7.7) in the macroeconomic context also concerns uncertainty. Recall from (7.1) that the profit-maximizing condition for a Clarke–Davies oligopolist i is

$$a_i = p\left\{1 - \frac{1}{\eta}[\lambda + (1 - \lambda)s_i]\right\}.$$

Average cost for enterprise i is known once price, the elasticity of demand, expectations of retaliation and the oligopolist's share s_i are known. All of this information is known to i's competitors in the profit-maximizing model, so they too can determine i's cost structure. Full knowledge of i's marginal or average costs being available to competitors is unlikely across the whole economy. In place of (7.7) in the model of Section 7.3, H will be determined from the definition (7.6). This does not explicitly introduce a role for uncertainty; rather, the certainty of the microeconomic optimization is curtailed.[2]

The model proposed in Section 7.3 relates the mark-up via a macroeconomic equation to H, λ and η, the determinants which emerge from the Clarke–Davies industry-level theory of profit maximization. In the short run this implies that firms respond quickly to changes in concentration and in collusive arrangements. But the profit-maximizing determination of H does not have a role, for the reasons already mentioned. A feature of the endogenous determination of H widely accepted in the structure, conduct and performance literature (see, for example, Geroski, 1991, p.177 and Davies, 1991, p.96) is the influence of collusion on H as the industry evolves. This may be seen in equation (7.7) when it is assumed that the industry demand schedule is not unit-elastic. In this case, H is positively related to λ, so that the greater the retaliation expected by an oligopolist, the greater will be the index of concentration. The explanation is that collusive restriction of output affects firms unequally. Large firms are able to obtain greater output expansions than smaller competitors. That is, collusive practices of the Clarke–Davies type produce greater differences in size between firms. Rejection of the profit-maximizing equation for *H* in the next section means that the model constructed there does not include such a direct relationship between structure and conduct. Collusion acts via changes in the price–cost margin to influence aggregate output in the model. This linkage is also apparent in the profit-maximizing theories at the industry level. Omission of the direct link may mean that the influence of collusion is under-valued. However, for the scenarios discussed in Section 7.3, inclusion of such a link would not nullify the conclusions reached. On the other hand, contributions by Hubbard suggest that the price–cost margins of US manufacturing are in fact closer to the value predicted by (7.2) when the collusion index is zero,

$$\frac{p-a}{p} = \frac{H}{\eta},$$

than when collusion is rigidly enforced to preserve output shares, that is, when λ = 1 and

$$\frac{p-a}{p} = \frac{1}{\eta}.$$

'Price–cost margins never approximate those predicted by collusion even in very highly concentrated industries' (Hubbard, in a comment on Hall, 1986, p.331).

Some of the empirical evidence on concentration and profitability was reviewed in Sections 6.2.2 and 6.2.3. Support for the Herfindahl index as a determinant of industry profitability emerged from some research. However, other measures of firm or industry concentration, such as the market shares of individual firms or *m*-firm concentration ratios, were found to be positively correlated with profitability. One explanation put forward in the earlier sub-sections for the lack of consistent evidence in favour of the Herfindahl index was that it may be closely correlated with other indicators for industries in which concentration is not high. Where a sector is highly concentrated the Herfindahl cannot be proxied satisfactorily by other indicators. A recent longitudinal study by Conyon and Machin (1991) for Britain measured concentration using the proportion of sales accounted for by the five largest firms in manufacturing industries. This was a proxy for the Herfindahl index which emerged from their profit-maximizing theory. In each year between 1983 and 1986 the average industry concentration was less than 45 per cent, suggesting that they had a valid proxy for the Herfindahl. The five-firm concentration ratio was shown in a series of instrumental variables regressions to be positively linked to profit margins. This does not necessarily mean that the relationship observed is based on the Herfindahl, rather than some other indicator. Other theories contain positive functional relationships between the margin and different indicators of concentration. One such theory has been proposed by Saving (1970), in which a group of large firms collude to maximize profits, while smaller firms behave as price takers. The results of Conyon and Machin might be interpreted as support for this approach.[3] A possible modification of the theory proposed in Section 7.3 would be to replace the Clarke–Davies industry sector with the approach proposed by Saving.

From their regressions, Conyon and Machin (1991, p.378) demonstrated that treating concentration as an endogenous variable may have a small but tangible effect in studies of the structure, conduct and performance of industry. The emphasis of the next section is rather to investigate the links between financial and imperfectly competitive commodity markets. Studies by Prais (1976) and Kay and King (1978) have stressed the importance of easier access to financial markets and the tax advantages available to large firms as causes of the growth in concentration at the level of the entire British macroeconomy. In the next section a simple relationship between activity in financial markets and the economy-wide price–cost margin is proposed.

7.2 The monopoly rents of firms and Tobin's q

A way in which the influence of industry organization on the macroeconomy operates through securities markets has been suggested by Lindenberg and Ross (1981). They viewed Tobin's q for a single enterprise as an indicator of the extent of monopoly rents accruing to the firm. For a competitive firm they concluded that the long-run value of q is unity, whereas:

> A monopolist ... who can successfully bar entry and is not adequately regulated will earn monopoly rents in excess of the ordinary returns on the employed capital. The market will capitalise these rents and the value of the firm will exceed the replacement cost of its capital stock, that is, q will persist above 1. (*Ibid.*, 1981, p.2)

The market value, MV, of the firm was perceived as having three components,

$$MV = RC + MV_A + MV_N,$$

where

RC = the value of the firm attributable to the capital stock,
MV_A = firm-specific factors which serve to reduce its costs relative to its competitors, and
MV_N = monopoly profits.

The difference between MV and RC is the capitalized value of the firm's monopoly profits plus its operating rent. Lindenberg and Ross calculated this as the present value of the difference between the streams of revenues and long-run costs. In period t they wrote

$$MV_t - RC_t = \int_t (p_\tau - AC_\tau)\, Q_\tau\, e^{-r(\tau - t)}\, d\tau,$$

where p_τ, Q_τ and AC_τ denote the price, output and average total cost confronting the firm in period $\tau > t$, and r denotes the discount rate applied in period t to all future earnings.

To use this idea in a simple way, it is assumed here that shareholders are myopic. Indeed, their vision is assumed to range over only the current short-run period. Each agent uses only the historical information embodied in the current replacement cost of the capital stock, and current information conveyed by the firm's profitability and securities price. This ignorance of the future might also apply when the information available to equities markets is generally regarded as unreliable or worthless. Here the market value of firm i, MV_i, is written as

$$MV_i = RC_i + (p - a_i)Q_i, \qquad (7.9)$$

where RC_i denotes the replacement cost of the capital stock in firm i, and a_i is the firm's short-run average cost.[4]

Householders who own firm i's equities incorporate into their estimate of MV_i the dividends they are to be paid. Further, following an idea of Samuelson and Modigliani (1966, p.274, n1), households are thought to regard retained profits as belonging ultimately to them. This deferred payment is also imputed into the valuation of firm i's shares by householders when deciding at which price to sell, or when deciding whether to purchase from new issues, or even when deciding to do nothing in the current period. Thus myopic households take into account current profitability $(p - a_i)Q_i$ when estimating MV_i. Presumably, equity owners view the current capital stock as the result of past investment programmes. Further, they may be assumed to be aware that these programmes were funded largely from retained profits. Also the level of profits was presumably great enough to induce households to contribute to past expansions.

Another explanation for households using (7.9) to value firms is that they apply very high discount rates to future earnings. This would be the case if all households indulged in pure speculation. Speculators are interested in quickly disposing of shares at a price higher than they paid. If over the period following their purchases a firm's q is higher, then speculators are able to realize gains. Should the q fall following a bad profit result, speculators are likely to cut their losses and sell. In summary, speculators are only interested in the short-run performances of firms.

Now consider management. Managers propose investment strategies and other decisions affecting corporate performance. Households respond by raising or lowering the price of securities. This does not mean that managers and shareholders are united in maximizing net worth. For example, corporations might seek funds from sources other than new issues. If this is retention of profits, it is not in the interests of management to set dividends too low as this might induce households to sell securities, so reducing net worth. Rather, it is supposed that management must monitor carefully the market for its securities before making decisions. (See also Section 5.1.) A new investment project will be undertaken when the firm's marginal q is at least one. Marginal qs cannot be observed, so the manager's decision rule is formulated in terms of the average q. Tobin and

Brainard (1977, p.243) took the view that, in the short run, average q and marginal q move together, except for temporary periods which may be ignored. The firm's average q will be at least one when, according to (7.9), the firm's current activities make a positive contribution to its market valuation. In these circumstances, the new equities issued by the firm will be taken up by the equities market. Why do managers include all of profits in their estimation of market value? After all, they only distribute a portion of it to shareholders, which on its own may be enough to raise the firm's q_i above unity. There are two reasons.

First, in the short-run neo-Pasinetti model proposed here, all retained profits are turned into additions to the capital stock. Second, by paying whatever level of dividends they settle on, a reliable indication of profitability is sent to equity markets. Here a constant fraction, s_c, of profits is retained. Once the proportion $(1 - s_c)$ has been distributed to households, the market is able to calculate the firm's total profits and, as was seen above, use this information in its estimations of the values of portfolios. Management would not place a value on the existing capital stock which was less than that settled on by the securities market. If they consistently did so, rivals would possibly attempt a takeover of the firm's assets and dismiss the incumbent management. Also, relative to the market, the firm would not over-value existing assets. When this happens the firm may incorrectly anticipate the mood of the equity market. For example, a firm might erroneously decide that its q was just less than one. This firm would not undertake investment, as the management would feel that funds would not be forthcoming from the market for an investment programme. Hence the firm would needlessly forgo investment opportunities and might begin to stagnate. The firm might also become the target of a takeover if its q was actually greater than one. Shareholders disgruntled by the lack of management activity might easily be induced either to sell their shares or to turn out the incumbent board of management at an annual meeting.

In (7.9) the price p of a unit of national income is also the replacement cost of a unit of the physical capital stock, M_i. Thus, for firm i, Tobin's q is given by

$$q_i = \frac{MV_i}{RC_i},$$

$$= 1 + \frac{(p-a_i)}{p}\frac{Q_i}{M_i}. \qquad (7.10)$$

These firm-level qs may be aggregated to obtain an expression for the economy-wide q as follows. At the aggregate level

$$q = \frac{MV}{RC},$$

$$= (\sum_{i=1}^{n} MV_i)/K,$$

$$= \sum_{i=1}^{n} q_i K_i / K.$$

Now, from (7.10)

$$\left| q = \sum_{i=1}^{n}(1 + \frac{p-a_i}{p}\frac{Q_i}{M_i})\frac{K_i}{K}, \right.$$

$$= \sum_{i=1}^{n} K_i/K + \sum_{i=1}^{n}(1 - a_i/p)(pQ_i/K),$$

$$= 1 + p(\sum_{i=1}^{n} Q_i)/K - \sum_{i=1}^{n}(a_i Q_i/Q)(Q/K),$$

$$= 1 + (p-a)\frac{Q}{K},$$

$$= 1 + \frac{(p-a)}{p}\frac{Q}{M}, \qquad (7.11)$$

where

$$a = \sum_{i=1}^{n} a_i Q_i / Q$$

is the output-weighted average of firm i's costs. This equation for q has the advantage that it is directly comparable with the formulation (7.10) for individual firms. From (7.11) it may be seen that the aggregate q varies around the value one with changes in the economy-wide price–cost margin, $(p-a)/p$, and with the aggregate output to capital ratio, $Q/M = pQ/pM = Y/K$. Only when average direct cost exceeds price can q be less than unity. Obviously (7.11) may be simplified to respecify q in terms of the profit rate P/K. By retaining (7.11) we are able to concentrate attention on the profit share, P/Y, given by

$$\frac{P}{Y} = \frac{(p-a)}{p}.$$

For a given output–capital ratio the greater the profit share the greater will be q. Further, as the share of profits is bounded above by unity, an upper bound on the value of q is given by

$$q = 1 + \frac{Q}{M}.$$

Thus the more unproductive is the capital stock, then the lower is the maximum value that q may attain. Suppose now that p is determined according to the mark-up strategy

$$p = (1+m)a.$$

In this case,

$$\frac{p-a}{p} = \frac{m}{1+m}$$

and when the mark-up is positive q cannot be less than one.[5]

Lindenberg and Ross (1981, p.23) observed that over the period 1960–73, US firms having some monopoly power often had qs of around 1.5. The aggregation procedure applied to a collection of firms' qs of this magnitude would clearly produce an aggregate q greater than unity. The empirical literature on Tobin's q has been reported in Section 5.1 and Sub-section 6.2.4. In the next section, equations (7.2) for the mark-up m and (7.11) for Tobin's q are incorporated into a short-run version of Kaldor's neo-Pasinetti system. The resulting version of the model will be used to study the impact of an increase in concentration on the distribution of income.

7.3   A short-run model of financial markets, industry structure and corporate behaviour

In Section 5.3 an extension of the neo-Pasinetti model was proposed in which investment was responsive to activities in financial markets and Tobin's q was set exogenously. There too the mark-up of price over marginal cost was related to a minimum value which would never be eroded by competition among corporations, and a component which ensured finance for planned investment. Here the mark-up equation is replaced with the oligopolistic approach discussed in Section 7.1, and the equation derived in Section 7.2 is used to endogenize q. These modifications to the earlier model provide a link between the securities market valuation of firms and corporate size and conduct. In this section the equations of the model are assembled and a short-run closure discussed. A study of the impact of increased concentration is presented in the next section.

The equations of the model to be analysed are:

$$s_h\{W + (1 - s_c)P\} = (1 - s_h)\,G + iI \qquad (7.12)$$

$$s_cP + s_h\{W + (1 - s_c)P\} = (1 - s_h)\,G + I \qquad (7.13)$$

$$q = p_sN/K \qquad (7.14)$$

$$p = \bar{p}(1 + p') \quad p_s = \bar{p}_s(1 + p'_s)$$

$$M = \bar{M}(1 + M') \quad N = \bar{N}(1 + N') \qquad (7.15)$$

$$q = \bar{q}(1 + q').$$

$$G = \bar{N}\Delta p_s = \bar{N}\bar{p}_sp'_s \qquad (7.16)$$

$$K = pM \qquad (7.17)$$

$$iI = p_s\Delta N = p_s\bar{N}N' = \bar{p}_s\bar{N}(1 + p'_s)N' \qquad (7.18)$$

$$p = (1 + m)a \qquad (7.19)$$

$$\frac{p-a}{p} = \frac{\lambda}{\eta} + \frac{(1-\lambda)}{\eta} H \qquad (7.20)$$

$$\frac{I}{K} = \frac{I_0}{K} + a(q-1) \qquad (7.21)$$

$$q = 1 + \frac{p-a}{p}\frac{Q}{M} \qquad (7.22)$$

$$Y = P + W \qquad (7.23)$$

$$W = wL = aQ \qquad (7.24)$$

$$Y = pQ \qquad (7.25)$$

$$H = \sum_{i=1}^{n}\left(\frac{Q_i}{Q}\right)^2 = \sum_{i=1}^{n} s_i^2. \qquad (7.26)$$

Compared with the system of Section 5.3, equation (5.19) for the mark-up has been replaced by (7.20) for the price–cost margin, equation (7.10) for q inserted as (7.22) and the definition of the Herfindahl index added as (7.26).

The elements of Kaldor's original specification of the neo-Pasinetti model are contained in equations (7.12) to (7.16). Equation (7.14) represents a departure from Kaldor's theory in line with the analysis of Section 3.3. Rather than use the valuation ratio which depends on an historical cost estimation of the value of the capital stock, an average measure of Tobin's q is employed here. This means that the occurrence of K in the denominator of (7.14) is a reference to the replacement cost of capital. In this one-good model, the replacement cost of a unit of capital is just the price, p, of a unit of current output and $K = pM$, where M denotes the stock of real capital. The numerator in the equation for q is the value of all N securities when the unit price is p_s, and q measures the market valuation of securities relative to the replacement cost of the physical assets they represent. With G defined as the change in the value of securities, $N\Delta p_s$, the other equalities in (7.16) may be deduced from (7.14). The handling of G differs from Kaldor's specification in three ways. First, the valuation ratio v, preferred by Kaldor, has been replaced by Tobin's q (see Section 3.3). Second, Kaldor (1966, p.318) set v to be constant in the golden age equilibria he studied. The emphasis in this section is again on the short run, and the equations of this version of the model attempt to capture the impact of variations in the preferred measure q abouts its long-run value of unity. Finally, because K denotes replacement cost, K now changes when the price p of a unit of capital changes, as well as when there is a variation in the stock of real capital, ΔM. From equation (7.17) for K, the change ΔK in total replacement cost is given by

$$\Delta K = K - \bar{K} = (\bar{p} + \Delta p)(\bar{M} + \Delta M) - \bar{p}\bar{M}$$

$$= (\bar{p} + \Delta p)\Delta M + \bar{M}\Delta p = I + \bar{M}\Delta p,$$

where a bar over a variable denotes its value immediately before the short-run period commences. In terms of growth rates,

$$K' = (1 + p')M' + p', \tag{7.27}$$

where p' is defined in (7.15), and similarly

$$K = \bar{K}(1 + K')$$

In his determination of the capital gain G, Kaldor assumed that the historical cost measure of capital grew at the constant rate g.

Equation (7.18) is copied directly from Kaldor. It formalizes his assumption that a given proportion, i, of total investment is financed by the issue of ΔN new shares. If investment were exogenously determined, then (7.18) would determine the value of newly-issued shares. But, as may be seen from (7.21), there is a component of investment which is responsive to variations in Tobin's q, so that the size and value of a new issue depends on conditions in financial markets as well as the plans of producers. The investment equation (7.21) models the notion put forward by Brainard and Tobin (1968, p.357) that 'the market value of equities, relative to the replacement cost of the physical assets they represent, is the major determinant of new investment'. This is the approach adopted in Sections 5.1 and 5.3.

It was shown in Section 7.2 that Tobin's q may be explained as the function of the economy-wide price–cost margin, $(p-a)/p$, and the output–capital ratio, Q/M, given by (7.22). The extension to the whole economy of the analysis by Clarke and Davies of the price–cost margin for an oligopoly, discussed in Sections 7.1 and 6.2, is given in (7.20). Following the discussion of Section 7.1, a denotes economy-wide average direct cost. Taken together (7.22) and (7.20) imply that Tobin's q is a function of the Herfindahl index of concentration, H, the measure of collusion between firms, λ, and the modulus of the economy-wide elasticity of demand, η, given by

$$q = 1 + \frac{Q}{M}\left\{\frac{\lambda}{\eta} + \frac{(1-\lambda)}{\eta}H\right\}. \tag{7.28}$$

The use of Clarke and Davies analysis of oligopoly led in Section 7.1 from (7.20) to equation (7.4) for the mark-up,

$$m = \frac{\Omega/\eta}{(1-\Omega/\eta)} = \frac{\Omega}{\eta-\Omega}, \tag{7.29}$$

where

$$\Omega = \lambda + (1-\lambda)H. \tag{7.30}$$

Aggregate wages, W, are defined by the first equality in (7.24), where w denotes the nominal wage rate, and L denotes employed labour. The second equality in (7.24) encapsulates the assumption that the model represents a closed, vertically integrated economy. As for the version of the model analysed in Section 5.3, it follows from Walras's law that the equation

$$W = aQ$$

may be derived from the other equations of the model.

To concentrate on the short run, the variables

$$M\ I_0\ a\ w\ \lambda\ \eta\ \bar{M}\ \bar{p}\ \bar{q}\ \bar{p}_s\ \bar{N}\ n \text{ and } s_i,\ i=1,\ldots,n$$

are taken to be exogenous. The assignment of M, I_0, a and w to this list is discussed in Section 5.3. Selection of λ as exogenous is reasonably straightforward. The thrust of the analysis is directed towards the determination of the profit share, which in the model is the relative price–cost margin. Thus the direction of linkages here should be from the structure and conduct variables to the performance indicator $(p - a)/p$. As there is no explanatory equation for λ, it is exogenous. For the structure index H there is equation (7.26) involving each oligopolist's share in output, s_i and the total number of firms, n. Specifying each share and the number of firms determines H. That η should be, or even can be, exogenous is not so clear. This is assumed here for simplicity. Variations in output and price as the model moves from one equilibrium state to another mean that the economy may operate at points on the aggregate demand schedule having different values for the elasticity of demand. The magnitude of the constant η has an effect on both the sign and magnitude of the mark-up. From (7.28)

$$m = \frac{\Omega}{\eta - \Omega}.$$

When η is greater than the structure–conduct composite,

$$\Omega = \lambda + (1 - \lambda)H,$$

the mark-up is positive. When the index λ takes values between zero and one, the minimum value of Ω is H (occurring when λ is 0) and its maximum is one (occurring when λ is 1). As the Herfindahl index can assume values between zero and unity, it follows that Ω lies in the range, $0 < H < \Omega < 1$ when $0 < \lambda < 1$ and H is less than 1. Hence $(\eta - \Omega)$ and the mark-up will be greater than zero for $\eta \geq 1$. Also $(\eta - \Omega)$, and therefore the mark-up, will be negative when $\eta < \Omega < 1$. When λ is less than 0 or λ is greater than 1, the composite variable Ω may lie outside the range $0 < \Omega < 1$. Clearly, in these cases there again arise the prospects of either positive or negative mark-ups, depending on the size of η relative to Ω. For example, with $\lambda = -1$ and $H = 1/4$, $\Omega = -1/2$ and m is negative for all values of η. With the same value of λ and $H = 3/4$, $\Omega = 1/2$ and the mark-up is positive for $\eta > 1/2$ and negative when $\eta < 1/2$. It should also be noted that the mark-up is indeterminate when $\eta = \Omega$. In the previous example this happens when $\eta = 1/2$. In the simulation described in the next section λ is confined to lie between zero and one, so that for values of η greater than or equal to one the mark up m is positive.

7.4 Increased industrial concentration and distribution

While the model described in the previous section might be used to study the impact of a change in any of the exogenous variables, here attention is confined to an increase in the composite Ω, which varies with the structure and collusion variables H and λ. One way in which

$$H = \sum_{i=1}^{n} s_i^2$$

will increase is when there is a reduction in the number of firms responsible for the production of the national product. This might happen as a consequence of successful cartel action to eliminate either a new entrant or a firm not observing its production quota. It might also happen in the period preceding the trough of a recession when some firms are forced out of production. This is the situation simulated here. When a firm ceases operation during a downturn, those oligopolists who continue to produce may be expected not to take decisions which would raise total output. They may fear reprisals from competitors so much, or believe they may be more easily detected in the process, that none try to increase output. In this case total output falls and the share of each oligopolist, and hence the concentration index, increases. Alternatively, managers may have sufficient confidence to try to acquire a small part of revenue lost when the number in the industry fell. If so, each firm may cautiously set about raising its output level a little, in line with prevailing agreements on production quotas. When all oligopolists understand why their competitors are raising output, and when each firm in turn does not raise its own output by too much, total output may be unchanged and then the share of each producer will increase. Again the Herfindahl index rises.

While firms may not want to raise total output in a slump, it can be argued that managers will not reduce output in a contraction when one firm ceases operation. It could be reasoned that managers may interpret the exit as evidence of a demand contraction and, as it were, with no other linkages operating, 'voluntarily' reduce output. However, protecting the firm from over-production by reducing output might allow a competitor to seize a larger share of the market. Reversing this may be very difficult during recovery within

the restrictions of collusive agreements. Further, a voluntary reduction of output at the time of an exit in this model is an admission by
management that investment plans will not be realized. Mismanage-
ment to the extent of losing market share and forgoing investment
will have an impact in the securities market. Thus the immediate
consequence of a firm retiring from production, it seems, is to raise
the index of concentration for the economy.

In this model an increase in the concentration index is predicted to
raise the mark-up. It is possible that other linkages operate to
override the impact on margins of an increase in H during a
recession. One possibility is that collusive agreements may be less
binding on those firms that continue to operate throughout the
trough, so ameliorating the effect on Ω of any increase in H. There is
evidence to suggest that the positive linkage between concentration
and price is stronger during periods of contraction, and when costs
are increasing rapidly, than during periods of prosperity (Dalton,
1973, p.519 and Sub-section 6.2.2 above). This suggests that the
influence of concentration dominates conjectures of attenuated retaliation, and the structure–conduct composite Ω grows during downturns. If it is anticipated that heightened fears of retaliation from
competitors induce an increase in λ, then changes in each of concentration and of competitors' anticipated responses act to increase the
composite Ω during a recession. Whatever the direction of change in
λ, it appears that the composite Ω increases with H. In the simulation reported here it is assumed that

$$\Omega = \lambda + (1-\lambda)H,$$

increases as a consequence of the change in H induced when a firm
ceases activity, while λ is fixed at its value prior to the downturn.
That is, oligopolists are assumed to observe rigidly the conventions
of expected output responses established in previous periods. The
effect of an increase in concentration on the margin in equation
(7.20) may be negated as firms move to operate on a high elasticity
portion of the aggregate demand curve. Like a reduction in collusive
agreements, this would act to reduce the mark-up. A downturn may
also be associated with a reduction in autonomous expenditure on
investment. Thus it is likely that a change in Ω is the result of shifts in
both H and λ, and is associated also with shifts in other variables
exogenous in this version of the model. Here we abstract from these

influences and consider only the effects of a change in H which results in an overall increase in the composite, Ω.

An increase ΔH in the Herfindahl index causes the composite Ω to grow by

$$\Delta\Omega = (1-\lambda)\Delta H, \qquad (7.31)$$

when $\lambda < 1$. In proportional change form this is

$$\Omega' = \frac{\Delta\Omega}{\Omega} = \frac{(1-\lambda)H}{\Omega} H', \qquad (7.32)$$

where $H' = \Delta H/H$. The proportional change in Ω is less than the growth in industry concentration. In (7.32) the weight on H' is the share prior to the exogenous shock of the term $(1-\lambda)H$ in Ω. Initially, the greater is H and the smaller is λ, the greater will be the proportional change in Ω induced by the increase in H. The occurrence of initial values for λ, H and Ω in the growth equation is a consequence of the way in which proportional changes have been defined. The appearances of λ, H and Ω in (7.32) are references to the values these entities had prior to the imposition of the exogenous change. To simplify the notation, starting values of variables are distinguished (using a bar) only when the possibility of confusion arises.

The solutions of the model for each endogenous variable are shown in Table 7.1. They are derived on the assumption that the closure of a firm does not alter nominal autonomous expenditure on investment. This would occur if the closing firm had planned not to invest, or if its competitors planned a greater expenditure (equal to that forgone by the closure) when they realized that a firm had closed its doors. In the event that autonomous investment is changed (perhaps departing from the long-run growth path planned by boards of managers) the solutions in Table 7.1 will require modification via a theory linking investment decisions and the structure–conduct composite. The assumption that managers plan autonomous investment in nominal terms matches the approaches taken in Sections 4.3 and 5.3. By making this assumption it is possible to investigate the effects which arise when investment managers first plan expenditure and this is built into corporate strategies on the values of new issues and dividend streams. After

Table 7.1 *Projections of an increase in industry concentration*

Variable	Solution	Growth rate
Ω	$\lambda + (1-\lambda)H$	$\{(1-\bar\lambda)\bar H/\bar\Omega\}H'$
$\dfrac{P}{Y} = \pi$	$\dfrac{\Omega}{\eta}$	Ω'
m	$\dfrac{\Omega}{\eta-\Omega}$	$(1+m)\Omega'$
p	$\dfrac{\eta}{\eta-\Omega}a$	$m\dfrac{\Omega'}{1+\Omega'}$
Q	$\dfrac{A}{a}I_0\dfrac{\eta-\Omega}{\Omega} = \dfrac{1}{a\,m}AI_0$	$-(1+\bar m)\dfrac{\Omega'}{1+\Omega'}$
Y	$AI_0\dfrac{\eta}{\Omega}$	$-\dfrac{\Omega'}{1+\Omega'}$
P	AI_0	0
W	$AI_0\dfrac{\eta-\Omega}{\Omega}$	$-(1+\bar m)\dfrac{\Omega'}{1+\Omega'}$
L	$\dfrac{A}{w}I_0\dfrac{\eta-\Omega}{\Omega}$	$-(1+\bar m)\dfrac{\Omega'}{1+\Omega'}$
I	BI_0	0
I_R	$\dfrac{B}{a}I_0\dfrac{\eta-\Omega}{\Omega}$	$-\bar m\Omega'$
M	$\bar M + I_R$	$-\{\dfrac{B}{a}\pi/M_0\}\Omega'$
K	$p\bar M + BI_0$	$\{m\,\bar M/M_0\}\dfrac{\Omega'}{1+\Omega'} = \bar M/M_0\,p'$
q	$A\dfrac{I_0}{K} + 1$	$-(1-1/\bar q)\dfrac{K'}{1+K'}$

Table 7.1 continued

G	$\bar{q}Kq' + \bar{q}\bar{K}K' - il$	
p'_s	$\bar{p}_s + G/\bar{N}$	$G/\bar{p}_s\bar{N}$
N'	$\bar{N} + il/p_s$	$il/p_s\bar{N}$

Notes

$A = \dfrac{(1-i)}{s_c - \alpha(1-i)}$ and $B = \dfrac{s_c}{s_c - \alpha(1-i)}$.

$\bar{M}_0$ = stock of real capital available for use in production.
M_0 = real capital stock available at the end of the period if all firms continued to operate.

this process is complete, it becomes clear to sales managers that price must rise as a consequence of the exit of a firm. The short run in this case is long enough for markets to adjust to the unanticipated price change and its impact on autonomous investment. Separation of management activities relating to sales from the other corporate functions is reminiscent of Hall's (1986, pp.301–2) distinction between marketing and production divisions. In the Clarke–Davies approach adopted here, marketing and production are more closely integrated, while a third division of management responsibility, investment, is distinguished.[6]

The model can be used to investigate the consequences of assuming that investment managers build into their plans the impact of price changes. When the closure of a firm precedes the formation of investment plans, managers may set a level of real investment which accounts for the expected effect of price. Underlying this scenario is the assumption that the investment division knows precisely by how much price will rise in the event of a firm leaving the industry. In the Clarke–Davies model of industrial organization, this means that sales managers know precisely how their market shares and their conjectural responses vary, and where on the aggregate demand curve they operate. Further, it must be assumed that this information is made available to their colleagues responsible for investment. In such a simulation, conjectural responses and the elasticity of the industry demand curve would be fixed, while the revenue shares of all producers would be decided immediately prior to the period under study, but before investment plans were finalized. Details of the solution of the system of equations for this scenario are similar to the steps involved in generating the solution of the model shown in Table 7.1.

The first row of the table shows the solution for Ω and, in the third column, is the corresponding growth rate. This is an expression for the growth in the structure–conduct composite when a firm ceases operation compared with the value Ω would have if all firms had continued to operate. When each firm expects that it has scope to raise its revenue share, λ is less than one, and the increase in the Herfindahl index H is translated into an increase in the composite. The constant $(1 - \bar{\lambda})\bar{H}/\bar{\Omega}$ is positive and less than one, indicating that the structure–conduct composite does not grow as much as H. The solutions for the other endogenous variables were obtained on the assumptions that:

1. the choice of exogenous variables is given in the list in Section 7.3;
2. corporations plan autonomous investment in nominal terms;
3. autonomous investment is unaffected by the closure of a firm;
4. the industry elasticity of demand η is at least unity, the conjectural response index λ is less than one and greater than zero, and the Herfindahl index is not one;
5. oligopolists react to the closure of one firm in such a way that the index of concentration increases; and
6. households include additions to the capital stock in the valuation of firms' assets at the end of the period.

Except for the last assumption, each of these has been covered already. The last is discussed below.

Reactions in securities markets may be sensitive to the assumptions made about the information households take into account in forming the valuation of paper assets. With assumption (6) households include current expenditure on investment in their valuation of securities. In Table 7.1, the capital gain is determined relative to the amount iI of new investment which households finance. This is consistent with a conclusion reached in Section 3.3. Recall that there

$$G = K\Delta v + (v - i)I, \qquad (3.37)$$

where v is the valuation of paper assets relative to the book value of the stock of the capital. When $\Delta v = 0$ and $v = 1$, then the neo-Pasinetti theorem yields

$$G = (1 - i)I = s_c P.$$

That is, eventually owners of securities realize a capital gain equal to the value of the dividends they forgo when corporations retain a proportion s_c of profits. This does not account exactly for the situation modelled here, as financial markets are assumed to operate in terms of replacement cost and Tobin's q, instead of the valuation ratio and historical cost. In these terms

$$\Delta K = (\bar{p} + \Delta p)(\bar{M} + \Delta M) - \bar{p}\bar{M},$$
$$= p\Delta M + \bar{M}\Delta p,$$
$$= I + \bar{M}\Delta p. \qquad (7.33)$$

That is, replacement cost grows by the value of nominal investment plus an allowance for the increase in replacement cost. Hence from Table 7.1

$$G = \bar{q}Kq' + \bar{q}\bar{K}K' - iI,$$
$$= \Delta K - iI \qquad \text{(when } q' = 0 \text{ and } \bar{q} = 1\text{),}$$
$$= (1 - i)I + M\Delta p \qquad \text{(from 7.33),}$$
$$= s_c P + M\Delta p.$$

Thus here the capital gain also includes retained profits plus a component accounting for inflation. Retained profits are used by corporations to purchase new capital in this model, and so the inclusion of investment expenditure in the determination of q allows for the long-run outcome that capital gains eventually include that part of profits which is not turned over to households in the form of dividends. This outcome is also consistent with the assumption in Section 7.2 that households do not look past the immediate period. They consider only the history of firms and their current profitability when determining market valuations via (7.9). It would be a relatively simple matter to amend the solutions in Table 7.1 to allow for the assumption that agents in securities markets are so myopic that they do not foresee the benefits which flow from the investment activity which they in part underwrite.[7]

Look now at the other solutions to the model. From the third and fourth rows of Table 7.1 it may be seen that the mark-up m and price p are increased. The share of profits in national income π increases at the same rate as the structure–conduct composite. These results may be derived from the income identities and the imperfectly competitive theory of price. The profit share and the mark-up are determined by the structure–conduct composite Ω and the elasticity of demand. In addition, price depends on average direct cost, which here has been fixed exogenously.[8]

Now consider the equilibrium equations for the two markets. Subtraction of (7.12) from (7.13) yields the neo-Pasinetti theorem,

$$P = \frac{(1-i)}{s_c} I.$$

Profit is also given by maQ. Together they may be manipulated to obtain an equation for real income Q as,

$$Q = \frac{1}{a\,m} \frac{(1-i)}{s_c} I.$$

This equation describes a family of combinations of output Q and nominal investment I which solve the model. It may be expanded as follows:

$$Q = \frac{1}{a\,m} \frac{(1-i)}{s_c} \{I_0 + \alpha(q-1)K\} \qquad \text{(from (7.21)),}$$

$$= \frac{1}{a\,m} \frac{(1-i)}{s_c} \left\{ I_0 + \alpha \left[\frac{p-a}{p} \frac{Q}{M} \right] K \right\} \qquad \text{(from (7.22)),}$$

$$= \frac{1}{a\,m} \frac{(1-i)}{s_c} \{I_0 + \alpha maQ\} \qquad \text{(from (7.19) and (7.17)),}$$

$$= \frac{1}{a\,m} \frac{(1-i)}{s_c} I_0 + \frac{\alpha(1-i)}{s_c} Q.$$

Hence

$$Q = \frac{1}{a\,m\,s_c - \alpha(1-i)} (1-i) I_0 = \frac{1}{a\,m} A I_0$$

$$= \frac{A}{a} I_0 \frac{\eta - \Omega}{\Omega} \text{ (from row 3 of Table 7.1)}$$

Real income is therefore the outcome of interactions between agents in both markets, and the influences of the theories of investment, Tobin's q and price. The growth rate for real income is shown in the table to be negative. That is, the increase in concentration induces a contraction of total output. This fall and the rise in price noted earlier are consistent with the behaviour of oligopolists facing a downward-sloping marginal revenue curve, although the general equilibrium effects on quantity and price involve more than a simple movement along the demand schedule.

Now we digress briefly to consider some investment multipliers. By writing nominal autonomous investment as

$$I_0 = p_0 I_0^R = (1 + m) a I_0^R = \frac{\eta a I_0^R}{\eta - \Omega},$$

the solution for Q can be converted to

$$Q = A \frac{\eta}{\Omega} I_0^R,$$

and the real autonomous investment multiplier is

$$\frac{\partial Q}{\partial I_0^R} = A \frac{\eta}{\Omega},$$

which is positive when

$$A = \frac{(1 - i)}{s_c - \alpha(1 - i)}$$

is greater than zero. This occurs when i is small and $s_c > \alpha(1 - i)$. Recall from Section 4.3 that combining Harcourt's rule with the basic Kaldorian system raised the possibility that the multiplier might be negative. For the extension of the neo-Pasinetti model analysed in Section 5.3, the income-investment multiplier could not be negative, but the magnitude was less than one. Here, not only is the multiplier always positive for realistic values of the parameters s_c, i and α, the magnitude exceeds one. To see this, recall that the structure–conduct composite Ω is less than one and the elasticity of demand is assumed to be at least unity. Thus the quotient η/Ω is greater than unity. The remaining quotient in the expression for the multiplier will be positive when the corporate retention rate s_c is less than one, the propensity of corporations i to seek finance from new issues is small, and the extent α to which investment is responsive to Tobin's q is small relative to s_c. For example, when α and i are zero the multiplier is

$$\frac{\partial Q}{\partial I^R_0} = \frac{1}{s_c}\frac{\eta}{\Omega}.$$

When managers decide autonomous investment in nominal terms (as is assumed here) the relevant multiplier is

$$\frac{\partial Q}{\partial I} = \frac{A}{a}\frac{\eta - \Omega}{\Omega}$$

which is also positive, but may be less than one.

From the definition $Y = pQ$ and row five of Table 7.1 for Q, national income may be written as

$$Y = \frac{(1-i)I_0}{[s_c - \alpha(1-i)]}\frac{\eta}{\Omega}.$$

Therefore the nominal investment multiplier is positive and it is greater than one.

Now return to the simulation reported in Table 7.1, where the structure–conduct composite increases and there is no effect of a firm closure on nominal autonomous investment. Income is projected to decrease relative to the value it would have attained if all firms had continued to produce. Here the growth in price is outweighed by the contraction in real income. Profits are unaffected by the change. The adjustment to the contraction falls entirely on labour. Aggregate nominal investment is unchanged, although, because of the increase in price, real investment contracts. Note that B in Table 7.1 is greater than unity and so nominal investment is projected to be greater than its autonomous component.

After a firm closes its doors the real capital stock is projected to contract in line with the contraction of real investment. By comparison the replacement cost of capital is projected to grow.[9] Note from the solution for q that the extent to which q exceeds its long-run value depends on the autonomous investment rate, I_0/K. For reasonable values of i, s_c, and α the coefficient of this rate is greater than one. This suggests that the initially favourable influence of planned autonomous investment on Tobin's q operates through the determination of the induced component of investment via

$$\frac{I}{K} = \frac{I_0}{K} + \alpha(q-1),$$

in a multiplier process to generate further increases in q. In terms of its growth rate,

$$q' = -(1 - 1/\bar{q})\frac{K'}{1+K'},$$

where $\bar{q}$ denotes the value attained by q when all firms are producing, and K' is the rate of change in replacement cost when one firm closes its doors. The change in replacement cost is positive, and q' will be negative for $\bar{q}$ greater than one. However, Tobin's q does not fall below its long-run value. On the other hand, if $\bar{q}$ is less than unity, q increases as a result of the closure, and the securities market becomes bullish. From Table 7.1 the capital gain available to households when a firm closes its doors is given by

$$G = \bar{q}Kq' + \bar{q}\bar{K}K' - iI.$$

Knowing the growth rates q' and K', this may be simplified to

$$G = -\bar{q}\bar{K}(1 - 1/\bar{q})K' + \bar{q}\bar{K}K' - iI,$$

$$= \bar{K}K' - iI,$$

$$= \Delta K - iI,$$

which is the change in replacement cost less the value of nominal investment funded by households. Whether a gain or a loss occurs depends on the effect of the change in concentration on unit replacement cost. If there is a capital gain the price of a security is bid up, while the number of new securities is reduced. In summary, with q greater than one when all firms operate (that is, when $\bar{q}$ is greater than one) the market value of capital declines relative to replacement cost, but there is scope for the securities price to rise and capital gains to be made. Households inflate their estimations of the rents available to remaining oligopolists (in line with the theory of Section 7.2), while firms are able to exploit the rise in the securities price to issue fewer new securities. Households involved in saving have good reason to bid up the securities price, as profit is not affected by the reduction in the number of firms, but income from wages bears the entire burden of the contraction of national income.

In the introduction to this chapter it was noted that this theory, like the theories of Weitzman and Solow, does not predict that the price mechanism alone can rescue an economy from an under-employment equilibrium. There is a striking comparison of the projections for profits with the empirical findings of Hall (1986): 'Hall's calculations of the relatively small impact of sales reductions on profits are very interesting. With constant marginal cost and a constant price elasticity of demand, there seems to be little sensitivity of profit to output movements' (Hubbard, in a comment, *ibid.*, p.336).

Notes

1. For a derivation of the expression, see Clarke–Davies (1982, p. 280).
2. In fact a different relationship between H and cost variations emerges if firms maintain their production levels when a competitor closes its doors. From the profit-maximizing condition firms remaining in operation will want an increase in price because their output shares have risen. Rimmer (1992) shows that each firm will want the same growth in price provided that the variation in firms' costs are mirrored in output shares. This linkage between shares and marginal costs does not invalidate equation (7.2) for the price–cost margin.
3. Or, rather, for a version of Saving's approach in which economies of scale matter (see Conyon and Machin, 1991).
4. Equation (7.4) was derived on the assumption that there are no indirect costs. Inclusion of an indirect component does not alter appreciably the solutions set out in Section 7.4 (see Rimmer, 1992).
5. The inclusion of indirect costs changes this (see Rimmer, 1992), and q will exceed unity only when the mark-up exceeds average indirect cost.
6. The rejection in Section 7.1 of the link between average costs and concentration separates price and production decisions further than is the case in the work of Clarke and Davies.
7. If the securities market valuation ignores additions to the capital stock, then a problem of timing arises. For in this case there must be a notional sub-period between short-run segments of time when the goods market is notionally in

suspension while the securities market continues its activities, evaluating actual investment outcomes.

8. Recall that in the Clarke-Davies profit-maximizing theory

$$a = \sum_{i=1}^{n-1} a_i s_i,$$

(A7.1)

where a_i denotes the average direct cost of the ith oligopolist. The exit of one producer raises firms' revenue shares. If it is the nth firm which stops producing, then the weighted sum of costs is not as small as

$$\sum_{i=1}^{n} a_i s_i.$$

Nevertheless, for accuracy, each a_i should be added to the exogenous list in Section 7.3, (A7.1) added to the list of equations, and a removed from the exogenous list. This technicality has not been incorporated into the scenario. In general, the possibility of a change in a should be accounted for in the growth rates given in Table 7.1, so complicating the formulae in the third column. Provided it is assumed that the adjustments due to variation in a are assumed small or non-existent, the further complications may be avoided. It is possible that the weighted sum of costs rises when one firm closes its doors.

9. When all firms operate and households include current investment in their valuations, write

$$\bar{K} = \bar{p}(\bar{M} + \bar{I}^R) = \bar{p}\bar{M} + \bar{p}\bar{I}^R = \bar{p}\bar{M} + I.$$

When one firm ceases activity,

$$K = p(\bar{M} + I_R) = p\bar{M} + pI_R = p\bar{M} + I.$$

Therefore

$$\Delta K = K - \bar{K} = (p - \bar{p})\,\bar{M},$$

and

$$\Delta K / \bar{K} = \frac{(p - \bar{p})}{\bar{p}} \frac{\bar{M}}{\bar{M} + I_R}$$

which therefore grows with price.

8. Conclusion

The subject matter of this book is the investigation of theories of income distribution. In the early chapters, post-Keynesian and neo-classical theories are explored. Starting-points for post-Keynesian analyses have often been the contributions made in the mid- and late 1950s by Kaldor. Here the approach has been to build on Kaldor's less frequently cited neo-Pasinetti model of 1966. The focus of the theory is the short run, and the model is augmented by equations explaining investment and price. In the preceding chapters closed models without government were specified. For extensions of the neo-Pasinetti model to be of greatest value in policy analysis, traded and government sectors should be added to the model.

Following Tobin and Brainard, a component of investment has been modelled as being responsive to the securities market valuation of capital relative to replacement cost. To do this the indicator of share market valuation used by Kaldor was replaced by Tobin's q. It was shown that the real-income/Tobin's q multiplier was positive for solutions of the extended model presented in Section 5.3. It was also shown that increases in the mark-up restrain the growth of national income, even when these are associated with expanded investment programmes. The impact of the increase in the margin, had no effect on profits, but wages and national income were reduced. Existing shareholders were insulated from this contraction. For a different model, comprising markets for money and securities under a short-run closure, Tobin (1969, pp. 329–30), constructed a money-market equilibrium curve along which q is a decreasing function of income. Extensions of the neo-Pasinetti model to include the money market would make it possible to simulate the effects of firms accumulating liquidity cushions, rather than relying on debt-financing or new issues to provide funds for investment purposes. In such a model it would be possible to study the effects of variations in the corporate savings ratio, s_c, and the propensity to seek finance on share

228

markets, i, as corporate preferences shifted from one source of finance to another. Two other approaches which might be used to analyse the impact of the composition of investment financing are given in Skott (1989) and Wood (1975) (see also the Appendix to Chapter 3). Skott's neo-Pasinetti model may be particularly suitable for the analysis of the impact of debt-financing policies.

Evidence on the influence of union power on market valuations and q was also reviewed in Chapter 5. If, as the evidence suggests, industry rents accrue in part to unions, then the relationship between profits and concentration may be diminished. It also appears that unionization distorts corporate choices among financial instruments. Linkages like these could be incorporated into the neo-Pasinetti model to further amplify the distribution process.

Another line of development of the neo-Pasinetti model would be possible with the extensions proposed in Chapters 5 and 7. Wood (1975, p.47) made the point that both managers and shareholders prefer the dividend stream to be stable over time. In the notation used here, the level of dividends, D, is given by $D = (1 - s_c)P$, so that, when the stream of dividends is regarded as stable, the corporate retention rate, s_c, must adjust to accommodate fluctuations in the profit stream. Retained profits are given by $s_c P = P - D$, and the neo-Pasinetti distribution result may be written as

$$\frac{P}{Y} = \frac{D}{Y} + (1 - i)\frac{I}{Y}. \tag{8.1}$$

When dividends are decided *ex post*, (8.1) is an accounting identity based on the requirement that the usage of corporate funds (that is, $D + I$ in this setting) must be equated with the total funds from all sources (that is, $P + iI$). When dividends are set *ex ante* by management, and independently of planned investment expenditure, it follows that the close post-Keynesian connection between the distribution of income and the investment–income coefficient is weakened.

With dividends and investments decided *ex ante*, an implication of equation (8.1) is that, for any planned expenditure on investment, the realized value of profits will be sufficient to finance any level of distributions. This result is similar to the Miller–Modigliani microeconomic theorem on the irrelevance of dividend payments, to the valuations of firms in a world without taxes or costs associated with equity transfers. There are a number of important differences between the corporations of the neo-Pasinetti model and the firms of the Miller–Modigliani world. The neo-Pasinetti corporations are prohibited from repurchasing shares, and the extent to which these corporations may raise finance in securities markets is limited, being linked to planned investment. The flexibilities which Miller–Modigliani firms have ensure the operation of the mechanisms which produce the theorem. Little account is taken of the demand side of the market for securities in the Miller-Modigliani analysis.

How is it that the neo-Pasinetti model also contains the implication that dividends are irrelevant to the investment decision? One explanation depends on a linkage between dividends and Tobin's q. For with the investment equation of Chapters 5 and 7,

$$\frac{I}{K} = \frac{I_0}{K} + \alpha(q-1), \text{ where } q = \frac{p_s N}{K},$$

and profit may be written as

$$P = D + (1-i)I,$$

$$= D + (1-i)\{I_0 + \alpha(q-1)K\},$$

$$= D + (1-i)\{I_0 + \alpha(p_s N - K)\}.$$

When market valuation $p_s N$ is greater than replacement cost K an increase in dividends induces a larger increase than is required to cover dividend payments. By simplifying the equation for P using the expressions for q and P in Table 7.1, the dividend multiplier can be written as

$$\frac{\partial P}{\partial D} = \frac{1}{1 - \alpha(1-i)}.$$

When α is zero the multiplier is one. This reflects the spirit of the Miller–Modigliani result that management need not be constrained by investment decisions in deciding dividends. But when α is not zero the multiplier is greater than one. That is, there is an extra source of revenue for firms, for not only is an increase in dividends translated into a matching increase in profit (as would be expected of the widow's cruse), but it also generates a further increase in profits, which in this model becomes investment. The added investment will in general have an impact on valuations.

The multiplier effect of dividends on profits depends on the linkages in the model of Chapter 7 which connect dividends, via Tobin's q, to the market valuation of paper assets. It is possible that, for individual firms, linkages which cause share prices to increase following the announcement of an increase in dividends are temporary, lasting for only a few days. In financial centres there may be further rounds of adjustment which realign market values and replacement costs. Managers of real-world, or maybe only Miller–Modigliani corporations could trade in equities to generate the extra funds required to pay promised dividends during the period of misalignment. According to the neo-Pasinetti equilibrium approach, they would reap an extra reward. To the extent that this mechanism has been expounded here, it seems that Tobin's q is increased for the duration of the entire short run.

Another approach to pricing was taken in Chapters 6 and 7, where profit-maximizing oligopolists colluded to preserve output shares. The economy-wide margin and Tobin's q are then functions of industry concentration and the extent to which firms strive to preserve their shares of output. A number of the models reviewed in Chapter 4 augmented Kaldor's 1955–6 theory with a perfectly competitive theory of factor usage. According to Blinder (1988, p.89) monopolistic competition is preferable:

It produces a Keynesian environment in two respects. First, it leads to theoretical models in which firms always want to sell more at current prices because price exceeds marginal cost. Second, output levels in monopolistic equilibria are generally below the social optima, which echoes the Keynesian idea that employment is typically too low.

Also the perfectly competitive model of Chapter 2 and some models in Chapter 4 imposed optimizing behaviour at a highly aggregated level. In aggregate, the output level achieved reflects individuals' cost-minimizing behaviour. Such an environment imposes a remarkable degree of uniformity and efficiency on economic agents. The approach adopted here specifies optimization at the lowest level, so that some macroeconomic indicators are determined by aggregating values of firm-specific variables. In Chapter 7, for example, the economy-wide q was obtained in this way. A case for not extending to the macroeconomy all the implications of profit-maximizing behaviour was argued in Section 7.1. Consequently, considerably greater diversity might be allowed within different sectors of the economy. The 1963 and 1965 papers of Harcourt (see Section 3.5) contain the suggestion that quite different microeconomic behaviour must occur in a Kaldorian two-sector model. It would be possible to incorporate into Harcourt's framework market behaviour of the type discussed in Chapter 5 for one sector. Consistent with his rejection of the idea of a representative firm, which replicates the whole economy at the microeconomic level, the other sector might be modelled, for example, as a Saving (1970)-type follower. Use of different industrial structures would provide further insights into the microeconomic conditions required for the working of the Keynesian distribution mechanism in a two-sector model. Models of this type might also resolve a doubt expressed by Blinder (1988, p.29) about the main finding of models involving monopolistic competition: 'output is normally *too low*, not that it is *too variable*. Hence the obvious policy intervention is an output subsidy, not macro stabilization policy.'

The version of the neo-Pasinetti model constucted in Chapter 7 includes linkages between an underlying imperfectly competitive industry structure and the macroeconomic aggregates of the model. A closure was developed in which indices of concentration and collusion, and the economy-wide elasticity of demand, were fixed. The extended model was solved to simulate the effects of an increase in the value of the Herfindahl index of concentration. It was argued that this might be expected to occur in a downturn when a firm closes its doors. As a result of the increase in concentration there was a redistribution of income to profits, but the level of profits was not affected. Wages and nominal and real income were projected to contract. For those projections obtained on the assumption that the securities market was initially bullish and that there was a positive mark-up of price over average direct cost, Tobin's q was projected to decline, and there arose in the simulation the possibility of further capital gains.

Out of these changes corporations obtained mixed blessings. Profits were maintained by the increase in price, but real investment was reduced. Further, managers were confronted with the problem of a decline in the securities market valuation of corporate assets. The holders of securities benefited from the capital gain associated with the increased price of capital goods, but those households which did not save had to endure, uncompensated, the problems associated with consumption during a period of inflation. Across all households there was projected a higher incidence of unemployment and falling real wages. Whether other theories of industrial organization and financial market behaviour also produce the same short-run redistributive processes is an issue that might be further pursued within the neo-Pasinetti paradigm.

Bibliography

Allen, R.G.D. (1968), *Macroeconomic Theory: Mathematical Treatment*, London: Macmillan.

Bain, J.S. (1951), 'Relation of profit rates to industry concentration', Quarterly Journal of Economics, **65**, 293–324.

Barroux, Y. (1988), Comment on Colin Mayer, 'New issues in corporate finance', *European Economic Review*, **32**, 1187–9.

Benzie, R.S. (1988), 'The financial behaviour of industrial and commercial companies, 1970–86', *Bank of England Quarterly Bulletin*, 75–82.

Berndt, E.R. (1991), *The Practice of Econometrics: Classic and Contemporary*, Reading, Massachusetts: Addison-Wesley.

Blinder, A.S. (1988), 'The fall and rise of Keynesian economics', *Economic Record*, **64**, 278–94.

Bodoff, J. (1975), 'Monopoly and Price Revisited', in Y. Brozen (ed.), 175–86.

Bohm, V. (1990), *General Equilibrium with Profit-maximising Oligopolists*, University of Mannheim Institut für Volkswirtschaftslehre und Statistik, Discussion Paper No 414/90.

Boulding, K.E. (1950), *A Reconstruction of Economics*, New York: John Wiley and Sons.

Boulding, K.E. (1953), 'The fruits of progress and the dynamics of distribution', *American Economic Review (Papers and Proceedings)*, **43**, 473–83, and in Boulding, K.E. (1962), 473–83.

Boulding, K.E. (1962), *A Reconstruction of Economics*, new edition, New York: Science Editions.

Brainard, W.C. and J. Tobin (1968), 'Pitfalls in financial model building', *American Economic Review (Papers and Proceedings)*, **58**, 99–122, and in Tobin, J. (1971), *Essays in Economics Vol. 1: Macroeconomics*, Amsterdam: North-Holland, 352–77.

Bronars, S.G. and D.R. Deere (1991), 'The threat of unionization, the use of debt and the preservation of shareholder wealth',

Quarterly Journal of Economics, **106**, 231–54.

Bronfenbrenner, M. (1960), 'A note on relative shares and the elasticity of substitution', *Journal of Political Economy*, **68**, 284–7.

Brozen, Y. (ed.) (1975), *The Competitive Economy: Selected Readings*, Morristown, New Jersey: General Learning Press.

Brozen, Y. (1982), *Concentration, Mergers, and Public Policy*, New York: Macmillan.

Campbell, T.S. (1982), *Financial Institutions, Markets, and Economic Activity*, New York: McGraw-Hill.

Cartter, A.M. (1959), *Theory of Wages and Employment*, Westport Connecticut: Greenwood Press.

Champernowne, D. (1958), 'Capital accumulation and the maintenance of full employment', *Economic Journal*, **68**, 211–44.

Champernowne, D. (1961), 'A Dynamic Growth Model Involving a Production Function', in F.A. Lutz and D.C. Hague (eds), 223–44.

Chen, P. (1990), 'Prices vs quantities and delegating price authority to a monopolist', *Review of Economic Studies*, **57**, 521–9.

Chirinko, R.S. (1987), 'Tobin's q and financial policy', *Journal of Monetary Economics*, **19**, 69–87.

Ciccolo, J.H. (1975), 'Four essays on monetary policy', unpublished doctoral dissertation, Yale University.

Ciccolo, J.H. (1978), 'Money, equity values and income: tests for exogeneity', *Journal of Money, Credit and Banking*, **10**, 46–64.

Ciccolo, J. and G. Fromm (1979), '"q" and the theory of investment', *Journal of Finance*, **34**, 535–47.

Clark, J.B. (1899), *The Distribution of Wealth*, London: Macmillan.

Clark, P.K. (1979), 'Investment in the 1970's: theory, performance and prediction', *Brookings Papers on Economic Activity*, No. 1, 73–124.

Clarke, R. (1985), *Industrial Economics*, Oxford: Basil Blackwell.

Clarke, R. and S.W. Davies (1982), 'Market structure and price–cost margins', *Economica*, **49**, 277–87.

Clarke, R., S.W. Davies and M. Waterson (1984), 'The profitability–concentration relation: market power or efficiency?', *Journal of Industrial Economics*, **32**, 436–50.

Collins, N.R. and L.F. Preston (1968), *Concentration and Price–cost Margins in Manufacturing Industries*, Berkeley: University of California Press.

Collins, N.R. and L.F. Preston (1969), 'Price–cost margins and industry structure', *Review of Economics and Statistics*, **51**, 271–86.

Conyon, M. and S. Machin (1991), 'The determination of profit margins in UK manufacturing', *Journal of Industrial Economics*, **39**, 369–82.

Coutts, K., W. Godley and W. Nordhaus (1978), *Industrial Pricing in the United Kingdom*, Cambridge: Cambridge University Press.

Cowling, K. (1982), *Monopoly Capitalism*, London and Basingstoke: Macmillan.

Cowling, K. and M. Waterson (1976), 'Price–cost margins and market structure', *Economica*, **43**, 267–74.

Dalton, J.A. (1973), 'Administered inflation and business pricing: another look', *Review of Economics and Statistics*, **55**, 516–19.

Davidson, P. (1968), 'The demand and supply of securities and economic growth and its implications for the Kaldor–Pasinetti versus Samuelson–Modigliani controversy', *American Economic Review (Papers and Proceedings)*, **57**, 252–69.

Davies, S. (1991), 'Concentration', in S. Davies, B. Lyons, H. Dixon and P. Geroski, 73–126.

Davies, S., B. Lyons, H. Dixon and P. Geroski (1991), *Economics of Industrial Organisation*, London: Longman.

Demsetz, H. (1974), 'Two Systems of Belief About Monopoly', in H.J. Goldschmid, *et al.*, 164–84.

Dixon, P.B., S. Bowles and D. Kendrick (1980), *Notes and Problems in Microeconomic Theory*, Amsterdam: North-Holland.

Dixon, R. (1988), *Concentration, mergers and collusion*, University of Melbourne Department of Economics Discussion Paper No. 209.

Dorward, N. (1987), *The Pricing Decision: Economic Theory and Business Practice*, London: Harper and Row.

Dougherty, C. (1980), *Interest and Profit*, New York: Columbia University Press.

Dunlop, J.T. (1950), *Wage Determination under Trade Unions*, Oxford: Basil Blackwell.

Eckstein, O. and G. Fromm (1968), 'The price equation', *American Economic Review*, **68**, 1159–83.

Eichner, A.S. (1973), 'A theory of the determination of the mark-up under oligopoly', *Economic Journal*, **83**, 1184–1200.

Eichner, A.S. (1976), *The Megacorp and Oligopoly: Micro Foundations of Macro Dynamics*, Cambridge: Cambridge University Press.

Eichner, A.S. (ed.) (1979), *A Guide to Post-Keynesian Economics*, London: Macmillan.

Fine, B. and A. Murfin (1984), *Macroeconomics and Monopoly Capitalism*, Brighton: Wheatsheaf.

Geroski, P. (1991), 'Competition Policy and the Structure–Performance Paradigm', in S. Davies, B. Lyons, H. Dixon and P. Geroski, 166–91.

Goldschmid, H. J., H.M. Mann and J.F. Weston (1974), *Industrial Concentration: The New Learning*, Boston: Little Brown and Co.

Goodwin, R.M. (1983), 'A note on wages, profits and fluctuating growth rates', *Cambridge Journal of Economics*, 7, 305–9.

Granger, C.W.J. (1969), 'Investigating causal relations by econometric models and cross-spectral methods', *Econometrica*, 37, 424–38.

Haache, G. (1979), *The Theory of Economic Growth*, London: Macmillan.

Hahn, F.H. and R.C.O. Mathews (1964), 'The theory of economic growth: a survey', *Economic Journal*, 74, 779–902.

Hall, R.E. (1977), 'Investment, interest rates and the effects of stabilization policies', *Brookings Papers on Economic Activity*, No. 1, 61–103.

Hall, R.E. (1986), 'Market structure and macroeconomic fluctuations', *Brookings Papers on Economic Activity*, No. 2, 285–338.

Hall, R.E. (1988), 'The relation between price and marginal cost in U.S. industry', *Journal of Political Economy*, 96, 921–47.

Hamouda, O.F. and G.C. Harcourt (1988), 'Post-Keynesianism: from criticism to coherence?', *Bulletin of Economic Research*, 40, 1–33.

Harcourt, G.C. (1963), 'A critique of Mr Kaldor's model of income distribution', *Australian Economic Papers*, 2, 20–36, and in G.C. Harcourt, (1982), 67–85.

Harcourt, G.C. (1965), 'A two-sector model of the distribution of income and the level of employment in the short run', *Economic Record*, 41, 103–17, and in G.C. Harcourt (1982), 86–103.

Harcourt, G.C. (1972), *Some Cambridge Controversies in the Theory of Capital*, Cambridge: Cambridge University Press.

Harcourt, G.C. (1982), edited by Prue Kerr, *The Social Science Imperialists*, London: Routledge and Kegan Paul.

Harcourt, G.C. and P. Kenyon (1976), 'Pricing and the investment decision', *Kyklos*, **29**, 449–77, and in G.C. Harcourt (1982), 104–126.

Harris, F.H. deB. (1984), 'Growth expectations, excess value, and the risk-adjusted return to market power', *Southern Economic Journal*, **51**, 166–79.

Harris, F. (1988), 'Testing competing hypotheses from structure-performance theory: efficient structure versus market power', *Journal of Industrial Economics*, **36**, 267–80.

Hart, P.E. and E. Morgan (1977), 'Market structure and economic performance in the United Kingdom', *Journal of Industrial Economics*, **25**, 177–93.

Hicks, J.R. (1932), *The Theory of Wages*, London: Macmillan.

Hirschey, M. (1982), 'Intangible capital aspects of advertising and R & D expenditures', *Journal of Industrial Economics*, **30**, 375–90.

Hirschey, M. (1985), 'Market structure and market value', *Journal of Business*, **58**, 89–98.

Howard, M.C. (1979), *Modern Theories of Income Distribution*, London: Macmillan.

Hunt, E.K. and H.J. Sherman (1975), *Economics: An Introduction to Traditional and Radical Views*, 2nd edition, New York: Harper International.

Intriligator, M. (1978), *Econometric Models, Techniques and Applications*, Amsterdam: North-Holland.

Johnson, H.G. (1973), *The Theory of Income Distribution*, London: Gray-Mills.

Jones, H.G. (1976), *An Introduction to Modern Theories of Economic Growth*, Tokyo: McGraw-Hill Kogakusha.

Kahn, R.F. (1959), 'Exercises in the analysis of growth', *Oxford Economic Papers (New Series)*, **11**, 143–56.

Kaldor, N. (1955–6), 'Alternative theories of distribution', *Review of Economic Studies*, **23**, 83–100, and in B.J. McCormick, and E.O. Smith (eds) (1968), *The Labour Market*, Harmondsworth: Penguin, 349–79.

Kaldor, N. (1957), 'A model of economic growth', *Economic Journal*, **67**, 591–624.

Kaldor, N. (1961), 'Capital Accumulation and Economic Growth', in F.A. Lutz and D.C. Hague (eds), 177–222.

Kaldor, N. (1966), 'Marginal productivity and the macro-economic theories of distribution: comment on Samuelson and Modigliani (1966)', *Review of Economic Studies*, **33**, 309–19.

Kalecki, M. (1938), 'The determinants of distribution of the national income', *Econometrica*, **6**, 97–112, and in American Economic Association (ed.) (1950), *Readings in the theory of Income Distribution*, London: George Allen and Unwin, 197–217.

Kalecki, M. (1954), *Theory of Economic Dynamics*, London: George Allen and Unwin.

Katz, L.F. and L.H. Summers (1989), 'Industry rents: evidence and implications', *Brookings Papers on Economic Activity: Microeconomics*, 209–290.

Kay, J.A. and M. King (1978), *The British Tax System*, Oxford: Oxford University Press.

Keynes, J.M. (1930), *A Treatise on Money*, London: Macmillan.

Keynes, J.M. (1936), *The General Theory of Employment, Interest and Money*, London: Macmillan.

Khalilzadeh-Shirazi, J. (1974), 'Market structure and price–cost margins in UK manufacturing industries', *Review of Economics and Statistics*, **56**, 67–76.

King, J.E. and P. Regan (1976), *Relative Income Shares*, London and Basingstoke: Macmillan.

King, J.E. and P. Regan (1988), 'Recent Trends in Labour's Share', in Y.S. Brenner, J.P.G. Reijnders and A.H.G.M. Spithoven (eds), *The Theory of Income and Wealth Distribution*, Sussex: Wheatsheaf, 54–86.

Kregel, J.A. (1972), *The Theory of Economic Growth*, London: Macmillan.

Kregel, J.A. (1977), 'Some Post-Keynesian Distribution Theory', in S. Weintraub, (ed.), Modern Economic Thought, Oxford: Basil Blackwell, 421–38.

Kregel, J.A. (1979), 'Income Distribution', in A.S. Eichner, (ed.), 46–60.

Kwoka, J.E. (Jr) and D.J. Ravenscraft (1986), 'Cooperation v. rivalry: price–cost margins by line of business', *Economica*, **53**, 351–63.

Layard, P.R.G. and A.A. Walters (1978), *Microeconomic Theory*, New York: McGraw-Hill.

Levacic, R. and A. Rebmann (1982), *Macroeconomics: An Introduction to Keynesian-neo-classical Controversies*, 2nd edition, Basingstoke and London: Macmillan.

Lindenberg, E.B. and S.A. Ross (1981), 'Tobin's *q* ratio and industrial organisation', *Journal of Business*, **54**, 1–32.

Lutz, F.A. and D.C. Hague (eds) (1961), *The Theory of Capital: Proceedings of a Conference held by the International Economic Association*, London: Macmillan.

Mains, N.E. (1980), 'Recent corporate financing patterns', *Federal Reserve Bulletin*, **66**, 683–90.

Marris, R. (1963), 'A model of the "managerial" enterprise', *Quarterly Journal of Economics*, **77**, 185–209.

Marris, R. (1964), *The Economic Theory of 'Managerial' Capitalism*, Glencoe, New York: Free Press.

Marris, R. and D.C. Mueller (1980), 'The corporation, competition and the invisible hand', *Journal of Economic Literature*, **18**, 32–63.

Mayer, C. (1987), 'The assessment: financial systems and corporate investment', *Oxford Review of Economic Policy*, **3**, i–xvi.

Mayer, C. (1988), 'New issues in corporate finance', *European Economic Review*, **32**, 1167–89.

Miller, M.H. and F. Modigliani (1961), 'Dividend policy, growth and the valuation of shares', *Journal of Business*, **34**, 411–33.

Nordhaus, W.D. and W. Godley (1972), 'Pricing in the trade cycle', *Economic Journal*, **82**, 853–82.

Norton, W.E. and P.M. Garmston (1984), *Australian Economic Statistics 1949–50 to 1982–83: Tables*, Sydney: Reserve Bank of Australia Occasional Paper 8A.

Odagiri, H. (1981), *The Theory of Growth in a Corporate Economy*, Cambridge: Cambridge University Press.

Oulton, N. (1981), 'Aggregate investment and Tobin's Q: the evidence from Britain', *Oxford Economic Papers*, **33**, 177–202.

Pasinetti, L.L. (1961–2), 'Rate of profit and income distribution in relation to the rate of economic growth', *Review of Economic Studies*, **29**, 267–79, and in A. Sen, (ed.) (1970), *Growth Economics*, Harmondsworth: Penguin, 92–111.

Phillips, A. (1972), 'An Econometric Study of Price-fixing, Market Structure, and Performance in British Industry in the Early 1950's', in K. Cowling, (ed.), *Market Structure and Corporate Behaviour: Theory and Empirical Analysis of the Firm*, London: Gray Mills, 175–92.

Poterba, J.M. and L.H. Summers (1983), 'Dividend taxes, corporate investment and "q"', *Journal of Public Economics*, **22**, 135–67.

Prais, S.J. (1976), *The Evolution of Giant Firms in Britain*, Cambridge: Cambridge University Press.

Qualls, D. (1972), 'Concentration, barriers to entry, and long-run economic profit margins', *Journal of Industrial Economics*, **20**, 231–42.

Qualls, D. (1974), 'Stability and persistence of economic profit margins in highly concentrated industries', *Economic Journal*, **40**, 604–12.

Rhoades, S.A. (1973), 'The effect of diversification on industry performance in 241 manufacturing industries: 1963', *Review of Economics and Statistics*, **55**, 146–55.

Riach, P.A. (1969), 'A framework for macro-distribution analysis', *Kyklos*, **22**, 542–65.

Rimmer, R.J. (1989a), 'Boulding's theory of distribution in a neo-Pasinetti framework', *Cambridge Journal of Economics*, **13**, 453–58.

Rimmer, R.J. (1989b), 'Employment implications of improved labour productivity in the Australian iron and steel industry', *Economic Record*, **65**, 114–25.

Rimmer, R.J. (1990), 'Kaldorian Distribution Theory', University of Melbourne, mimeo.

Rimmer, R. J. (1992), 'Industry Structure, Conduct and a Keynesian Theory of Distribution', Deakin University, Melbourne, mimeo.

Ripley, F.C. and L. Segal (1973), 'Price determination in 395 manufacturing industries', *Review of Economics and Statistics*, **55**, 263–71.

Robinson, J. (1933), *The Economics of Imperfect Competition*, London: Macmillan.

Robinson, J. (1953–4), 'The production function and the theory of capital', *Review of Economic Studies*, **21**, 81–106.

Robinson, J. (1956), *The Accumulation of Capital*, London: Macmillan.

Robinson, J. and J. Eatwell (1973), *An Introduction to Modern Economics*, revised edition, London: McGraw-Hill.

Salinger, M.A. (1984), 'Tobin's *q*, unionization, and the concentration–profits relationship', *Rand Journal of Economics*, **15**, 159–170.

Samuelson, P.A. (1962), 'Parable and realism in capital theory: the surrogate production function', *Review of Economic Studies*, **29**, 193–206.

Samuelson, P.A. (1963), 'A Brief Survey of Post-Keynesian Developments', in R. Lekachman, (ed.), *Keynes' General Theory: Reports of Three Decades*, New York: St Martin's Press, 331–47.

Samuelson, P.A. (1966), 'A summing up', *Quarterly Journal of Economics*, **80**, 568–83.

Samuelson, P.A. (1973), *Economics*, 9th edition, New York: McGraw-Hill.

Samuelson, P.A. and F. Modigliani (1966), 'The Pasinetti paradox in neoclassical and more general models', *Review of Economic Studies*, **33**, 269–301.

Sargent, T.J (1987), *Macroeconomic Theory*, 2nd edition, Boston: Academic Press.

Saving, T.R. (1970), 'Concentration ratios and the degree of monopoly', *International Economic Review*, **11**, 295–306.

Sawyer, M.C. (1985), *The Economics of Industries and Firms*, 2nd edition, London: Croom Helm.

Schmalensee, R. (1972), *The Economics of Advertising*, Amsterdam: North-Holland.

Schmalensee, R. (1985), 'Do markets differ much?', *American Economic Review*, **75**, 341–51.

Schmalensee, R. (1987), 'Collusion versus differential efficiency: testing alternative hypotheses', *Journal of Industrial Economics*, **35**, 399–425.

Schwartzman, D. (1959), 'The effect of monopoly on price', *Journal of Political Economy*, **67**, 352–62.

Schwartzman, D. (1961), 'The effect of monopoly: a correction', *Journal of Political Economy*, **69**, 494.

Semmler, W. (1984), *Competition, Monopoly and Differential Profit Rates: On the Relevance of the Classical and Marxian Theories of Production Prices for Modern Industrial and Corporate Pricing*, New York: Columbia University Press.

Sen, A.K. (1963), 'Neo-classical and neo-Keynesian theories of distribution', *Economic Review*, **39**, 53–64.

Sensenbrenner, G. (1991), 'Aggregate investment, the stock market and the q model: robust results for six countries', *European Economic Review*, **35**, 769–832.

Shepherd, W.G. (1972), 'The elements of market structure', *Review of Economics and Statistics*, **54**, 25–37.

Sims, C.A. (1972), 'Money, income and causality', *American Economic Review*, **62**, 540–52.

Skott, P. (1981), 'On the "Kaldorian" saving function', *Kyklos*, **34**, 563–81, and in P. Skott (1989), 33–47.

Skott, P. (1989), *Kaldor's Growth and Distribution Theory*, Frankfurt am Main: Verlag Peter Lang.

Sleuwaegen, L. and W. Dehandschutter (1988), 'The critical choice between the concentration ratio and the H-index in assessing industry performance', *Journal of Industrial Economics*, **35**, 193–208.

Smirlock, M., T. Gilligan and W. Marshall (1984), 'Tobin's *q* and the structure–performance relationship', *American Economic Review*, **74**, 1051–60.

Smith, A. (1982), *A Mathematical Introduction to Economics*, Oxford: Basil Blackwell.

Solow, R.M. (1955–6), 'The production function and the theory of capital', *Review of Economic Studies*, **23**, 101–8.

Solow, R.M. (1957), 'Technical change and the aggregate production function', *Review of Economics and Statistics*, **39**, 312–20.

Solow, R.M. (1958), 'A sceptical note on the constancy of relative shares', *American Economic Review*, **48**, 618–31.

Solow, R.M. (1969), *Price Expectations and the Behaviour of the Price Level*, Manchester: Manchester University Press.

Solow, R.M. (1986), 'Monopolistic competition and the multiplier', in W.P. Heller, R.M. Starr and D.A. Starret (eds), *Equilibrium Analysis: Essays in Honour of Kenneth J. Arrow*, Cambridge: Cambridge University Press.

Stigler, G.J. (1964), 'A theory of oligopoly', *Journal of Political Economy*, **72**, 44–61.

Stiglitz, J.E. and H. Uzawa (1969), *Readings in the Modern Theory of Economic Growth*, Cambridge Massachusetts: MIT Press.

Swann, T.W. (1956), 'Economic growth and capital accumulation', *Economic Record*, **32**, 334–61.

Sylos-Labini, P. (1979a), 'Industrial pricing in the United Kingdom', *Cambridge Journal of Economics*, **3**, 153–63.

Sylos-Labini, P. (1979b), 'Prices and income distribution in manufacturing industry', *Journal of Post-Keynesian Economics*, **2**, 3–25.

Thomadakis, S.B. (1977), 'A value-based test of profitability and market structure', *Review of Economics and Statistics*, **59**, 179–85.

Tobin, J. (1969), 'A general equilibrium approach to monetary theory', *Journal of Money, Credit and Banking*, **1**, 15–29, and in J. Tobin (1971), *Essays in Economics Vol. 1: Macroeconomics*, Amsterdam: North-Holland, 322–38.

Tobin, J. (1974), 'Monetary policy in 1974 and beyond', *Brookings Papers on Economic Activity*, No. 1, 219–32.

244 Income Distribution in a Corporate Economy

Tobin, J. and W.C. Brainard (1977), 'Asset Markets and the Cost of Capital', in B. Balassa and R. Nelson (eds), *Economic Progress, Private Values and Public Policy: Essays in Honour of William Fellner*, Amsterdam: North-Holland, 235–62.

Tobin, J. and W. Brainard (1990), 'On Crotty's critique of *q*-theory', *Journal of Post-Keynesian Economics*, **12**, 543–49.

Udea, K. and Y. Yoshikawa (1986), 'Financial volatility and the *q* theory of investment', *Economica*, **53**, 11–27.

Von Furstenberg, G.M. (1977), 'Corporate investment: does market valuation matter in the aggregate?', *Brookings Papers on Economic Activity*, No. 2, 347–408.

Von Furstenberg, G.M., B.G. Malkiel and H.S. Watson (1980), 'The Distribution of Investment Between Industries: A Microeconomic Application of the "*q*" Ratio', in G.M. Von Furstenberg, (ed.), *Capital, Efficiency and Growth*, Cambridge, Massachusetts: Ballinger, 395–460.

Wallis, K.F. (1974), 'Seasonal adjustment and relations between variables', *Journal of the American Statistical Association*, **69**, 18–31.

Waterson, M. (1980), 'Price-cost margins and successive market power', *Quarterly Journal of Economics*, **94**, 135–50.

Waterson, M. (1984), *Economic Theory of the Industry*, Cambridge: Cambridge University Press.

Waterson, M. (1988), 'Recent US evidence on concentration–profitability relationships and its implications for merger policy', University of Reading, mimeo.

Weiss, L.W. (1974), 'The Concentration–Profits Relationship and Anti-trust', in Goldschmid *et al.*, 184–233.

Weiss, L.W. (1975), 'The Role of Concentration in Recent Inflation', in Y. Brozen, (ed.), 206–9.

Weitzman, M.L. (1974). 'Prices vs quantities', *Review of Economic Studies*, **41**, 477–91.

Weitzman, M.L. (1982), 'Increasing returns and the foundations of unemployment theory', *Economic Journal*, **92**, 787–804.

Wernerfelt, B. and C. Montgomery (1988), 'Tobin's *q* and the importance of focus in firm performance', *American Economic Review*, **78**, 246–50.

Wilder, R.P., C.G. Williams and D. Singh (1977), 'The price equation: a cross-sectional approach', *American Economic Review*, **67**, 732–40.

Williams, D., C.A.E. Goodhart and D.H. Gowland (1976), 'Money, income and causality: the UK experience', *American Economic Review*, **66**, 417–23.

Williams, P. (1982), 'Market Structure and the Conduct of Firms in the Private Sector', in L. Webb, and R. Allan, *Industrial Economics: Australian Studies*, Sydney: Allen and Unwin.

Wood, A. (1975), *A Theory of Profits*, Cambridge: Cambridge University Press.

Index

in neo-Pasinetti model, 51,
123–4, 128–9, 130–32
influence on capital gains, 50
influence on profits, 133
long-run value, 51–2, 112–13
marginal, 112–13
proxy for monopoly rents, 186,
190
short-run impact on income,
135–6
structure and collusion, 7, 188
theory of investment, 5, 111–16,
143–53

Udea, K. and Yoshikawa, Y.,
150–51, 193n
UK,
price formation, 160
profitability and concentration,
172
propensity for external finance,
120–21
trading profits and dividends,
118–19
see also Britain
unemployment, 6–7, 27, 31n, 67–9,
71, 83, 85, 87, 103, 233
and stability, 67–8
unionization, 114–15, 160, 173, 229
and choice of finance, 115
US,
advertising, 182–3
aggregate household savings
propensity, 56
determination of investment,
144–8, 150, 152
determination of q, 187, 189,
190–91
employment, 81
external finance, 120–21
functional shares, 19
influence of q on profits, 133
investment elasticity, 134
investment rates, 144–7
investment–income coefficient, 56
monopoly profits, 190–91
price formation, 154–63

profitability and concentration,
164, 166–73
profits, retained earnings, and
dividends, 119–20
propensity to retain profits, 56
q, 133
structure of finance, 120

valuation ratio, 48, 110
influence in securities and
commodity markets, 55–7
solution in neo-Pasinetti model,
49–50, 52–4
vertical integration, 130, 165
von Furstenberg, 49, 133, 147–8

wage rate, nominal, 41, 61–2,
69–71, 82, 85, 132
real, 10, 12, 36, 61, 72, 83–8, 103
wage–rental ratio, 16–19, 26–7
wages and salaries, fixed, 102–3
waiting, and the return to
capitalists, 25–6
Walras's law, 130, 213
Waterson, M., 182, 194n
see also Cowling, K.
Weiss, L. W., 164, 166, 169–72,
183, 191
Weitzman, M. L., 6, 127, 196, 226
Wenerfelt, B., and Montgomery,
C., 115–16, 186
widow's cruse, 1, 32, 42, 105
Williams, D., Goodhart, C. A. E.,
and Gowland, D. H., 193n
Wood, A., 54–5, 140n, 229
collusion, 80
finance frontier, 54, 76
neo-Pasinetti result, 54–5
nonprice competition, 80
opportunity frontier, 76
workers,
active and saving, 46
retired and dissaving, 46

Yoshikawa, Y., *see* Udea, K.

New Directions in Modern Economics

Post-Keynesian Monetary Economics
New Approaches to Financial Modelling
Edited by Philip Arestis

Keynes's Principle of Effective Demand
Edward J. Amadeo

New Directions in Post-Keynesian Economics
Edited by John Pheby

Theory and Policy in Political Economy
Essays in Pricing, Distribution and Growth
Edited by Philip Arestis and Yiannis Kitromilides

Keynes's Third Alternative?
The Neo-Ricardian Keynesians and the Post Keynesians
Amitava Krishna Dutt and Edward J. Amadeo

Wages and Profits in the Capitalist Economy
The Impact of Monopolistic Power on Macroeconomic
Performance in the USA and UK
Andrew Henley

Prices, Profits and Financial Structures
A Post-Keynesian Approach to Competition
Gokhan Capoglu

International Perspectives on Profitability and Accumulation
Edited by Fred Moseley and Edward N. Wolff

Mr Keynes and the Post Keynesians
Principles of Macroeconomics for a Monetary Production
Economy
Fernando J. Cardim de Carvalho

The Economic Surplus in Advanced Economies
Edited by John B. Davis

Foundations of Post-Keynesian Economic Analysis
Marc Lavoie

The Post-Keynesian Approach to Economics
An Alternative Analysis of Economic Theory and Policy
Philip Arestis

Income Distribution in a Corporate Economy
Russell Rimmer

The Economics of the Profit Rate
Competition, Crises and Historical Tendencies in Capitalism
Gérard Duménil and Dominique Lévy

Printed and bound by CPI Group (UK) Ltd, Croydon, CR0 4YY

23/04/2025

14661001-0002